INTERCULTURAL BUSINESS COMMUNICATION

SECOND EDITION

Intercultural Business Communication

Lillian H. Chaney

The University of Memphis

Jeanette S. Martin

The University of Mississippi

Prentice Hall
Upper Saddle River, New Jersey 07458

Editor-in-Chief: Natalie Anderson
Editorial Assistant: Sue Galle
Assistant Editor: Kristen Imperatore
Managing Editor: Bruce Kaplan
Marketing Manager: Debbie Clare
Production Manager: Gail Steier de Acevedo
Production Coordinator: Kelly Warsak
Permissions Coordinator: Monica Stipanov
Manufacturing Buyer: Natacha St. Hill Moore
Manufacturing and Prepress Manager: Vincent Scelta
Cover Design: Bruce Kenselaar
Cover Art: DigitalSTOCK
Full Service Composition: BookMasters, Inc.

Library of Congress Cataloging-in-Publication Data

Chaney, Lillian H.
    Intercultural business communication / Lillian H. Chaney, Jeanette
S. Martin. — 2nd ed.
        p.   cm.
    Includes bibliographical references and index.
    ISBN 0-13-013700-6
    1. Business etiquette.   2. Corporate culture.   3. Business communication.
    4. Intercultural communication.   I. Martin,
    Jeanette S.   II. Title.
    HF5389.C47   2000
    395.5′2—dc21   99-21946
                                                                            CIP

Prentice-Hall International (UK) Limited, London
Prentice-Hall of Australia Pty. Limited, Sydney
Prentice-Hall Canada, Inc., Toronto
Prentice-Hall Hispanoamericana, S.A., Mexico
Prentice-Hall of India Private Limited, New Delhi
Prentice-Hall of Japan, Inc., Tokyo
Prentice-Hall (Singapore) Pte Ltd.
Editora Prentice-Hall do Brasil, Ltda., Rio de Janeiro

Printed in the United States of America

10 9 8 7 6 5 4 3 2 1

Contents

Foreword

With the globalization of the world economy, it is imperative that managers, both present and future, be sensitive to differences in intercultural business communication. Professors Lillian H. Chaney and Jeanette S. Martin have done an admirable job in addressing a broad range of issues and skills that are crucial to effective intercultural encounters. In the book, the most significant issues pertaining to cross-cultural interaction are covered: culture, intercultural (both verbal and nonverbal) communication, and cultural shock. In addition, the book contains practical guidelines and information on how to conduct negotiations across countries and write business letters in different societies, as well as other general do's and don'ts in international business. College students and businesspeople new to the international business scene can certainly benefit from such practical advice.

This book can also sensitize readers to the dynamics of international diversity. With the increasing multiethnic composition of the North American labor force and the growing participation of women in the professional and managerial ranks of organizations, it is equally important that students, the managers of the future, be attuned to the issues associated with managing and valuing diversity within a domestic context. The book addresses the issues of gender differences and how these impact on communication styles and patterns.

While recognizing the significant differences that can exist across cultures and subcultures, it is important to acknowledge the existence of individual differences within any given society. Just as it is naive to assume that all cultures are similar, it is equally fallacious to fall into the trap of "cultural stereotyping." To quote Lao Tzu, the famous Chinese philosopher who is usually considered to be the spiritual leader of Taoism, "The one becomes the many." Although people in a given society may share certain common values and characteristics, there can be important differences in how these are applied and exhibited in specific situations. In addition, these intranational differences can be exacerbated by religious influences, exposure to Western philosophies and ideas through education at universities abroad, overseas travel, and social and business contacts with peoples from other cultures. Furthermore, it is significant to note that cultural values and norms do evolve over time, however slowly. Some of the cultural characteristics alluded to in this book may be changing or have changed. A cursory review of the dramatic upheavals that have taken and are still taking place in virtually all aspects of societal and organizational functionings in many socialist and former socialist countries will attest to the fact that culture is not static; rather, it evolves over time.

Judicious application of the principles and techniques introduced in this book will enable readers to develop a proficiency in managing diversity, both cross-nationally and internationally.

Rosalie L. Tung
The Ming & Stella Wong Professor
of International Business
Simon Fraser University
Canada

Preface

Purpose

With the increasing number of multinational corporations and the internationalization of the economy, intercultural business communication continues to become more important. Government leaders, educators, and businesspersons agree that internationalizing the curriculum is important to maintaining the competitive position of the United States in the world economy. Since all international activity involves communication, students need a knowledge of intercultural business communication to prepare them for upward mobility and promotion in tomorrow's culturally diverse domestic and international environments.

Contents

Topics selected for *Intercultural Business Communication* were those considered important or essential by three Delphi panels of experts: international employees of multinational corporations, college professors who teach intercultural communication, and members of the Academy of International Business.* We know of no other book on intercultural communication that has used research involving experts' perceptions of the importance of topics to be covered as a basis of content selection.

The topics include

- The nature of intercultural communication
- Universal systems
- Contrasting cultural values
- Cultural shock
- Language
- Oral and nonverbal communication patterns
- Written communication patterns
- Global etiquette
- Business and social customs
- Intercultural negotiation process
- Intercultural negotiation strategies
- Laws affecting international business and travel

*Martin, J. S. (1991). Experts' Consensus Concerning the Content for an Intercultural Business Communication Course. (Doctoral dissertation, The University of Memphis). Major professor, L. H. Chaney.

Each chapter contains objectives, terms, questions and cases for discussion, and activities. Also provided are exercises to be used for self-evaluation of material covered and illustrations to depict various aspects of the content.

Both authors have traveled or worked in a number of countries or multinational corporations and, therefore, have firsthand knowledge of many of the topics covered.

Changes to the Second Edition

- Including anecdotes from neophytes and experienced travelers and from other sources in a boxed format throughout the book to add realism to principles presented in the chapters. Boxes also contain additional related facts to validate or explain text materials.
- Deleting the chapter on Country-Specific Information and adding the chapter on Business and Social Customs, including:
  –Greeting and handshaking customs
  –Verbal expressions
  –Male and female relationships
  –Humor in business
  –Superstitions and taboos
  –Dress and appearance
  –Customs associated with holidays and holy days
  –Office customs and practices
  –Customary demeanor/behavior
  –Bribery
  –Special foods and consumption taboos
- Updating of all information presented in the first edition to reflect changes which have taken place in the various countries identified, especially in economic and political situations. More recent references were used for all chapters.
- Rearranging, revising, and expanding of selected chapters. For example, Cultural Shock and Language are presented earlier in the second edition; Dress and Appearance has been expanded to reflect the current trend toward business casual attire in some countries; technology was included as appropriate.
- Adding cases for discussion to all chapters.
- Incorporating the emerging role of women in international business into various chapters as appropriate.
- Including country-specific information in a majority of chapters.
- Revising the Instructor's Manual to include a sample syllabus and suggested videos and references.
- Preparing PowerPoint slides to make available to those adopting the textbook.

Proposed Use

Intercultural Business Communication is designed to be used as a text for a college-level course in intercultural business communication or to augment courses in which intercultural communication is a major component.

Acknowledgments

Appreciation is expressed to the following persons who reviewed the manuscript and offered helpful suggestions: Maryann Albrecht, University of Illinois–Chicago, Chicago, IL; Roberta Allen, Western Michigan University, Kalamazoo, MI; Marie Dalton, San Jacinto College, Pasadena, TX; Lynn Fitzgerald, New England Banking Institute, Boston, MA; Marie Flatley, San Diego State University, San Diego, CA; Clifford Hurston, Bethune-Cookman College, Daytona Beach, FL; Carolyn Rainey, Southeast Missouri State University, Cape Girardeau, MO; Roblyn Simeon, San Francisco State University, San Francisco, CA; Carol Smith, Fort Lewis College, Durango, CO; and Richard F. Tyler, Anne Arundel Community College, Arnold, MD.

About the Authors

Lillian H. Chaney is a Professor of Management and Distinguished Professor of Office Management at The University of Memphis. She received both the M.S. and the Ed.D. from the University of Tennessee. She is coauthor of a textbook on office management and has published numerous articles on communication and office management in professional journals. Dr. Chaney teaches graduate/undergraduate courses in business communication, executive communication, and international business communication and negotiation. She has teaching experience at a South American university and has conducted training programs on communication, corporate etiquette, and business ethics for international corporations, educational institutions, and government agencies.

Jeanette S. Martin is an Associate Professor at the University of Mississippi. She received her B.A. from Michigan State University, M.B.A. from the University of Chicago, and her Ed.D. from The University of Memphis. She has considerable corporate experience in both U.S. multinational corporations and foreign multinational corporations. Dr. Martin has published several articles involving intercultural business communication, education, and management information systems. Her current research and consulting interests include NAFTA and the effects intercultural communication has on such international agreements.

CHAPTER

1

The Nature of Intercultural Communication

Objectives
Upon completion of this chapter, you will:

- be able to define such terms as intercultural, international, intracultural, multicultural, and ethnocentric.

- understand how communication barriers affect intercultural communication.

- understand the differences between norms, rules, roles, and networks.

- be able to distinguish between subcultures and subgroups.

- understand the concept of business globalization.

- be able to differentiate between ethnocentric, polycentric, regiocentric, and geocentric management orientations.

More than 2 million North Americans work for foreign employers, and the number of foreign companies who have built plants in the United States is increasing. Evidence that the world is becoming more cosmopolitan can be seen in the number of international businesses such as Coca-Cola, McDonald's, Sony, and Honda that are common around the world. The new economic bonanza is apparent in the universal appreciation of food such as sushi, fashion such as jeans, and music such as U.S. jazz and rock. Because of the global boom, more and more business will involve international activities, which will require the ability to communicate across cultures.

Because communication is an element of culture, it has often been said that communication and culture are inseparable. As Alfred G. Smith (1966) wrote in his preface to *Communication and Culture,* "culture is a code we learn and share, and learning and sharing require communication. Communication requires coding and symbols that must be learned and shared. Godwin C. Chu (1977) observed that every cultural pattern and every single act of social behavior involves communication. To be understood, the two must be studied together. Culture cannot be known with a study of communication, and communication can only be understood with an understanding of the culture it supports" (Jandt, 1995, p. 22).

Not only are North Americans working for foreign employers, but the complexion of the workforce in the year 2000 is five-sixths nonwhites, women, and immigrants; in 1988 they made up only half of the workforce. By the year 2010 Hispanic Americans will become the largest minority group; by 2050 the number of minorities will almost equal that of whites (Weaver, 1998).

To gain a better understanding of the field of intercultural communication, a knowledge of frequently used terms is important. Such terms as intercultural, international, and multicultural are often used interchangeably. However, certain distinctions should be made.

The term intercultural communication was first used by Edward T. Hall in 1959. Hall was one of the first researchers to differentiate cultures based on how communications are sent and received. Hall defined **intercultural communication** as communication between persons of different cultures.

Intercultural business communication is a relatively new term in the business world and is defined as communication within and between businesses that involves people from more than one culture. Although we generally think of the United States as one culture, a great deal of culture diversity exists. For example, more than 30 percent of residents of New York City are foreign born, Miami is two-thirds Latin American, and San Francisco is one-third Asian. In fact, African Americans, Asians, and Latin Americans make up 21 percent of the U.S. population. An increase in the Asian and Latin American populations is expected during the next decade. Many U.S. citizens communicate interculturally almost daily because the communication is between people of different cultural backgrounds (Copeland, 1988).

As contact occurs between cultures, diffusion takes place. **Diffusion** is the process by which the two cultures learn and adapt materials and adopt practices from each other. This practice is exemplified by Columbus' joining of the Old and New Worlds. The Old World gave the New World horses, cows, sheep, chickens, honeybees, coffee, wheat, cabbage, lettuce, bananas, olives, tulips, and daisies. The New World gave the Old World turkeys, sugarcane, corn, sweet potatoes, tomatoes, pumpkins, pineapples, petunias, poinsettias, and daily baths (Jandt, 1995).

With the increased globalization of the economy and interaction of different cultures, the concept of a world culture has emerged. A **world culture** is the idea that as traditional barriers among people of differing cultures break down, emphasizing the commonality of human needs, one culture will emerge, a new culture to which all people will adhere. So why do we study intercultural business communication? Because it addresses procedural, substantive, and informational global problems. Intercultural business communication allows us to work on the procedural issues of country-to-country contacts, diplomacy, and legal contexts; it allows us to become involved with the substantive, cultural level and helps sensitize us to differences. It also allows us to gather information to make decisions when we are in an intercultural environment (Rohrlich, 1998).

The United States continues to welcome a large number of immigrants each year and has been referred to as a melting-pot society. **Melting pot** means a sociocultural assimilation of people of differing backgrounds and nationalities; the term implies losing ethnic differences and forming one large society or **macroculture.** While the idea of everyone's being the same may sound ideal, the problem with this concept is that many U.S. citizens wish to maintain their ethnic-cultural heritage. Rather than being one melting-pot society, therefore, the reality in the United States is that many U.S. cities are made up of neighborhoods of people with a common heritage who strive to retain their original culture and language. If you travel to San Francisco, a visit to Chinatown with its signs in Chinese and people speaking Chinese will verify this reality. Many street signs in other U.S. cities such as New York, Miami, or Honolulu, are in another language in addition to English. The result has not been the melding of various cultures into one cultural group as idealists believed would happen. Because we have cultures within cultures (**microcultures**), communication problems often result. In reality the United States is a salad bowl of cultures. While some choose assimilation, others choose separation.

America as a cultural melting pot which assumes assimilation as the acculturation pattern is no longer valid (Differences, 1996).

Intracultural communication is defined as communication between and among members of the same culture. Generally, people who are of the same race, political persuasion, and religion or who share the same interests communicate intraculturally. Having the same beliefs, values, and constructs facilitates communication and defines a particular culture (Gudykunst & Ting-Toomey, 1988). However, due to distance, cultural differences may exist within a culture such as differences in the pace of life and regional speech patterns between residents of New York City and Jackson, Mississippi. Distance is also a factor in the differences in the dialects of the people of other cultures, such as in northern and southern Japan.

The terms intercultural communication and international communication should not be used interchangeably. **Intercultural communication,** as stated previously, involves communication between people of different cultures. **International communication** takes place between nations and governments rather than individuals; it is quite formal and ritualized. The dialogue at the United Nations, for example, would be termed international communication.

Since all international business activity involves communication, a knowledge of intercultural communication and international business communication is important to prepare you to compete successfully in international environments. In fact, upward mobility and promotion in tomorrow's corporate world may depend on your knowledge of intercultural business communication.

Globalization

Although globalization has come to the world, most of the world's businesses are not globalized. Business **globalization** is the ability of a corporation to take a product and market it in the entire civilized world. International firms have subsidiaries or components in other countries; however, control of the foreign operations is maintained at the home country headquarters. Multinational firms allow their foreign operations to exist as domestic organizations. Most firms are international, either sourcing, producing, or exporting. Many times the product may also be partially or completely manufactured somewhere other than the United States. The top ten multinational firms listed in *The Economist* (Emmott, 1993) earned 31 to 93 percent of their total revenues from foreign sales. The United Nations estimated there were 35,000 multinationals; and the largest 100 multinationals, excluding banking and finance, accounted for $3.1 trillion of worldwide assets in 1990. U.S. dependency on exports is confirmed by the fact that one of every six manufacturing jobs is related to exports. Export crops account for 40 percent of farm production, and exports account for one-third of all U.S. corporate profits. In the past some U.S. corporations have been largely insulated from globalization due to a strong domestic market and an absence of foreign competitors. However, this trend is changing as foreign corporations enter the U.S. market.

The personnel of an organization must have a global mindset in order for the firm to succeed in the international marketplace. Laurent (1986), in a study of multinational corporations, found that successful multinational corporations do not submerge the individuality of different cultures completely in the corporate culture, that intercultural contact can promote a determination not to adjust to other cultures, and that new management theory and practice can be presented only to individuals who are culturally able and willing to accept it. Rhinesmith (1993) states, "The corporate culture contains the values, norms of behavior, systems, policies, and procedures through which the organization adapts to the complexity of the global arena" (p. 14). Successful corporations have found that the values, beliefs, and behaviors of the parent corporation do not need to be the beliefs, values, and behaviors of the offices in other cultures. Hofstede's (1991) study of IBM determined that managers had to adjust the corporate management philosophy to fit the beliefs, values, and behaviors of the country in which they were working. Companies with franchises abroad have had to make certain adjustments to accommodate the tastes and preferences of individual countries; for example, Tex-Mex cuisine is prepared kosher in Israel. According to Rhinesmith (1993), "Diversity—both domestic and international—will be the engine that drives the creative energy of the corporation of the twenty-first century. Successful global managers will be those who are able to manage this diversity for the innovative and competitive edge of their corporations" (p. 5). Evans, Doz, and Laurent (1990) state that the five elements critical to building a successful corporate culture are 1) a clear and simple mission statement, 2) the vision of the chief executive officer, 3) company-controlled management education, 4) project-oriented management training programs, and 5) emphasis on the processes of global corporate culture (p. 118).

Lopez-Vasquez, director of multicultural affairs at the Oregon Health Sciences University and a consultant with IEC Enterprises, Decatur, Georgia, believes that well-meaning managers who become supervisors of Hispanic workers often make the mistake of attempting to adopt a "color-blind" approach. "The cultural disparities are obvious," he says.

Lopez-Vasquez argues for what he calls "essential treatment" of some special consideration for Hispanic employees. "I suggest that companies recognize that today it's essential to take steps to recruit and retain Hispanics, because Hispanics in the United States represent a fast-growing market and because Central and South America are key areas for success in international markets," he says (Staa, 1998, p. 8).

Although the United States is dependent upon foreign economic opportunities, the multinational firms have had problems with U.S. citizens working in foreign assignments. The failures to adapt included differences in lifestyle, language, and business philosophy as well as financial problems, government problems, cultural shock, and problems with housing, food, gender, and family. Ruch (1989) found the ability to blend with the host culture and explain one's own culture is more important than having product, price, or quality advantages. Although many of the people sent on foreign assignments know their U.S. market, they do not have the ability to accept another culture on that culture's terms even for short periods.

Culture

Whereas communication is a process, **culture** is the structure through which the communication is formulated and interpreted. Culture deals with the way people live. When cultures interact, adaptation has to take place in order for the cultures to communicate effectively. In dealing with intercultural business communication, awareness of the symbols of each culture, how they are the same, and how they are different, is important.

DIMENSIONS OF CULTURE

In order to communicate effectively in the intercultural business environment, being knowledgeable about all cultural factors that affect the situation is essential. The following graphical representation of culture (Figure 1.1) has three primary dimensions—languages, physical, and psychological (Borden, 1991, p. 171).

The languages, physical, and psychological dimensions of culture are interdependent. As we are born into a society, no one dimension is more important than the others. The individual dimensions develop in harmony with each other.

First, the language dimension is used to communicate with other people who have values and beliefs like our own. Second, the physical dimension relates to the physical reality of our environment and the cultural activities of the people. The physical dimension is measured objectively. Third, the psychological dimension relates to our knowledge, our beliefs, and our mental activities. The psychological dimension is measured subjectively. While we can alter these characteristics and our way of communicating with others, we must first understand our own personal dimensions and understand why we are the way we are.

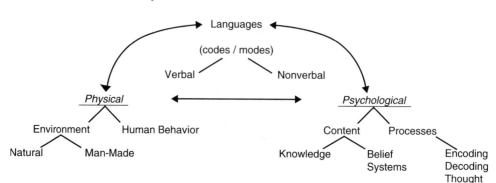

FIGURE 1.1 Dimensions of Culture

Culture is learned through perception. Perceptions are formed in various ways: where we are born and raised, the language we learn, the people and environment with which we live, and the psychological stimuli we encounter. No two individuals will view the external world the same because no two individuals will receive exactly the same stimuli nor do they share the same physical sensory receptors. Since we only know what we have personally perceived and cannot know for sure what someone else has perceived, intercultural communication involving different cultures becomes particularly difficult (Singer, 1998).

Glen's (1981) cognitive approach to studying culture suggests that different cultures structure knowledge differently and that these differences determine aspects of behavior and communication such as information that is accepted as proof for an opinion or argument, the syntax of the information, and the topics that are considered appropriate to discuss.

If you find that a particular cultural attitude is constant across cultures, then you do not have to be concerned about that particular cultural trait. However, if you find that a particular cultural attitude varies for specific cultures, you will want to consider the effect it will have on communications with cultures that possess this attitude. A **cultural symbol** is a word or object that represents something in the culture. Cultural symbol variability may be included in social cognitive processes such as information processing, persuasive strategy selection, conflict management styles, personality, social relations, and self-perceptions as well as habits, norms, rules, roles, networks, language, and environment. All of the factors interact and influence each other. In order to communicate effectively in the intercultural business environment, a knowledge of all cultural factors that affect the situation are important.

STEREOTYPES OF U.S. CULTURE

Stereotypes, perceptions about certain groups of people or nationalities, exist with U.S. persons and those of other cultures. Although stereotyping is a guide to a national culture, it does not work well with individuals, particularly those who have worked in international business or who have lived or studied abroad. Individuals generally will have differences from their national culture (Lewis, 1996).

In *American Ways,* Althen (1988) describes typical U.S. businesspersons as people who tend to

- be informal in their relationships.
- be rather formal in their business attire (suits for men and dresses or suits for women); however, many firms are becoming more relaxed in their dress codes or have a casual day when employees can dress less formally.
- be workaholics because they spend more time working than they do with their family or social engagements; U.S. executives tend to put in long hours at the office.
- embarrass foreign businesspeople by doing manual labor (for example, mowing their own lawns) or tasks that would be done by the lower class or servants in their country.
- be overly concerned with time, money, and appointments; people of other cultures interpret the need of U.S. businesspeople to begin meetings on time and start business discussions immediately as an indication that they are unfriendly, impersonal, and cold.
- make decisions on hard, objective facts rather than on personal feelings, social relationships, or political advantage.
- consider contracts and the written word as very important and to be taken very seriously.
- be aware of the status differences within the organization; however, generally no display of superiority or inferiority is made which tends to make rank-conscious foreigners very uneasy.
- be mobile; they rarely work for one company all their life which is very different from many countries in the world.
- convey superiority in their actions because they feel the United States is a superior nation.*

Axtell (1991) identified these stereotypes of persons in the United States: arrogant, loud, friendly, impatient, generous, hard working, and monolingual. These descriptions, admittedly, are stereotypes.

STEREOTYPES OF PERSONS IN OTHER CULTURES

Axtell (1991, pp. 83–84) asked people in the United States who conduct business with persons outside the United States to give one-word descriptors of their impression of people of other nationalities. Some of these stereotypes follow:

Culture	*Image*
English	conservative, reserved, polite, proper, formal
French	arrogant, rude, chauvinistic, romantics, gourmets, cultural, artistic
Italians	demonstrative, talkative, emotional, romantics, bold, artistic
Latin Americans	mañana attitude, macho, music lovers, touchers
Asians	inscrutable, intelligent, xenophobic (fear/hatred of strangers/foreigners), golfers, group oriented, polite, soft-spoken

Source: Adapted from *American Ways: A Guide for Foreigners* (p. 6–7), by Gary Althen, 1988, Yarmouth, ME: Intercultural Press, Inc. Used by permission.

By recognizing differences as well as similarities, businesspersons can adjust their mode of communication to fit the individual culture with which they are communicating.

Enculturation

Enculturation is the socialization process you go through to adapt to your society. When you grow up in one culture, you learn one way of classifying, coding, prioritizing, and justifying reality. Cultural information that you are willing to share with outsiders is considered **frontstage culture,** while cultural information that is concealed from outsiders is considered **backstage culture.** An example of frontstage culture would be a sales representative who loudly announces: "We got the Hunter Fan account." This information is readily shared. An example of backstage culture would be the sales representative who conceals the fact that his child is mentally retarded. Frontstage and backstage culture vary by culture and by individuals within the culture because some people are inherently more open than others. As a representative of your company, you need to learn what the culture with which you are working considers acceptable frontstage information that can be shared and what is considered backstage information that is not to be shared with others.

Datan, Rodeheaver, and Hughes (1987) use the concept of scripts to explain the cognitive imprinting that happens during enculturation.

> Individuals experience events in their lives as "scenes"—organized wholes combining people, places, time, actions, and in particular, affects that amplify these experiences and provide a sense of urgency about understanding them. Out of early scenes, the individual develops sets of rules for interpreting, evaluating, producing, predicting, or controlling future scenes. These rules— "scripts"—are initially innate but are supplemented and replaced by learned scripts. Higher-order scripts are created when scenes are combined and instilled with fresh affect—"psychological magnification" .... The order in personality development, then, derives from the individual's need to impose order—the script—on the critical events or scenes, in life. And, finally, scripts that initially arise from scenes begin to give rise to scenes instead, as the individual's construction of experience affects experience itself (p. 164).

Examples of such scripts are the inability of the Japanese to say the word "no" directly but instead to say "it would be difficult," and the difficulty for someone of a strong Christian background to lie to save face when for a Christian lying is never condoned.

Acculturation

People do not want to abandon their past; therefore, they acculturate new ideas into their existing culture. **Acculturation** is the process of adjusting and adapting to a new and different culture (Hazuda, Stern, & Hoffner, 1988). If people of two different cultures absorb a significant number of each others' cultural differences and have a number of similarities, **cultural synergy** takes place with the two cultures merging to form a stronger overriding culture. Corporate cultures are examples of the synergy of diverse cultures.

Marcia A. Smith, president of Columbia Cascade, tells of the following incident when on a trip to France in 1992:

As a woman, Smith faced an additional dilemma. She quickly realized she was butting heads with foreign corporate executives who had a customary requirement—no dealing with women. "He did not want to talk to me, so I had to send my (male) vice president," she says. "I don't care who goes in to negotiate the deal. I just think you need to be absolutely aware of the cultural differences."

Smith didn't let being a woman keep her from succeeding abroad: Columbia's clients today include foreign governments, some 50 foreign companies, and 25 academic institutions (Przybla, 1997, p. 25).

A manager, in order to be productive and creative, must make his/her workers realize that the corporation is more important than individual differences. Differences are not to be suppressed but managed to maximize the group's productivity and creativity (Weaver, 1998). Hofstede's (1991) work shows that what motivates a worker in one country may or may not be important to a worker in another country. For corporations to get the most from their people, they will have to have managers who can work effectively with many cultural groups.

People who learn more than one culture are **multicultural** and can move between cultures very comfortably. An example of mutlicultural persons is the Royal Grimaldi family of Monaco. Princess Grace was a U.S. citizen and married Prince Ranier of Monaco. The Grimaldi children were raised in Monaco; however, due to the time they spent in the United States, they were acculturated to this country. Although acculturation increases the interconnectedness of cultures, differences are sources of potential problems. All differences will probably not be absorbed by either culture.

Acculturation has four dimensions: integration, separation, assimilation, and deculturation. When a minority moves into a majority culture, he or she will choose one of these modes either consciously or subconsciously. Although as a majority culture we may feel assimilation is the correct acculturation process, the individual may not feel this fits his or her needs. Assimilation takes place when individuals are absorbed into their new culture and withdraw from their old culture. Integration takes place when individuals become an integral part of the new culture while maintaining their cultural integrity. Separation happens when individuals keep their culture and stay independent of the new culture. Deculturation occurs when individuals lose their original culture and do not accept the new culture, leading to confusion and anxiety (Alkhazraji, 1997). The acculturation mode that an individual chooses will be governed by the individual's views and desired ways of life.

Ethnocentrism

Ethnocentrism is the belief that your own cultural background, including ways of analyzing problems, values, beliefs, language, and verbal and nonverbal communication, is correct. Ethnocentrists believe their culture is the central culture and other cultures are incorrect, defective, or quaint. When we evaluate others, we do it through our self-reference criterion because it is what we know. Fisher (1997) in his research refers to ethnocentrism as mindsets. **Mindsets** are ways of being that allow us to see, perceive, and reason through our own cultural awareness. Mindsets are learned by growing up in a particular culture. We learn to be open or closed to others and their way of living; however, these mindsets can be altered.

Mindsets include the psychological and cultural factors that make us individuals and make us different or similar. We are predisposed due to enculturation to perceive and reason according to our cultural upbringing. Our reactions to situations are preprogrammed until we decide to change. Every culture in the world has a different mindset, and every individual within that culture has a variance to that mindset.

The U.S. mindset includes the concept that the American way is best. ("American" as used in the United States is an example of ethnocentrism because the term "American" actually refers to all the people in North, South, and Central American countries.) Although this is mainly a U.S. concept, people who are born in smaller countries feel the same about their own country—that it is the best place to live. The belief that one's own culture is best is a very natural phenomenon common to all cultures. Although it is natural to be ethnocentric and have a particular mindset, when we judge other mindsets we need to look at them from the perspective of the people who hold them before we judge them as good or bad. However, we must be careful about generalizing about other cultures or making assumptions about how they view the United States.

The term *Ugly American* was derived from the behavior of U.S. travelers observed by persons in other cultures who judged them to be inconsiderate of the culture they were visiting. This term came from the 1958 book by William Lederer and Eugene Burdick and the subsequent 1963 movie by the same name. The book and movie depict an incompetent, ignorant U.S. ambassador in a fictional Southeast Asian country. The term quickly caught on to describe rude, sef-centered people who have no sensitivity for those who are different from themselves. In reality, most U.S. Americans, when traveling to other countries, do not fit this stereotype of the *Ugly American*. They want to understand people of other cultures but are simply uninformed (Bosrock, 1995).

Norms, Rules, Roles, and Networks

Norms, rules, roles, and networks are situational factors that influence encoding and decoding of both verbal and nonverbal messages within a culture. They are unwritten guidelines people within the cultural group follow. **Norms** are culturally ingrained principles of correct and incorrect behaviors which, if broken, carry a form of overt or covert penalty. **Rules** are formed to clarify cloudy areas of norms. The U.S. Supreme Court is an excellent example of an organization that looks at the intent of a rule and determines how strongly or loosely it should be followed. A **role** includes the behavioral expectations of a position within a culture and is affected by norms and rules. **Networks** are formed with personal ties and involve an exchange of assistance. Networks and the need to belong are the bases of friendships and subgroups. An example of a political network is the exchange of votes between U.S. legislators needed to support their projects. When the United States decided to help the people of Kuwait defend themselves against Iraq in 1992, the U.S. ambassador to the United Nations called in the other ambassadors within his network for their concurrence. The ability to develop networks in intercultural situations can enable you to do business more effectively in multicultural environments. In some cultures such as the Arab, Spanish, and Japanese, networking is essential since they prefer to conduct business with people they know or with associates of people they know (Gudykunst & Ting-Toomey, 1988).

Subcultures and Subgroups

Subcultures are groups of people possessing characteristic traits that set apart and distinguish them from others within a larger society or macroculture. The macroculture may be a country, a city, or a business. For example, U.S. citizens belong to many different religions, yet belong to the macroculture of U.S. citizens. Examples of subcultures (or microcultures) in the United States include senior citizens, teenagers, baby boomers, African Americans, Latin Americans, Catholics, Jews, disabled individuals, trade associations, and self-help groups. All these groups will have similarities to the macroculture but will also have some differences. The subculture members will have the same self-perception and agree that they belong to the subculture (Dodd, 1987).

Intercultural business communication necessitates working with subcultures. The subcultures form a diversity of ethnic identities with which managers will have to learn to work harmoniously. Women are one such subculture. As Adler (1993) states, "Although women represent over 50 percent of the world's population, in no country do women represent half, or even close to half, of the corporate managers" (p. 3). In some Middle East, Far East, and South American countries, business is male oriented. Because North American women have progressed in the business world faster than their counterparts in most other countries of the world, they may expect to automatically be accepted by men who would be offended by women in business in their own culture. Although men in some countries are still apprehensive about conducting business with women, Bosrock (1995) states that "regardless of the attitude toward women in a given country, most women are treated politely. Much of the resistance to women in business is directed at local women, not Westerners" (p. 109). Even in Asian and South American cultures where women are traditionally seen as nurturers of the family, attitudes are changing. Many employers now are less concerned with gender than performance (Bosrock, 1994, 1997). Women sent abroad have a very high success rate. A self report showed 97 percent of the female expatriate managers were successful, a much higher percentage than reported by male expatriates (Adler, 1994).

Subgroups, although also part of the macroculture, are groups with which the macroculture does not agree and with which it has problems communicating. Members of these groups often engage in communication behavior that is distinctively different from that of the dominant culture. Examples of subgroups include youth gangs, prostitutes, saboteurs, embezzlers, and other groups that have unique experiences and/or characteristics not sanctioned by the macroculture (Dodd, 1987).

Communication Barriers

When encountering someone from another culture, communication barriers are often created when the behavior of the other person differs from our own. **Communication barriers** are obstacles to effective communication. An example of such a barrier is the head nod. The nod indicates understanding in the United States, but in Japan it means only that the person is listening. By understanding intercultural communication, we can break down barriers and pave the way for mutual understanding and respect.

Bell (1992) identified the following barriers to communication:

1. Physical—time, environment, comfort and needs, and physical medium (e.g., telephone, letter)
2. Cultural—ethnic, religious, and social differences
3. Perceptual—viewing what is said from your own mindset
4. Motivational—the listener's mental inertia
5. Experiential—lack of similar life happenings
6. Emotional—personal feelings of the listener
7. Linguistic—different languages spoken by the speaker and listener or use of a vocabulary beyond the comprehension of the listener
8. Nonverbal—nonword messages
9. Competition—the listener's ability to do other things rather than hear the communication

Several cultural iceberg models exist. What you do not see culturally can be a barrier to your ability to communicate effectively and complete your agenda. As shown in Figure 1.2, the values that are below the "waterline" represent those upon which behaviors are based; however, we respond to the surface values that we can sense. In order to truly understand a culture, we must explore the behaviors below the "waterline." The common elements of trust, sincerity, and integrity are necessary to building successful business relationships when cultural differences exist (Funakawa, 1997).

Intercultural Constructs

Borden (1991) lists seven constructs that individuals must possess if they are going to succeed interculturally. The degree to which we can understand intercultural communication depends upon the degree to which:

FIGURE 1.2 Cultural Iceberg

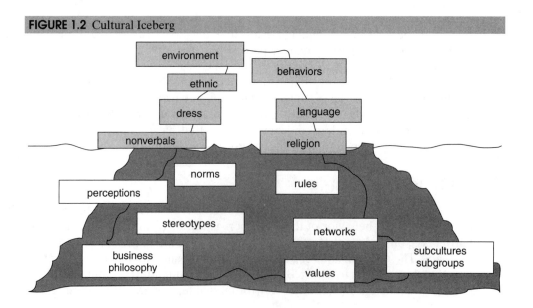

1. We are aware that our intent to communicate, either as communicator or communicatee, may result in only expressive behavior or information gathering, respectively.
2. Our cybernetic (self-concept) in one culture can operate independently of our cybernetic in another culture.
3. We are competent in the language of other cultures.
4. We are able to work within the constraints (personal, situational, and cultural) of the human communication system established by the communication from other cultures.
5. We are culturally literate in our own and other cultures.
6. We know the position of our culture and other cultures on the four universal values dimensions and their interaction with the cultural orientation model.
7. We know the cultural orientation of our culture and other cultures on the associative-abstractive, particularistic-universalistic, and closed-minded/open-minded dimensions and can use it as the first approximation of the cognitive style of the communicants (pp. 210–213).

The components of Borden's constructs will be discussed in later chapters.

Multinational Management Orientations

To compete successfully in a global economy, a knowledge of management styles used by international corporations is also important. With the emergence of the concept of world culture has come a heightened awareness of the interdependence of nations and the need to break cultural barriers and find ways to work harmoniously with people of all cultures.

Multinational firms, those located in more than one nation, generally will follow either an ethnocentric, polycentric, geocentric, or regiocentric form of management. Multinational firms such as Sony, Quaker Oats, Exxon, Robert Bosch, and Nissan may follow a single management style at all global locations or may use various styles of management to increase productivity while maintaining worker morale. All multinational or global corporations are **transnational,** which means they cross the borders of countries in conducting their business (Moran & Stripp, 1991).

Not all of these management styles consider the diversity of cultures working within them nor are they managed to take advantage of the surprises that surface in multinational management. As Rhinesmith (1993) has stated, global managers have a mindset that allows them to take advantage of and manage the complexity, adaptability, teams, uncertainty, and learning that the global organization requires. Since people are the most critical factor for an organization to succeed globally, people are also the restraining factor in the firm's ability to survive and grow. Human resource development personnel must be involved in the education and changing of the mindsets. The global mindset differs from the domestic mindset as illustrated in Table 1.1 (Rhinesmith, 1993, p. 27).

The person who can manage a domestic operation does not necessarily have the competencies to manage a global operation. People who have a global mindset tend to live life in many ways that may be physically, intellectually, emotionally, or spiritually different depending upon the culture with which they are interacting.

When a firm is located in one country and all its sales are in the same country, **ethnocentric management** practices will be employed. Ethnocentric management does not account for cultural differences in the workforce. All workers will be treated the same.

TABLE 1.1 Comparison of Domestic and Global Mindsets	
Domestic Mindset	*Global Mindset*
Functional expertise	Bigger, broader picture
Prioritization	Balance of contradictions
Structure	Process
Individual responsibility	Teamwork and diversity
No surprises	Change as opportunity
Trained against surprises	Openness to surprises

Source: From *A Manager's Guide to Globalization* (p. 27), by S. H. Rhinesmith, 1993, Homewood, IL: Richard D. Irwin, Inc. Used with publisher's permission.

Many times the management practices employed will rely on one person's views of how the organization should be run. Some domestic corporations that purchase goods from abroad for resale at home, that are financed from abroad, or that buy technology abroad still need to think globally due to their international activities (Moran & Stripp, 1991). For example, U.S. car manufacturers complained that their cars were not selling in Japan. These manufacturers, however, had not changed the position of the steering wheel from the left to the right for driving on the opposite side of the road from the United States, and they had not downsized their cars in consideration of the limited space available to park cars in Japan. When a company expands internationally, they have to consider the consumers who are targeted to buy their products.

Werner G. Hennecker (Pegasus Gold): We run our business on a certain set of standards, regardless of whether we're in the United States or Kazakhstan. Our in-house environmental policy is much more stringent than that required by any of the areas in which we operate, but it's inviolate. It's been interesting getting people in some parts of the world that haven't worried much about environmental issues to focus on them. Our solution was to base a large part of our bonus program on employees' avoidance of environmental incidents (Donlon, 1996, p. 3).

Polycentric management practices consider the culture of the country in which the firm is located. The people in charge consider the cultural needs of the workers in the area in which the firm is located. A melting-pot effect may seem to exist because the majority's culture is considered in management decisions. In the United States, you will see this particularly in small firms. Leaving the familiar polycentric management practices behind is part of the problem employees have when they move to a foreign country to work because they were comfortable with the old management style (Moran & Stripp, 1991).

Regiocentric management considers the region rather than the country in which the firm is located, realizing that countries can and often do have many different cultural backgrounds. The regional theory acknowledges that in the United States all areas are not the same. For example, running a production facility in Michigan with high unionization and a facility in Mississippi with low unionization and different ethnic bases calls for different management strategies. Management strategies will consider the diversity of the workforce (Moran & Stripp, 1991). Unions tend to keep the workers from interacting directly with management. Many firms now wish to use Total Quality Management (TQM) which utilizes interaction between workers and management. Saturn automotive built their plant in Springfield, Tennessee, because they could start the plant without a union and implement TQM. Although Saturn now has a workforce which is unionized, the union works with management and the quality and sales of the Saturn automobile have been better than any other General Motors' product.

Shepard: We've also developed a program called Aegon University, in which we put managers in their 30s and 40s from different countries into a dormitory setting and bring in international executives to speak to them. Even more important, this gives them the opportunity to network individually. They are building an e-mail system among the graduates of Aegon University that lets them share practices they think might work across borders in addition to potential customers that operate globally in the pension business (Donlon, 1996, p. 4).

Geocentric management requires a common framework with enough freedom for individual locations to operate regionally in order to meet the cultural needs of the workers. Geocentric refers to synergy of ideas from different countries of operation. The most successful multinational corporations use integrated geocentric management. Corporations have common control practices which the individual locations are free to modify. To compete successfully in a global economy, being able to recognize the management style used is helpful (Moran & Stripp, 1991).

Claude I. Taylor (Air Canada): When we first started to go international, we had Canadians everywhere. We found that didn't work, because they weren't accepted and they didn't understand the local culture. That meant we had two levels of labor problems: We had a management problem and a contract problem.

Today, we're expanding rapidly in the United States, and we have the odd Canadian in there part time. But our philosophy for outside markets is to bring foreigners—from France, Germany, Hong Kong, and South Korea, for example—into Canada for six months, indoctrinate them about what we do, and then send them back (Donlon, 1996, p. 3).

The ability of different cultures to communicate successfully in a business environment, to assimilate their cultures and conduct business, and to do this either within the United States or abroad is the emphasis of intercultural business communication. Different cultures do present communication problems; differing business practices and negotiation strategies pose additional problems. Intercultural business communication involves a knowledge and understanding of other cultures including their subcultures and subgroups and standards of behavior. With the emergence of the concept of a world culture has come a heightened awareness of the interdependence of nations and the need to break the cultural barriers in order to find ways to work harmoniously with people of all cultures.

Bosrock (1995) offers the following Ten Commandments for Going International:

1. Be well prepared.
2. Ask questions, be observant, and listen.
3. Make an effort; trying and making a mistake is better than not trying at all.
4. When problems develop, assume the main cause is miscommunication.
5. Be patient; accomplishing your goals in another country/culture usually requires more time and effort.
6. Assume the best about people; most people act based upon their learned values and traditions.
7. Be sincere.
8. Maintain a sense of humor.
9. Make an effort to be likeable; when people like you, they will forgive your mistakes.
10. Smile.

Terms

- Acculturation
- Backstage culture
- Communication barriers
- Cultural symbol
- Cultural synergy
- Culture
- Diffusion
- Enculturation
- Ethnocentric management
- Ethnocentrism
- Frontstage culture
- Geocentric management
- Globalization
- Intercultural business communication
- Intercultural communication
- International communication
- Intracultural communication
- Macroculture
- Melting pot
- Microculture
- Mindsets
- Multicultural
- Multinational firm
- Networks
- Norms
- Polycentric management
- Regiocentric management
- Roles
- Rules
- Stereotypes
- Subculture
- Subgroup
- Transnational
- World culture

Questions and Cases for Discussion

1. The United States has long been called a melting pot. What does this term mean?
2. What does it mean for a firm to be global?
3. Give examples of how products have been globalized.
4. Explain the differences between norms, roles, rules, and networks.
5. Define a subculture and give examples of U.S. subcultures.
6. What is cultural synergy?
7. Distinguish between intercultural communication and intracultural communication.
8. Identify the dimensions of culture.
9. Identify types of barriers to communication.
10. Are business cultures necessarily aligned to national cultures?

CASE 1

At a reception for a U.S. political candidate, the guests appear to be divided into groups. People in some groups are all African American, others are Latin American,

---

EXERCISE 1.1

Instructions: Match the following terms with their definition.

___ 1. Belief that your own culture is superior

___ 2. The socialization process we go through to learn a culture

___ 3. A sociocultural assimilation

___ 4. Cultural information concealed from outsiders

___ 5. Absorption of new ideas into existing culture

___ 6. Between members of same culture

___ 7. Between persons of different cultures

___ 8. Between nations and governments

___ 9. Groups having traits differing from the macroculture

___ 10. Culturally ingrained principles of correct/incorrect behavior

A. Acculturation

B. Backstage culture

C. Enculturation

D. Ethnocentrism

E. Frontstage culture

F. Intercultural

G. International

H. Intracultural

I. Melting pot

J. Norms

K. Subcultures

---

and others are Asian. Explain the cultural phenomena that are operating at this political gathering.

CASE 2

The U.S. automotive manufacturers have complained about Japanese automotive imports and that the U.S. car firms are locked out of the Japanese market. The Japanese have countered that the U.S. firms have not done their homework; they offer cars that are too big or are not fuel efficient. While U.S. car sales have decreased in the United States, Japanese car sales have increased. Japanese manufacturers have begun to assemble cars in the United States; many U.S. firms are moving part of their operations to Mexico. Discuss the implications to these firms as they globalize.

CASE 3

In 1979, the Shah of Iran was admitted to the United States for medical reasons. The Iranians reacted by holding all the diplomatic personnel hostage in the embassy in Iran. The secretary of state was Henry Kissinger, and the president was Jimmy Carter. The United States took the position that the Iranians should not be upset with the Shah being allowed into the United States for the humanitarian reason of medical need. The Shah had been a friend to the United States and the United States to the Shah; therefore, the U.S. government felt a certain obligation to the Shah. The revolution in Iran was based on Islamic religious assumptions. Give two position statements, one using the mindset of the United States and the second using the mindset of Iran to show how and why each viewed their position as correct. Is objectivity difficult to maintain when writing the Iran position statement?

CASE 4

The United States has globalized faster than it has paid attention to mindsets that differ from the U.S. mindset. The world is connected by news satellites, and that allowed the Gulf War Crisis to be viewed as it unfolded—the world literally watched the war happen. Explain how the world and public opinion have been affected by mass media. Include how world negotiations have changed for governments, diplomats, politicians, and businesses.

Activities

1. Clip a story from the local newspaper that is related to some aspect of intercultural communication such as problems encountered by persons of other cultures in the acculturation process or problems between subgroups; give a short report to the class.
2. Ask a member of the class who is from another culture to discuss how cultural norms and rules in his or her culture differ from those in the United States.
3. Invite a member of the business community who conducts business globally to address problems encountered when dealing with representatives of other cultures whose form of management (ethnocentric, polycentric, geocentric, or regiocentric) may be different from that in the United States.
4. Interview a foreign student on roles of women and children in his or her culture. In a report to the class, make comparisons between these roles and those in the United States.
5. Write a one-page proposal for improving relationships between U.S. students and students from other cultures in your school.
6. Analyze a multinational corporation's annual report and determine where it is producing and selling goods and what the profit margins of those goods are compared to other multinational firms.

References

Adler, N. J. (1993). Competitive frontiers: Women managers in triad. *International Studies of Management and Organization, 23* (2), 3–23.

Alkhazraji, K. M. (1997). *Immigrants and cultural adaptation in the American workplace.* New York: Garland Publishing.

Althen, G. (1988). *American Ways.* Yarmouth, ME: Intercultural Press, Inc.

Axtell, R. E. (1991). *The do's and taboos of international trade.* New York: John Wiley & Sons, Inc.

Axtell, R. E. (1990). *Do's and taboos of hosting international visitors.* New York: John Wiley & Sons, Inc.

Axtell, R. E., Briggs, T., Corcoran, M., & Lamb, M. B. (1997). *Do's and taboos around the world for women in business.* New York: John Wiley & Sons, Inc.

Bell, A. H. (1992). *Business communication: Toward 2000.* Cincinnati, OH: South-Western Publishing Co.

Borden, G. A. (1991). *Cultural orientation: An approach to understanding intercultural communication.* Upper Saddle River, NJ: Prentice Hall.

Bosrock, M. M. (1994). *Put your best foot forward: Asia.* St. Paul, MN: International Education Systems.

Bosrock, M. M. (1995). *Put your best foot forward: Europe.* St. Paul, MN: International Education Systems.

Bosrock, M. M. (1997). *Put your best foot forward: South America.* St. Paul, MN: International Education Systems.

Copeland, L. (1988). Making the most of cultural differences at the workplace. *Personnel, 65,* 52.

Datan, N., Rodeheaver, D., & Hughes, F. (1987). Adult development and aging. In M. R. Rosenzweig & L. W. Porter (Eds.), *Annual Review of Psychology, 38,* 153–180.

Differences between sexes are shrinking. (1996). *USA Today, 124* (2608), p. 10.

Dodd, C. H. (1987). *Dynamics of intercultural communication.* Dubuque, IA: Wm. C. Brown.

Donlon, J. P. (1996, September). Managing across borders. *Chief Executive, 117,* 58–68.

Emmott, B. (1993). Multinationals: The non-global firm. *The Economist, 326* (7804), 5–20.

Evans, P., Doz, Y., & Laurent, A. (Eds.) (1990). *Human resource management in international firms: Change, globalization, innovation.* New York: St. Martin's Press.

Fisher, G. (1997). *Mindsets* (2nd ed.). Yarmouth, ME: Intercultural Press, Inc.

Funakawa, A. (1997). *Transcultural management: A new approach for global organizations.* San Francisco: Jossey-Bass Publishers.

Glen, E. S. (1981). *Man and mankind.* Norwood, NJ: ABLEX Publishing Corporation.

Gudykunst, W. B., & Ting-Toomey, S. (1988). *Culture and interpersonal communication.* Newbury Park, CA: Sage Publications.

Hall, E. T. (1959). *The silent language.* Garden City, NJ: Doubleday.

Hazuda, H. P., Stern, M. P., & Hoffner, S. M. (1988). Acculturation and assimilation among Mexican Americans: Sales and population-based data. *Social Science Quarterly, 69,* 687–706.

Hofstede, G. (1991). *Cultures and organizations.* London: McGraw-Hill Book Company.

Jandt, F. E. (1995). *Intercultural Communication.* Thousand Oaks, CA: Sage Publications.

Laurent, A. (1986). The cross-cultural puzzle of human resource management. *Human Resource Management, 25* (1), 91–102.

Lewis, R. D. (1996). *When cultures collide: Managing successfully across cultures.* London: Nicholas Brealey.

Moran, R. T., & Stripp, W. G. (1991). *Dynamics of successful international business negotiations.* Houston, TX: Gulf Publishing Company.

Przybla, H. (1997, September 5). Women face tough road doing business overseas. *Washington Business Journal, 16* (17), 25, 2p, 2bw.

Rhinesmith, S. H. (1993). *A manager's guide to globalization.* Homewood, IL: Richard D. Irwin, Inc.

Rohrlich, P. E. (1998). Why do we study intercultural communication? In Weaver, G. R. (Ed.) *Culture, communication and conflict: Readings in intercultural relations.* Upper Saddle River, NJ: Simon & Schuster.

Ruch, W. V. (1989). *International handbook of corporate communication.* Jefferson, NC: McFarland.

Singer, M. R. (1998). The role of culture and perception in communication. In Weaver, G. R. (Ed.), *Culture, communication and conflict: Readings in intercultural relations.* Upper Saddle River, NJ: Simon & Schuster.

Staa, D. (1998). No need for inter-American cultural clash. *Management Review, 87* (1), 8.

Weaver, G. R. (Ed.) (1998). *Culture, communication and conflict: Readings in intercultural relations.* Upper Saddle River, NJ: Simon & Schuster.

CHAPTER

Universal Systems

Objectives
Upon completion of this chapter, you will:

■ increase your understanding of systems that are universal to all cultural groups and their relationship to communicating and negotiating in a global setting.

■ understand the role that economic and political systems play in communicating interculturally in business settings.

■ see the relationship between educational systems and global communication.

■ gain insight into social systems and hierarchies that affect effective intercultural business communication.

Cultural systems have an impact on multicultural communication. **Cultural universals** are formed out of the common problems of all cultures. The following systems are found in all cultures: economic, political, education, marriage and family, and social hierarchies and interaction. A knowledge of how cultural systems in the United States differ from those of other cultures can enhance communication effectiveness when conducting business with people of other cultures. Although these systems are universal to all cultures, different cultures may deal with an issue in a significantly different way. In communicating interculturally, the variabilities are equally as important as the similarities.

Economic Systems

A culture develops an economic system in order to meet the material needs of its people. The way in which the products that meet the material needs of the people are produced, distributed, and consumed is referred to as the **economic system.** All societies not only work out ways of producing or procuring goods, they must also determine the procedure for distributing them.

The different economic systems in the world today include capitalism, socialism, agrarianism, and barter. The United States and Japan are capitalistic; Sweden and China are socialistic; Belize and Cambodia are agrarian; and Laos and the Marshall Islands

CHAPTER 2   *Universal Systems*   **21**

use the barter system. The relationship between the public and private sectors and which sector dominates may make some economic systems a blend of the first three systems. No single correct economic system exists. The U.S. method of distributing goods is based on the capacity to pay while such countries as Cuba distribute goods according to need.

Economic ISMs
- **Socialism**—You have two cows. Give one cow to your neighbor.
- **Communism**—You have two cows. Give both cows to the government, and they may give you some of the milk.
- **Nazism**—You have two cows. The government shoots you and takes both of the cows.
- **Anarchism**—You have two cows. Keep both of the cows and shoot the government agent and steal another cow.
- **Capitalism**—You have two cows. Sell one cow and buy a bull.

In addition to identifying the type of economic system a country follows, it is also important to understand other aspects of the country's economy, including **imports** (goods brought into the country) and **exports** (goods sent out of the country). This knowledge may prove useful in the negotiation process.

A brief description of the economic systems of the United States and the six countries with which the United States conducts most of its international business follows. Also included are other details of the economies of these countries (*Culturgram '98*, 1997).

UNITED STATES

The U.S. economic system is capitalistic with socialistic overtones. Free market principles tempered by government regulations operate the economy. In addition, the United States is a financial center, and its economy affects the world. The U.S. capitalistic system is affected by inflation (brought about by the change from an industrially oriented economy to a service and technical economy), unemployment, and the economy of other countries since many U.S. corporations have become multinational.

The economy in the United States is the largest and most technically advanced in the world with an average real gross domestic product (GDP) per capita of $26,397. (GDP is the value of goods and services earned per capita.) Unemployment in the United States in 1998 was the lowest in 25 years. The U.S. exports include capital goods, cars, consumer goods, food, and machinery. Tourism is important to many state economies. U.S. citizens believe materialism is an important aspect of life. This materialism encourages replacement of possessions. Much of this purchasing is done with credit cards, and credit card debt is very high.

The United States is part of the North American Free Trade Agreement (NAFTA) that is expanding markets, services, and manufacturing between the United States, Canada, and Mexico. (NAFTA is discussed in greater detail in chapter 11.)

The unit of currency is the U.S. dollar.

CANADA

Canada's economy is very strong worldwide. The economy is capitalistic with socialistic controls in the areas of health care and the retirement system. The economy is driven by manufacturing, mining, fishing, farming, and food processing. Canada is the world leader in supplying wood pulp and timber.

Canada has a real GDP per capita of $21,459. (Dollars in text are U.S. dollars unless specified.) Unemployment varies by region, with Quebec having the highest rate of the provinces; in 1996 it was almost 12 percent.

Canada is ranked second in the world in the production of gold and uranium, third in silver, and fourth in copper. Canada exports wheat, barley, oats, and other agricultural products. Tourism is an important source of revenue in recent years. Canada exports more products to the United States than it imports.

In 1993, Canada joined Mexico and the United States in signing NAFTA which provides expanded markets for goods.

The unit of currency is the Canadian dollar.

GREAT BRITAIN

Great Britain, which includes England, Ireland, The Isle of Man, and the Channel Islands, has one of the largest economies in Europe. Great Britain's economy is based on capitalism; however, many sectors of the economy were nationalized or socialized between 1945 and 1980. Since the 1980s, some of the sectors have been privatized, and less regulation of industry has been encouraged. Great Britain is still a major industrial power in the world.

The average annual real GDP per capita is $18,620. Unemployment is about 6 percent. Exports include manufactured goods, crude oil, and consumer goods. Great Britain's natural resources include coal, oil, natural gas, tin, iron ore, and salt.

The pound sterling is the unit of currency.

FRANCE

The French economy which is the world's sixth largest is a free market system and one of the most highly developed in the world. Also, France is the United States' tenth largest trading partner.

The French standard of living is quite high with an average annual real GDP per capita of $20,510. Unemployment is usually high; it was 12 percent in 1997.

France is a major producer of such products as wine, milk, butter, cheese, barley, and wheat. The principal exports are machinery and transport equipment, steel products, and agricultural goods.

The French franc is the unit of currency.

GERMANY

Germany is one of the largest economies in Europe and the third largest in the world behind the United States and Japan. The German economy is based on principles of free enterprise and private ownership; however, government and business work together closely. The former communist system of East Germany is now being changed; emphasis is now on deciding what is best for the economy of the unified Germany (Morrison, Conaway, & Douress, 1997).

Germany has an average annual real GDP per capita of $19,675; however, the figure for the east is almost half of that for the west. Since the unification of Germany, the east is making significant progress in its shift to a market economy. Both regions have a combined unemployment rate of nearly 12 percent (18 percent in the east and 10 percent in the west).

Germany's main exports are cars, steel, aluminum, televisions, and other manufactured goods, making it one of the largest exporters in the world.

The German deutsche mark, one of the strongest in the world, is the unit of currency.

JAPAN

Japan's economy is a capitalistic/free market one based on manufacturing, fishing, and exporting. Except for fish, Japan must import over half of its food supply. Japan must also import most of its raw materials for manufacturing, and over 95 percent of exports are manufactured goods. An early 1990s recession caused businesses to have to lay off or retire employees early.

Japan is one of the world's most productive nations. The average annual real GDP per capita is $21,581. Unemployment is less than 3 percent. Machinery, electronics, engineering, textiles, and chemicals are major industries in Japan. Japan exports much more to the United States than it imports; this trade imbalance is a source of friction between Japan and the United States.

The yen is Japan's unit of currency.

MEXICO

Mexico's economy is dependent on that of other countries. The oil industry, agriculture, tourism, and *maquiladoras* (Mexican assembly facilities often near a major U.S. market) employ most of the working people. The government is attracting foreign investments, privatizing state-owned companies, and deregulating trade in order to combat unemployment, high inflation, and debt.

Mexico is beginning to recover from its worst recession in over 50 years. U.S. companies such as General Motors, Sam's Wholesale Clubs, Hunter Fan, and Blockbuster Video have shown their faith in Mexico's economic stability by investing billions of dollars there. When the economy shrank by 7 percent in 1995, inflation rose to 52 percent, and over a million people lost their jobs. Export industries have been growing since 1993 with the passage of NAFTA with the United States and Canada. NAFTA resulted in lowered trade barriers and led to an increase in maquiladoras. By 1996, Mexico's unemployment rate had dropped to 6 percent. Mining and petroleum are the two most important industries, but tourism is a source of employment for many people. Mexico exports oil, coffee, agricultural products, and engines. Mexico is also a major supplier of marijuana despite costly efforts to curb the drug trade. Real GDP per capita is $7,384.

The unit of currency is the peso.

Political Systems

The **political system** is the governing system of the country and can be based on dictatorship, inherited rights, elected procedures, consensus, or conquest. A person's age, economic expertise, or marital status may be considered when selecting people for political positions in some countries. In other countries, oratory skills and the ability to sway public opinion may be factors. Group members may even select a political leader because they believe the person to have supernatural powers. A description of a few political systems follows.

UNITED STATES

The U.S. political system is a democratic federal government with individual states having designated rights. The president is elected by the electoral college, and other positions are voted on by the people. Congress, which is dominated by the Democratic and Republican parties, has two houses: the 435-seat House of Representatives and the 100-seat Senate. U.S. Americans tend to be very proud of their political system yet may not be well informed about politics. However, U.S. citizens do not like their system to be criticized. The voting age is 18.

> Americans tend to embody what to many is a curious combination of admiration for their political system in general and disdain for its particular operations. They criticize their leaders but do not want foreigners to do so. They think about politics as a separable aspect of life, one they can choose to ignore (Althen, 1988, p. 47).

CANADA

Canada is officially a confederation with parliamentary democracy, a system partially patterned after that of Great Britain and that of the United States. The Parliament includes up to 104 senators who are appointed as well as 301 members of the House of Commons who are elected. The people elect the prime minister who is the leader of the dominant political party in the House of Commons. The central government has power in the areas of national health insurance, trade, the military, and development. The country is divided into provinces; each province controls its region. The Queen of England is represented by a governor-general. The voting age is 18.

GREAT BRITAIN

Great Britain is ruled by a constitutional monarchy with a parliament. Although the monarch (Queen Elizabeth II) is head of state, elected officials govern through Parliament. The main legislative body is the 659-member House of Commons, elected by citizens over the age of 18. The party with the most members in Parliament governs; that party's leader becomes the prime minister who, along with the cabinet, governs as the executive body. The 1,200-member House of Lords makes up Parliament's upper chamber; two-thirds are hereditary members and one-third are appointed life members.

IRAN

Religious and lay leaders make up the Council of Guardians which approves presidential candidates as well as appoints judicial authorities. While the president is the official chief of state, Iran's supreme religious leader often wields ultimate political power. The voting age is 15.

JAPAN

Japan, a constitutional monarchy, has an emperor with no governing power as its head of state. The prime minister who heads the government and his cabinet make up the executive branch. Legislative power rests with the *Diet,* a 252-seat House of Councillors or upper house and the 512-seat House of Representatives or lower house. The 47 prefectures or provinces have governors who are elected by the people. The voting age is 20.

MEXICO

Mexico has a federal government with the president elected by all voters over 18 years of age. The legislation is made up of a 128-seat Senate and a 500-seat Chamber of Deputies. While voting is compulsory, it is not enforced. Though technically autonomous, the 31 states of Mexico are heavily controlled by the federal government in the areas of education, security, and national industries.

SAUDI ARABIA

The Saudi Arabian political system is comprised of 14 regions called governorates. Each governorate is headed by an emir (governor) who answers to the king. The king, who is chief of state, rules with the Council of Ministers. The system of governance issued in 1992 changed the political structure; the new system provides for a consultative council made up of 60 appointed members who serve as advisors to the king and Council of Ministers. After the current crown prince serves, all future kings will be elected by the princes (now numbering over 500); new crown princes will be appointed and subject to dismissal by the king. This new system will eliminate inherited rule.

World Economics

Companies worldwide have become increasingly affected by economic, political, and competitive pressures from companies in other countries. Whereas it is well known that the automobile, steel, textile, and electronic industries face worldwide competition, it may not be as well known that many small- and medium-sized firms are also having to compete in world markets (Nath, 1988).

The United States maintained a substantial technological lead after World War II during the 1950s, 1960s, and the beginning of the 1970s. Today this competitive edge is gone, and the macroeconomy of the world affects the performance of U.S. industry. Many U.S. industries were not prepared for this change in the macroeconomy, and the U.S. government had to provide temporary protection for industries and negotiate with foreign firms to limit their exports to the United States. In addition, the justice department relaxed antitrust rules allowing more joint ventures. When a particular industry is caught in the growing complexity of global economics, many smaller firms, regions, and communities may face adverse economic times. Although U.S. companies are facing intensive foreign competition, the groundwork has been laid to increase productivity, reduce capacity requirements, and increase flexibility making the United States able to compete in the long run.

Although the United States had a trade deficit of $86.6 billion in 1991, direct foreign investment in the United States that year was $66.98 billion (*Economic Indicators,* 1992). During the 1980s, the inflow of foreign funds was due to high interest rates in the

United States, the value of the dollar, stock prices of U.S. firms, and the formation of joint ventures. The influx of foreign investments have made it difficult to distinguish a U.S. firm from a foreign firm. Many companies now have no allegiance to a given nation but are truly multinational firms in their thinking and actions. The actions multinational firms take are in the best interest of their corporation rather than the best interest of their originating country. If a corporation can manufacture a product cheaper in another country, it will do so by closing the current plant and opening a new plant in another country. Many product lines are produced almost entirely outside of the United States today including televisions, camcorders, electronic components, tires, and clothing.

The multinational firm also has to deal with a very complex political environment. A successful domestic firm learns and operates within the existing political situation. A firm that moves into the international environment has to learn how to manage and predict politics in other nations. The multinational firm deals successfully with many diverse and conflicting political environments. Some people are concerned that because of the size, wealth, resources, and knowledge of some multinational companies, they will become political bodies themselves. In many countries, the multinational firm exercises power that parallels the powers of the country's government. For example in the Middle East, corporations within the oil cartels exert power that equals the government's power. Some multinational managers view the world as a single marketplace ignoring national boundaries. The multinational company may well be an agent of change in the future.

Multinational companies also must be concerned with supernationalism, international politics, and international relations of the nations in which they operate. Decrees by such organizations as the United Nations, the European Economic Community, and NAFTA are only a few examples of supernationalism today. Regionalism and economic interdependency are common in international politics, and it is projected that more regional trade agreements will be formed in the near future (Reich, 1991).

Companies also have to be concerned with subnationalism and the strife and political havoc that can result. **Subnationalism** exists when a political body attempts to unite diverse people under one government. With the discarding of communism in Eastern Europe, one of the results has been that subnationals want their own countries and their own government once again (Reich, 1991).

Nationalism, supernationalism, and subnationalism are all active forces multinational companies have to consider because such factors affect the politics and the economics of the areas of the world in which they operate. Although the form and content of the "-isms" may vary from region to region, the possibility of upheaval is something multinational companies must consider. A company must analyze the political environment's positive and negative aspects before expanding into the environment. Other economic differences that may need to be considered before doing business in another nation include chronic high inflation versus low inflation, developed banking systems versus primitive systems, agricultural economy versus an industrial economy versus a technological economy, low employee productivity versus high employee productivity, favorable versus unfavorable balance of payments, and currency exchange rates. To secure additional information related to conducting business in other countries, the following sources are recommended:

The Economist Business Traveller's Guides (Upper Saddle River, NJ: Prentice Hall, 1987) are available for Great Britain, Japan, and the Arabian Peninsula. The guides provide maps of key cities; names of hotels and restaurants; and economic and political background, such as business structure, major industries, and social factors that affect business.

Culturgram '99 (Provo, Utah: Brigham Young University, 1998) provides information for a number of countries. The *Culturgram* covers a variety of topics, such as greetings, visiting, eating, gestures, the people, the lifestyle, land and climate, history, commerce, government, economy, education, transportation, communication, health, and information for the traveler.

Educational Systems

The educational system of a country may be formal, informal, or a combination of the two. People in societies such as the Maoris of New Zealand and the Aleuts of Alaska, still pass on a great deal of information concerning their cultural heritage by word of mouth; people in other societies, as in the United States and Canada, include most of their cultural heritage in textbooks. Other societies have some of both. However it is accomplished, every society has a way of passing on its cultural heritage. **Cultural heritage** is the body of customary beliefs, social forms, material traits, thoughts, speech, and the artistic and intellectual traditions of a society.

There are many different and legitimate ways of thinking; we in the West value one of these ways above all others—the one we call "logic," a linear system that has been with us since Socrates.... We have been taught to think linearly rather than comprehensively.... Given our linear, step-by-step, compartmentalized way of thinking, fostered by the schools and public media, it is impossible for our leaders to consider events comprehensively (Hall, 1976, p. 255).

FORMAL EDUCATION

Because societies are different, formal education varies between countries. The types of educational training in business also vary between and within countries and may include liberal arts, technical training, and apprenticeships. Liberal arts training teaches the humanities and considers learning important in its own right. Technical business training is generally narrowly focused along specialized lines such as marketing, management, finance, economics, accounting, or management information systems. A problem with technical training is that there is very little human training and thought given to the people part of the business process. The apprenticeship program offers students practical experience and theory.

As the population of third world nations receive training beyond the secondary level, these nations become more developed and similar in their use of technologies (Victor, 1992). One of the arguments for NAFTA is that it will help Mexico train and educate its population and will prevent foreign companies from taking advantage of an illiterate workforce. NAFTA requires that a company going into Mexico from the United States or Canada provide the same safety standards within its plants as in its home country and contribute to water treatment facilities and sewage treatment plants.

The costs of such standards make the advantages of a workforce willing to work for low wages deteriorate quickly.

Accessibility to education varies from country to country. Much of Europe operates on a two-track system in which, at approximately the age of 12, children are assigned to a vocational track or a university track. While the United States, Japan, and the Russian states have open access to the educational system for all children, the importance the family places on education, the child's ability, and the quality of the child's teachers all play an important role in how far a child will go in the educational system (Victor, 1992).

How people are expected to learn may be seen as a continuum from very involved in the learning process (much interaction between teachers and students) to little involvement (no interaction between teachers and students). In the Israeli kibbutz, for example, children are expected to react spontaneously, and the classrooms are noisy. Chinese classrooms, on the other hand, are silent due to the reverence paid to knowledge, truth, and wisdom (Samovar & Porter, 1991).

The value of an education, once it is received, varies again from country to country. A description of educational systems in the United States and other selected countries is given in the following sections.

UNITED STATES

In the United States, education for those who are 5 to 16 years of age is compulsory and free. Although not highly competitive up to the secondary level, the U.S. educational system is somewhat competitive at the postsecondary level at such schools as Harvard, Massachusetts Institute of Technology (MIT), and Yale, where intellectual demands may be quite rigorous. Since education is a state's right, competition between and within state educational systems may vary. The literacy rate in the United States is 99 percent. However, variations exist by region, and functional illiteracy exists in the adult population. Even though graduating from certain prestigious institutions of higher learning may help in securing initial corporate positions, what a person does on the job determines the person's career and the companies for which the person will work. University ties then become less important (Victor, 1992).

Anybody can get into college in the United States, according to Malaysian students. Malaysians, remarking on the easy accessibility of American colleges and universities, compared U.S. schools unfavorably to those of the British who once ruled Malaysia and provided the model for their educational system. However, the Malaysians observed, "You Americans put men on the moon, so there must be something right about your system" (Althen, 1988, p. 53).

CANADA

In Canada the provinces are responsible for their educational system; however, all the provinces provide free and compulsory education for persons between the ages of 6 and 16. The literacy rate is 99 percent. In Newfoundland, the primary and secondary education is free but operated by different religious groups. In Quebec, Catholic and Protestant school boards are supported by the government to direct school curricula. While the government subsidizes a university education, students pay for tuition. About 10 percent of the population have university degrees, and other students may complete a two-year technical program or attend a two-year university preparatory program.

GREAT BRITAIN

The educational systems of Great Britain and Canada are similar. Great Britain has free and compulsory education for those between the ages of 5 and 16, and its literacy rate is 99 percent. The General Certificate of Secondary Education Exam is taken at age 16 to allow students to earn the General Certificate. At age 18, after earning the General Certificate of Education, they may attend one of over 40 universities or attend one of the various professional schools. Members of the British upper class tend to go to the elite educational institutions. Although it is possible for someone in the lower classes to attend such schools, primarily those with alumni connections attend the elite educational institutions. Therefore, one's position in society determines one's education.

FRANCE

France's educational system has several unique aspects. Education is free and compulsory for those between the ages of 6 and 16. The literacy rate is 99 percent. The Catholic schools, partially subsidized by the state, enroll 20 percent of the children. Secondary school begins at age 11 and lasts seven years to age 18. Secondary education is offered by lycées and colleges. The lycée is the equivalent of a U.S. junior college. Upon completing secondary school, students take a comprehensive exam for one of the 60 universities. Except for marketing schools, most university training is also free in France.

The French consider the university graduated from to be very important. While positions in business and government are not limited to a few institutions, alumni of the Grandes Écoles are considered more favorably. In France, where one goes to school determines his or her own position in society. The Grandes École and the alumni of the Grandes Écoles control business in France; and to be successful in business dealings in France, one must network through alumni (Victor, 1992).

GERMANY

In Germany's educational system, people must determine their careers early in life. Education is free from kindergarten through the university. School begins with preschool at age 4; however, school is mandatory from age 6 to 15. Literacy is 99 percent in Germany. People of Germany are required to choose between technical training and college training at the age of 13. The entrance exam to universities is very difficult; acceptance into the university can only be gained by passing a rigorous exam after finishing a college preparatory school.

IRAN

Elementary schooling is compulsory for children age 7 to 12 years. About 74 percent go on to secondary school. Following secondary school, students choose to either go into a trade or attend an additional year of preuniversity schooling. Higher education is provided by the University of Tehran and numerous smaller universities. Iran's educational system has only recently included females, but the genders are segregated—a fundamental Islamic principle. In Iran the literacy rate for the adult population is 69 percent.

Religious instruction receives more emphasis than secular education. Studies in science and mathematics are popular when they are available.

JAPAN

The educational system in Japan is very competitive; entrance exams to private schools and universities are rigorous. Competition is keen for acceptance to the prestigious schools since graduating from these schools usually assures the person a position in a top corporation. Japan's literacy rate is 99 percent. Education for persons between the ages of 6 and 15 is generally free and compulsory; after age 15 tuition must be paid. Math and science are stressed.

> In Japan, education is expected to be difficult and sometimes unpleasant.
> The story goes that an elderly Japanese college professor took a student's paper, rolled it, and hit the student over the head with it yelling "It's no good!" When asked why he had done that rather than offering the student some suggestions for improving the paper, he replied, "If I told him what to do, that would be too easy and he would forget. If I make him find it himself, he will always remember" (Dillon, 1990).

In addition, the heavy intellectual demand on the students occurs during the primary and secondary education years rather than in the college years. After high school, the students take a very competitive university entrance exam. Since the university a student graduates from determines the company for which he or she will work, the better the university the better that person's career will be. A close allegiance (i.e., sense of loyalty) is maintained between graduating classes, employee careers, alma mater, and year of graduation.

MEXICO

Education in Mexico has only recently reached the masses. Mexico has compulsory and free education for persons between the ages of 6 and 14. Although the literacy rate reported is 89 percent overall, figures on various subcultures such as the Amerindian vary. Following six years of primary education and three years of secondary education, students choose either a preuniversity education or a technical education program. College entrance exams are quite difficult; only one-third of the students pass the exam. A university degree takes from three to seven years to complete.

SAUDI ARABIA

Saudi Arabia's educational system, including university instruction, is funded by the government. In Saudi Arabia, the literacy rate is increasing and is currently 62 percent. Children age four to six attend kindergarten with boys and girls in the same classroom. After age six, boys and girls attend separate schools. Six years of primary school are followed by three years of intermediate school and three years of secondary school. During the second year of secondary school, the student follows either a science or literary track. Although males and females attend the same university, they have separate classes and are given hours when they can each use such common facilities as the library.

INFORMAL EDUCATION

Countries that do not have an entrenched formal educational infrastructure for all people will tend to have two classes of people: the small wealthy upper class and the lower class in which the majority live in poverty. The wealthy who attend school, and in many cases go to college abroad, will have a very different view of the world and their cultural heritage. The masses will hold a strong allegiance to the cultural past. Depending on the country involved, the literacy level of the masses can vary widely. A person cannot take for granted that everyone can read, has a knowledge of mathematics, or is familiar with technology. Many times what is important in one nation may be very unimportant in another nation (Victor, 1992).

Examples of cultures that place more emphasis on informal rather than formal education include: Gambia, with 37 percent adult literacy, no universities; Mali, with a literacy rate of about 29 percent, their first university currently being built in Bamako; and Bangladesh, with a literacy rate of 35 percent which is higher for men (48 percent) than women (24 percent). Only 3 percent of the people complete three or more years at a university compared to almost 24 percent of U.S. citizens who complete degrees (*Culturgram '98*, 1997).

Marriage and Family Systems

Marriage and family systems are made up of attitudes, beliefs, and practices related to marriage and the family, which are held by people in a particular culture. In order to survive, all societies must procreate. Since human infants must depend on adults for their basic needs, cultures have defined how the young children in their culture will be reared and who is responsible for their care. Consequently, all cultures have devised rules concerning who can marry and have set procedures to be followed when people marry and raise families. Anthropologists have researched and categorized much of this information for us (Ferraro, 1990).

Although many different ways of being a family exist, people will tend to consider their own background first when they consider the concept of family. In many parts of the world, the concept of family is so strong that it is of paramount importance in each person's life. This is particularly true in the Japanese, Chinese, Spanish, African, Arabic, Indian, Italian, and Turkish cultures. In some cultures, the association of the family is so strong that sharing the family wealth with outsiders or protecting outsiders is an unknown concept. In the United States and parts of Europe, work and family life are often combined; business guests are invited to the home. The Japanese, Taiwanese, and people of many Arabic nations, on the other hand, would not invite business guests to their home.

The word *family* has very different connotations around the world. In the United States, the definition of a family encompasses the nuclear family and the extended family. The **nuclear family** consists of the father, mother, and children; the **extended family** consists of grandparents, uncles, aunts, and cousins (Samovar & Porter, 1991).

In many countries, the family may include second-, third-, and fourth-generation relationships. Arab families may have over a hundred close relatives, and in Mexico even godparents are considered family. Family can mean your immediate biological family, or it can mean the entire culture. In some parts of the world, the children are reared and taught communally as in parts of Israel. Each community member takes part in raising and educating each child. The family unit, as the culture views "family," will help to foster individual and/or group dependency (Victor, 1992).

In Italy, the most important affiliation is to the family which is also responsible for a large number of self-employed people and small businesses. A necessity of Italian life is an affiliation with at least one prime interest group (such as a political party or trade union) in order to live and work.

The ability to be hired and to work in many countries depends on your relatives. Nepotism and favoritism are considered a way of life. However, in U.S. corporations nepotism and favoritism are viewed with disfavor because the person being hired under such circumstances is often considered unqualified or corrupt. Corporations may need to adjust their views of family relationships in multinational business relationships in order to be successful (Victor, 1992).

Family systems originally evolved to meet the needs of the society, subsequently, the following forms developed: **polygyny** (or **polygamy**), one man with many wives; **polyandry,** one woman with many husbands; **monogamy,** one husband and one wife; and **serial monogamy,** a number of different monogamous marriages (Dodd, 1987).

Many Arabic countries and followers of Islam practice polygyny. The Arabic countries currently have the highest birth rate in the world; however, they also have a very small population base. In the United Arab Emirants (UAE), 80 percent of the people who live there are not Arabian. The UAE has had to import people to fill the jobs that are available; therefore, the government encourages men to have large families and many wives. Polyandry would help reduce the birth rate and has been practiced by many of the Polynesian nations. Monogamy is practiced in North America, South America, the Orient, Europe, and parts of Africa. Serial monogamy is practiced where people are able to remarry after divorce or death of a spouse; the United States practices serial monogamy.

Another aspect of family is establishing who is in control or who plays the role of the authority figure. Families can be **patriarchal** (father-oriented) or **matriarchal** (mother-oriented). Inheritance rights and the naming of children help to determine whether a society is matriarchal or patriarchal (Dodd, 1987).

FIGURE 2.1 Family Systems

FIGURE 2.2 Family Authority Figures

Jewish families are matriarchal due to the Judaic code of inheritance through the mother although the father's name is used. Christians and followers of Islam tend to be patriarchal, and the father's name is given to the children. Spanish women, however, maintain their maiden name by hyphenating it to their married name, but the Spanish culture is patriarchal. Many professional women in the United States are now retaining their maiden name when they marry.

A brief description of marriage and family customs in the United States and in other selected countries follows to give you an idea of how family structure and customs vary from culture to culture.

UNITED STATES

Dating in the United States begins as early as age 13. Premarital sex is common, and many couples choose to live together prior to or in place of marriage. The average age for marriage is 26 for men and 24 for women. In the United States you will find a nuclear family, which consists of either monogamous or serial monogamous parents or single-parent families. The nuclear family generally maintains a close relationship with members of the extended family. The traditional family includes a mother, father, and one or more children. However, one out of three children is born out of wedlock. Some women are choosing not to marry the father of the baby or are using sperm banks if they prefer to be solely responsible for a child. Almost half of all women work which affects decisions on family size. Many older members of the extended family live in private or government institutions rather than with their immediate families, partly due to the mobility of the family and changes in living conditions.

CANADA

The Canadian family system is similar to that of the United States in that dating begins before age 16. Canada is generally a patriarchal society. Frequently, both parents work outside the home. The divorce rate is low in Canada, which results in a predominantly monogamous society (*Culturgram '98*, 1997).

FRANCE

France tends to have an elitist attitude toward the family. Dating begins around age 15. In France, social class, wealth, and educational level are important when choosing a spouse (Harris & Moran, 1996). The nuclear family is common in France; however, living together before or instead of marrying is also common. The average family has only one child, with many couples choosing to have no children. Many of the French have moved away from their extended family in order to work or to study.

GERMANY

The German family system includes dating which is dutch treat (each gender pays his or her own expenses). Marriage occurs generally after the age of 20, but Germans usually believe they must have some financial security prior to marriage. Living together before marriage is not unusual. The family is generally patriarchal, and one to two children are the norm. In the former East Germany, it is common for both parents to work, while in what was West Germany, it is less common for both parents to work.

JAPAN

In Japan, the family system is quite different. In the past, most marriages were arranged; now, however, many of the people from Western cultures choose their own spouse. Dating begins around age 15, but the average age for marriage is 27 for men and a little younger for women. Men feel they must be financially secure before marriage and they assume financial responsibility for the wedding. The family includes the extended family and has a strong sense of obligation and responsibility. One's actions reflect strongly on the family as well as on one's self. While the father is the breadwinner, the mother runs the household. In the past, it has been considered improper for women to work outside the home; however, many of the younger women have chosen to have a career rather than marriage and a family. Families tend to be small with fewer than three children. Having a male heir is important in Japan as well as in most other Asian countries. The divorce rate is very low, and the marriages are monogamous.

MEXICO

In the Mexican family system, dating is allowed; however, a boy often meets the girl at a prearranged place rather than picking her up at her home. Marriage follows the customary Catholic traditions. The Mexican family tends to be large by U.S. standards (more than three children), and family unity is very important. The divorce rate is low, so monogamous families are the norm. In the rural areas, particularly, households include members of the extended family. While the family is patriarchal, the mother runs the household. Family responsibilities take precedence over all other responsibilities.

SAUDI ARABIA

The family system in Saudi Arabia is very different from that of the United States. Saudi Arabian marriages are arranged, although a minority of men and women are being allowed to choose their mates. Because of the separation of the genders, there is no dating. Islamic law allows a man to have four wives with the wives' permission; however, most Saudi men have only one wife. Most Saudi families live with extended families and have strong patriarchal authority but are matriarchal in the home. The family is the most important part of a Saudi's life. Women and men are separated in most aspects of life. Women do not socialize in public with men but are always accompanied by a male relative when in public. Women do not interact with men outside their family and may not drive a car or ride a bicycle.

Social Hierarchies and Interaction

Although human behavior is never totally controlled, society, through social order, limits its randomness. People learn through enculturation what is and is not proper social behavior. Generally the learning is introduced by the older family members to the younger family members; however, most of the social ideals arise in society in general and not in the family directly. Many times there are family and nonfamily orientations. A good starting point to learn about another culture is from children's literature, television shows, and games that are enjoyed by the culture. The social structure of a society tends to be enduring and is shared by the members of the culture. Social values are changed very slowly when dealing with an entire society. What are considered proper **social hierarchies** and **social interactions** are being tested as business becomes multinational and as people meet and deal with other ways of living. We either adapt or remain restricted in the cocoon of our own culture. If you are to communicate successfully in a multicultural environment, you will have to learn that different is simply different, not better or worse. The actions of the people of other cultures are correct for them.

In examining social hierarchies and social interactions, consideration must be given to the five sets of structures into which society can be divided: social reciprocity, group membership, intermediaries, formality, and property (Condon & Yousef, 1975).

Social reciprocity refers to the way formal and informal communications are handled. Someone who believes in independent social reciprocity tries to avoid commitment; under symmetrical-obligatory social reciprocity, people have an equal obligation; and under complementary-obligatory social reciprocity, people are forever indebted to others.

Group membership has two extremes: People can belong to many groups or very few groups, and there is also a middle ground between the two. People belonging to many groups generally are not strongly associated with any of them and do not want to give up their personal freedom; likewise, people who belong to few groups for a long time may tend to subordinate themselves to the group. The people in between try to balance group affiliation and personal freedom.

The use of intermediaries in societies can tell you a great deal about the makeup of the society. **Intermediaries** are people who act as go-betweens with other people. If no use is made of intermediaries, you will have a great deal of directness and independence. If intermediaries are always used, you will have a society that dislikes confrontation and is very group oriented. In the middle are the people who can sometimes be direct and sometimes want someone else to intervene.

Formality is the degree of preciseness, regularity, or conformity expected within the society. Formality is particularly troublesome between cultures because even the most formal culture also has some informality, and the most informal culture has some formality. Selective formality, which is the middle ground between the two extremes, can be very different in various cultures.

The last structure is **property** which is something that is or may be possessed. Property can be viewed as private, utilitarian, or community. U.S. Americans think of property as an extension of the self; Mexicans think of property ownership in relation to feelings and need. In the past, communist countries had community property. Native Americans also believed that land was community property. Even in private property cultures, there will be common property such as parks, land grant colleges, and hospitals. The three values of the five structures discussed are capitalism, socialism, and communism.

True equality does not exist in any country in the world due to power, wealth, or privilege that exist in all countries. While the United States considers equal opportunity important, the differences in children's lives make it clear that not all will grow up with an equal opportunity to achieve wealth or position. Human beings do not choose their cultural interaction and social hierarchial foundations; they are born or adopted into them. Hierarchial divisions can be social classes, gender, ethnic groups, castes, or tribes. Although aristocracies or monarchies may not be active in many nations in the world, they still form a very large network. Through this network, many members are still in positions to influence the public. Religious and legal systems are used in many cultures to enforce class distinctions.

No nation in the world treats women and men equally. The Human Development Index (HDI) was developed by the United Nations Development Program to measure individual purchasing power, health, and education for the population as a whole and for women in particular. Table 2.1 shows the percentage difference in the HDI national score and the score for women (Jandt, 1995).

Although Sweden has the lowest difference between the overall HDI and the women's HDI, its HDI overall is fifth in the rankings. Japan is first in the overall HDI but is seventeenth on the women's HDI scale. Employment and wages are the main differences in industrialized countries whereas health care, nutrition, and education are the main differences in developing countries (Jandt, 1995).

Laws, rules, or religion may preserve or dictate social interaction and the social hierarchies that may evolve within a given culture. All cultures have punishments that are administered when cultural norms are violated. Although punishment is universal, the scope of punishment for the same crime may vary significantly between cultures and include fines, incarceration, or death.

When working interculturally, you may need to adjust your approach to work to match that of the people in the host country. Differences may occur in such areas as speed and efficiency, time, rules of work, kinesics, friendships, work-role expectations, social acceptance, the showing of respect, correct body posture, knowledge, the showing of empathy, role behavior, management interaction, and ambiguity tolerance. By taking the time to learn about the characteristics of a culture, you show your sincerity and friendship. Management skills that consider differences among cultures will solve business problems more successfully. Friendships in many cultures are necessary before any business will ever be conducted. In fact, friendship and work may be interrelated.

TABLE 2.1	Percentage Difference between Overall HDI and Women's HDI in 32 Countries*		
Country	*Percentage*	*Country*	*Percentage*
Sweden	−5.7	Portugal	−21.2
Norway	−9.9	Switzerland	−21.5
Denmark	−9.9	Ireland	−22.2
Finland	−10.0	Japan	−22.4
New Zealand	−10.9	Greece	−23.4
France	−11.0	Myanmar	−23.8
Australia	−12.3	Luxembourg	−24.4
Paraguay	−14.8	Sri Lanka	−24.7
The Netherlands	−14.8	Swaziland	−24.9
Great Britain	−15.1	Philippines	−25.2
Belgium	−15.1	Costa Rica	−25.8
United States	−15.6	Cyprus	−26.3
Canada	−16.9	Singapore	−31.1
Italy	−17.3	Hong Kong	−32.3
Austria	−17.9	Kenya	−34.7
Germany	−19.7	South Korea	−36.4

Source: From United Nations Development Program, *Human Development Report,* 1993 (In Jandt, 1995).

Examples of social hierarchies and interactions for the United States and other selected cultures follow.

UNITED STATES

In the United States, people like to believe that they can rise above cultural bias and change their status; yet at the same time many find security in the social hierarchy and social interaction patterns into which they were born. In the United States, wealth is related to social class. However, the U.S. society still admires achievement above all else. People who invent, discover, or "make it on their own" are widely admired. U.S. Americans enjoy socializing and are frank and outspoken; they will discuss most subjects except personal issues. U.S. Americans tend to be informal, belong to very few groups, do not use intermediaries, and are possessive of property (Althen, 1988).

CANADA

Canadians view their society as separate from the United States and do not like being considered as U.S. people living in Canada. French-Canadians are very proud of the cultural heritage that they maintain. Canadians in general are very proud to be Canadian and they take special pride in their own province. Canadians are generally more formal than U.S. residents but are very friendly and kind to guests. They tend to be very social but conservative, and etiquette is important.

CHINA

Family is very important to the Chinese and comes before the individual. Sons are valued more than daughters. With the family planning campaign of 1971 (of one child per urban family and two per rural family), the Chinese no longer have large families to care for them in their old age, and the only children are very spoiled. Even with this effort, in 1992 there were 24 million children born, approximately the total population of Canada. China has the lowest ratio of women to men (Jandt, 1995).

JAPAN

The Japanese are very concerned with social reciprocity which can be seen in the importance of gift giving. Gift giving signifies respect for the recipient. The peak of gift giving is at the end of each year. Formality and conformity in life, work, and family are all very important aspects of the social hierarchy of the society. The Japanese are very social and are devoted to their families, employers, and superiors. Friendships are not made easily but are made for life and not taken lightly. The Japanese like to use intermediaries particularly when trying to resolve negative situations in order to help everyone save face. Property is very important but very expensive since so many people live in such small geographic areas (Condon & Yousef, 1975; *Culturgram '98*, 1997).

The Japanese have one or two children. The Japanese women have long served the men in their lives. The role of the women in Japan is changing although sexual harassment is still normal in the workplace. With increasing education and economic opportunities, Japanese women are postponing marriage. The birth rate is currently 1.53 children. Once a woman marries, she basically has to stay home. The Japanese wife handles the family's finances (Jandt, 1995).

Japanese men have a saying: To have the best of all worlds is to have an American house, eat Chinese food, and have a Japanese wife. To have the worst of all worlds is to have a Japanese house, eat British food, and have an American wife.

MEXICO

Mexicans view social reciprocity as very important. Mexicans are good hosts and place great importance on being a good employer, a good employee, and a good friend. People of Mexico involve religion in their social interactions. The majority of Mexicans are Catholic and take their religion and religious celebrations very seriously. Much of their life is informal with the exception of their religion. Their attitude toward property is an aspect of their social attitude of sharing. Property is viewed in a utilitarian way as belonging to those who need it. A possessive attitude toward property is infrequent (Condon & Yousef, 1975).

SAUDI ARABIA

For the people of Saudi Arabia, life moves at a slower pace than that of Western nations. Social reciprocity is very important. Although the people are very friendly and hospitable, their personal privacy is important. The social hierarchy has been maintained by formal and conservative traditions. Saudi Arabians are devoted to their extended family and to their religion. The Islamic religion is their way of life (*Culturgram '98*, 1997).

The women in Saudi Arabia are considered equal to men; however, the Muslim's definition of equality and sameness are different. A woman can obtain an education, work, and own property. A woman who works serves other Saudi women only and may not speak to men other than blood kin. Her husband is responsible for her needs as his wife and mother of his children; however, if she divorces her husband or he divorces her the children remain in his custody. Children descend only from their father's paternal family. The family patriarch makes all the decisions in the family. A woman may not go out without a male relative or the husband's written permission, and no women may drive cars or ride bicycles. The dress code only pertains to appearances while in public and many wear jeans and haute couture under the *abaya* or *chador*. The abaya and veil (the covering that Islamic women wear) are a physical display of honor, dignity, and chastity (Jandt, 1995).

Terms

- Cultural heritage
- Cultural universals
- Economic system
- Extended family
- Exports
- Formality
- Imports
- Intermediaries

- Marriage and family system
- Matriarchal
- Monogamy
- Nuclear family
- Patriarchal
- Political system
- Polyandry
- Polygamy

- Property
- Serial monogamy
- Social hierarchies
- Social interaction
- Social reciprocity
- Subnationalism
- Supernationalism

EXERCISE 2.1

Instructions: Match the currencies on the right with their country on the left.

___ 1. Australia

___ 2. Great Britain

___ 3. France

___ 4. Hong Kong

___ 5. Japan

___ 6. Mexico

___ 7. Norway

___ 8. Russian States

___ 9. Taiwan

___ 10. Germany

A. dollar

B. drachma

C. franc

D. krone

E. lira

F. mark

G. peso

H. pound

I. ruble

J. rupee

K. yen

L. yuan

EXERCISE 2.2

Instructions: Circle the T for true and the F for false.

1. T F   Most countries have similar economic systems.
2. T F   No true universal governmental body exists.
3. T F   Political systems in England and Japan are dissimilar.
4. T F   Multinational companies are responsible only to the country in which they are based.
5. T F   Enculturation means learning about other cultures.
6. T F   Educational systems throughout the world vary widely.
7. T F   The university from which a person graduates is very important in France.
8. T F   A major family system in the United States is serial monogamy.
9. T F   Islamic believers tend to be matriarchal.
10. T F   Social reciprocity is relatively unimportant in Japan and Saudi Arabia.

Questions and Cases for Discussion

1. Define universal cultural systems and identify them.
2. Why do societies develop economic/political systems and what do these systems do for the members of a society?
3. Compare the economic systems of Japan and Canada.
4. Compare the political systems of Great Britain and Mexico.
5. Discuss differences in educational systems in various cultures.
6. Explain how marriage and family systems in the United States are different from those of other cultures.
7. How important is social reciprocity in Mexico, Japan, and Saudi Arabia?
8. What are intermediaries? In which countries are intermediaries used?
9. Explain cultural variations in the way property is viewed.
10. Explain what is meant by equality in the United States. Does the term mean the same thing in other countries?

CASE 1

Education is offered to everyone in the United States; however, 25 percent of the people who enter school as five-year-olds never graduate from high school. In Japan the high school graduation rate is 95 percent, and in Germany and Great Britain it is equally as high. However, in countries such as Mexico and third-world nations many people never complete the equivalent of a high school education. The percentage of people who attend college after high school varies from country to country as described in the text. Currently many nations are sending a large number of students to U.S. universities, and many foreign companies are giving grants to the United States "think tank" universities (such as MIT, Stanford, Chicago, and Harvard).

1. In light of this information, what do you see as the future role of U.S. universities in the world?

2. Is the fact that 25 percent of the U.S. population does not graduate from high school important in light of what is happening in other countries in the world?
3. Is the fact that so many foreign students are attending college in the United States positive or negative? What do you see as the long-term effects?

CASE 2

Many Korean children and children of other nationalities have been adopted by U.S. Americans. Generally these children were reared in homes where the parents were not of the nationality of the adopted child. Sometimes after the children become adults they return to their native country to learn about people of their own ethnic heritage. Would language differences pose a problem? What cultural problems would they have?

CASE 3

Many of the former communist countries are trying to change their economic and political systems. Examples are the Russian states, Czechoslovakia, and the former East Germany. What cultural changes will be necessitated in their educational system in order to have a smooth transition?

CASE 4

Since more and more firms are becoming multinational and must deal with a number of monetary systems, what is the feasibility of developing one monetary system to do away with exchange rates? Do multinational firms have the ability to help bring about a world currency?

Activities

1. Interivew an Asian or Latin American student to learn about the educational system in his/her country and the relationship between educational training and their positions in business and society. Be prepared to share your findings with the class.
2. Research the economic system of a country you would like to visit. Prepare a one-page summary for class discussion and submission to the instructor.
3. Research the marriage and family system of a country of your choice. In a one-page written summary, make comparisons with the family life-style in the United States.
4. Prepare a list of countries with patriarchal family systems and those with matriarchal family systems in order to gain a better understanding of the role of women in various cultures.
5. List at least two countries that practice the following family systems: polygyny, polyandry, monogamy, and serial monogamy.

References

Althen, G. (1988). *American ways*. Yarmouth, MA: Intercultural Press.

Condon, J. C., & Yousef, F. (1975). *An introduction to intercultural communication*. New York: Macmillan Publishing Company.

Culturgram '98. (1997). Provo, UT: Brigham Young University, Publications Division of the David M. Kennedy Center for International Studies.

Dodd, C. H. (1987). *Dynamics of intercultural communication*. Dubuque, IA: Wm. C. Brown Publishers.

Dillon, L. S. (1990, May). The occidental tourist. *Training & Development Journal*, 72–80.

Economic Indicators. (1992, September). Prepared for the Joint Economic Committee by the Council of Economic Advisers. Washington, DC: U.S. Government Printing Office.

Ferraro, G. P. (1990). *The cultural dimension of international business.* Upper Saddle River, NJ: Prentice Hall.

Hall, E. T. (1976). *Beyond Culture.* New York: Anchor Books.

Harris, P. R., & Moran, R. T. (1996). *Managing cultural differences* (4th ed.). Houston: Gulf Publishing Company.

Jandt, F. R. (1995). *Intercultural communication.* Thousand Oaks, CA: Sage Publications.

Morrison, T., Conaway, W. A., & Douress, J. J. (1997). *Dun & Bradstreet's guide to doing business around the world.* Upper Saddle River, NJ: Prentice Hall.

Nath, R., (Ed.) (1988). *Comparative management.* New York: Ballinger Publishing Company.

Reich, R. B. (1991). *The work of nations: Preparing ourselves for 21st century capitalism.* New York: Alfred A. Knopf.

Samovar, L. A., & Porter, R. E. (1991). *Intercultural communication: A reader.* Belmont, CA: Wadsworth Publishing Company.

Victor, D. A. (1992). *International business communication.* New York: HarperCollins Publishers, Inc.

CHAPTER

Contrasting Cultural Values

Objectives
Upon completion of this chapter, you will:

■ appreciate the role that values play in communicating effectively with persons from other cultures.

■ understand differences in word meanings among cultures.

■ learn how attribution and perception play a role in cultural values.

■ appreciate attitude differences toward men and women in various cultures.

■ understand how attitudes toward work and ethics vary with the culture.

■ learn how religious influences impact cultural values.

■ understand how individualism and collectivism play a role in cultural values.

Values, according to Thiederman (1991), form the core of a culture. **Values** are social principles, goals, or standards accepted by persons in a culture. They establish what is proper and improper behavior as well as what is normal and abnormal behavior. Values are learned by contacts with family members, teachers, and religious leaders. What people hear, read, and see on television influences their value system.

People in various cultures have different attitudes toward women, ethical standards, and work. Semantic differences and attributions affect cultural values as do religious influences. Since the U.S. workplace is becoming increasingly diverse culturally, managers need to be aware of the values of all workers. They will then understand what motivates people of different cultures and will be able to deal effectively with problem situations.

Some values held by people in the United States are not shared by people in other cultures. In his book, *American Ways,* Althen (1988) identifies a number of U.S. values

43

and assumptions including equality, informality, individualism, directness, and attitude toward the future, time, and work.

People in the United States may claim that all persons are equal and that no person is superior to another simply because of wealth, education, or social status. In reality, subtle distinctions are made within a group to acknowledge status differences, many of which are nonverbal. Because of this belief in equality, U.S. Americans are uncomfortable with displays of respect, such as bowing, that are common in some cultures. In the United States, men and women are considered equal. Although inequalities do exist, many women hold positions of power and influence in education, government, and industry.

People in the United States also are rather informal when compared to people of other cultures. They often dress more casually. It is not unusual to see the president of the United States in jeans or jogging attire. The posture of U.S. people is often informal; assuming a slouched stance or putting feet on a desk or chair is not uncommon. Their speech is also rather informal; they often address people they hardly know by their first names.

Another quality that people in the United States value is directness. They prefer that people be open and get to the point. Such sayings as "What is the bottom line?" and "Put your cards on the table" illustrate the importance placed on directness in the United States. In some cultures such as those found in Asia, people do not value directness. They will not reveal their emotions using the same nonverbal cues as westerners; therefore, people in the United States have difficulty reading Asian body language (the reverse is also true). U.S. Americans generally believe that honesty and truthfulness are important unless the truth would hurt a person's feelings or unless they did not know the person well enough to be candid. They are less concerned than people in Asia with saving face.

People in the United States value time and study time-management principles to learn how to get more work done in a day. They are concerned with punctuality for work and appointments, and they study ways of working more efficiently. The success of the fast-food industry in the United States is directly related to eating on the run rather than wasting time by lingering over meals. In other parts of the world, mealtime is very leisurely. In many South American countries, businesses close for two hours in the middle of the day for a long meal and a siesta (rest), but people often work into the evening.

The importance of time to different cultures is directly related to religious dogma. The Puritans who came to the United States were very concerned with wasting time and with the future, more than the past or present. Native Americans, African Americans, Latin Americans, and Asians, however, come from a different combination of religious biases and cultural differences and are occupied with the past and present. One of the reasons Deming's theory of management was adopted in Japan before it was in the United States was the amount of time it takes to formulate group decisions as opposed to individual decisions. The Japanese have always been team oriented; therefore, it was easier for Deming to sell them on his theories.

People in the United States do not place as great an emphasis on history as do people of many other cultures; they look to the future and consider change to be desirable, particularly if they are Christians. In the Asian, Arabic, and Latin cultures, the past is revered. Their future is determined by fate or, in some religions, by the Almighty. People of the Islamic faith believe that if they work very hard and pray, everything will be as Allah desires. They simply try to live in harmony with whatever changes occur, rather than seeking change as is true in the U.S. culture. The following list contrasts the priority of cultural values of U.S. Americans, Japanese, and Arabs [("1." represents the most important value); Elashmawi & Harris, 1993, p. 63].

U.S. AMERICANS	JAPANESE	ARABS
1. Freedom	1. Belonging	1. Family security
2. Independence	2. Group harmony	2. Family harmony
3. Self-reliance	3. Collectiveness	3. Parental guidance
4. Equality	4. Age/seniority	4. Age
5. Individualism	5. Group consensus	5. Authority
6. Competition	6. Cooperation	6. Compromise
7. Efficiency	7. Quality	7. Devotion
8. Time	8. Patience	8. Patience
9. Directness	9. Indirectness	9. Indirectness
10. Openness	10. Go-between	10. Hospitality

In the United States, companies are having to recognize the differences in values that exist in their workforces as the number of Asians, Arabs, and Latin Americans increases.

Semantic Differences

Semantics is the study of the meaning of words; it involves the way behavior is influenced by the use of words and nonverbal methods to communicate.

Words in the English language often have multiple meanings, some of which are contradictory. The word *sanction,* for example, may mean either to restrict a particular activity or to authorize it. Semantic differences are compounded when interacting with people of other cultures. Even when both speak the same language, a word may have a different meaning and implication in another culture.

Although England and Australia are English-speaking countries, words are often used in a different way in these countries from the way they are used in the United States. The word *homely,* for example, means plain in the United States while in England, it means friendly, warm, and comfortable. To the English, a *sharp* person is one who is devious and lacking in principles rather than one who is quick, smart, and clever which is its meaning in the United States. The expression *quite good* has a different meaning to the English than to U.S. Americans. The English interpretation is less than good, whereas the U.S. meaning is very good. Australian English also holds some surprises for people in the United States. In Australia, you would hear such terms as *bloke* for man, *lollies* for candy, and *sandshoes* for sneakers.

A misunderstanding over the meaning of one word during an important meeting in World War II caused quite an argument between U.S. Americans and the British. The problem was caused by the British interpretation of the phrase "to table an item," which to them means to bring up the item for immediate consideration. The U.S. interpretation, on the other hand, was to shelve or postpone the subject (Axtell, 1991).

Language problems are compounded when conducting business with persons in non-English-speaking countries. Differences in the meanings of words are often lost in translation. Sometimes a word has no real counterpart in the other language, and the translator must select a word that he or she believes is similar to the meaning intended.

Semantic differences can be seen in the meaning of the word "stop" in the United States and in South America. A U.S. American while traveling in Bolivia observed that drivers rarely stopped at the red octagonal sign with the word "alto," the Spanish word for "stop." A local Bolivian explained that in that country, the stop sign is more a recommendation than a traffic law.

Brand names for U.S. products have caused problems when translated into another language. For example, the Spanish translation of Ford Motor Company's *Fiera* truck means ugly old woman, not a very flattering name for a vehicle. U.S. firms have had to exercise greater care when introducing products in non-English-speaking countries because of marketing errors made in the past when product names and slogans were translated into another language (Axtell, 1991).

When conversing with people of other cultures, be sure your meaning is clear by avoiding slang, contractions, and idioms; by paraphrasing what the other person has said; and by speaking slowly and distinctly.

Attribution and Perception

Attribution, or the ability to look at social behavior from another culture's view, can cause communication problems since known experiences from your own culture are used in explaining unknown behaviors of those in another culture. **Perception,** the learned meaning of sensory images, may involve learning a new reaction to an old learned stimulus.

To lessen anxiety when communicating with someone of an unfamiliar culture, reducing uncertainty and increasing predictability about your own and the other person's behavior are important. The **uncertainty-reduction theory,** according to Gudykunst and Ting-Toomey (1988, p. 22), "involves the creation of proactive predictions and retroactive explanations about our own and others' behavior, beliefs, and attitudes." People who have high uncertainty avoidance prefer to specialize, avoid conflict, want clear instructions, and do not want competition. Some ways to reduce uncertainty about other people are to observe them, try to get information about them, and interact with them.

Uncertainty avoidance can be used to determine whether people who have different convictions can be personal friends. People from countries with weak uncertainty avoidance are more likely to remain close friends in spite of differing opinions while those in countries with strong uncertainty avoidance would be less likely to remain friendly following open disagreements. Some key differences between weak and strong uncertainty avoidance societies follow (Hofstede, 1991).

Weak Uncertainty Avoidance	*Strong Uncertainty Avoidance*
Citizen protest is acceptable.	Citizen protest should be repressed.
Civil servants are positive toward the political process.	Civil servants are negative toward the political process.
Positive attitudes toward young people are evident.	Negative attitudes toward young people are evident.
One group's truth should not be imposed on others.	There is only one truth—ours.
Human rights: nobody should be persecuted for their beliefs.	Religious, political, and ideological fundamentalism and intolerance are practiced.
Scientific opponents can be personal friends.	Scientific opponents cannot be personal friends.

Source: From *Cultures and Organizations* (p. 134), by G. Hofstede, 1991, London: McGraw-Hill Book Company. Copyright © 1991. Reproduced with permission of McGraw-Hill.

Attribution training involves making people aware of their own cultural context and how it differs from the cultural context of the country to which they will travel. Measuring employees' attributional confidence, then training them to be cognizant of their personal differences with the assignment culture, is often used to prepare employees for overseas assignments. The training is accomplished by forcing participants to evaluate behavior from the viewpoint of people of the host nation. This is done by providing scenarios that summarize problems they may encounter while living in another country. Participants are then asked to select the one response considered correct from the viewpoint of the native of the country being studied. With feedback from the trainer and exposure to numerous situations, participants are better able to understand cultural variations in behavior and to look at the situation from the other culture's viewpoint.

Attitudes Toward Women

Attitudes are our likes (or affinities) and dislikes (or aversions) to certain people, objects, or situations. Attitudes are rooted in our behavior and in our emotions (Weaver, 1998). Sometimes our personal attitudes may differ from those of the macroculture or dominant culture. For example, a U.S. American male may have the attitude that women belong in the home and not in the workplace. The attitude of the macroculture, however, is that women may choose to work or to stay home and take care of the family.

A society's attitudes toward women are influenced by cultural roots. In some countries such as the United States, women are supposed to have the same rights as men. In other countries such as Libya and Kenya, women are considered subordinate to men. In fundamental Islamic cultures, women are allowed to work only with other women.

This attitude toward a woman's role in society is carried into the workplace. In the United States, gender differences in the workplace are deemphasized. The women's rights movement has worked for such legislation as fair employment laws requiring that men and women must be given equal pay for equal work. Even though differences in pay still exist, treating men and women equally is expected in U.S. firms. The acceptance of women at higher levels of responsibility is evidenced by the appointments of Sandra

Day O'Connor and Ruth Bader Ginsburg to the U.S. Supreme Court and of Janet Reno as U.S. Attorney General. The number of women appointees to top national and state level governmental positions continues to increase. In large corporations, the number of women executives is also on the increase. Women-owned businesses are making a significant economic contribution. In fact, 6.5 million businesses owned by women generate more jobs than do Fortune 500 firms (Aburdene & Naisbitt, 1992).

Naisbitt and Aburdene (1990) in their book, *Megatrends 2000,* have identified the 1990s as the decade of women leadership positions in business. They point out that during the past two decades, women in the United States have taken two-thirds of the new jobs created and that women are starting new businesses at twice the rate of men. Compared to this U.S. trend, in France one-fifth of small businesses are owned by women while in Canada the rate is one-third. In Great Britain, the number of self-employed women has increased three times as fast as the number of self-employed men in the past decade.

Following the collapse of communism and the rise of the Pacific Rim, a New World order is emerging. Projections are that by the year 2000, 90 percent of the world will be ruled by democracies. With democracy comes increased opportunities, especially for women and especially in government and politics. Women are having a more powerful voice as they are assuming an increasing number of leadership positions throughout the world (Aburdene & Naisbitt, 1992). The United States and Canada lead the world in the number of women who have executive positions. North American women have advanced faster and farther than women in any other part of the world. According to research conducted by Adler, an authority on women in international business, women's presence in U.S. management has risen from 14 percent of all managers in 1950 to 42 percent in 1992. However, the number of women executives compared to men is still very low (Axtell, Briggs, Corcoran, & Lamb, 1997). While women represent over half of the population in the world, in no country do they represent half of its corporate managers (Adler & Israeli, 1994). In fact, Axtell, et al. (1997) report that worldwide only 14 percent of top managerial positions in business and only 10 percent of national legislative seats are held by women. In addition to the United States and Canada, most women managers are found in Northern and Western Europe, Australia, and New Zealand (Axtell, et al., 1997).

In many countries of the world, women are just beginning to be accepted at managerial levels. Progress in the advancement of women is slow in the Middle East. In such countries as Saudi Arabia, the Islamic belief in the subordination of women has impeded the progress of working women. Women in Mexican businesses are respected, but they are expected to compete on an equal footing with men and prove their competence. Although Mexican businesses have historically been male dominated, this seems to be changing as many Mexican businesswomen are now enjoying success at managerial levels.

According to a Labor Ministry survey published in May 1993, women in Japan hold only 1.2 percent of senior company positions. Only 6.4 percent of women employed had reached low-management positions, and 2.3 percent had advanced to section chief. Worthy of mention, however, is the fact that the highest ranking person in a Japanese international agency is a woman (Aburdene & Naisbitt, 1992). Even though the 1986 equal employment law clearly bars firms from discriminating against women, no penalties are involved for companies that do not comply with the law. Japanese professional women, therefore, still face many hurdles in their climb up the corporate ladder (Rossman, 1990). With mounting global competitiveness, companies need to examine their current attitudes and practices toward women to ensure that they are making maximum use of their resources and that selection and promotion decisions are based solely on qualifications rather than along gender lines. Fortunately, people in many other countries, including those where women are not treated as equals, are beginning to change their sexist attitudes and are less concerned with gender than performance.

INDICATIONS OF CHANGING ATTITUDES TOWARD WOMEN:

Results of a 1993 survey of female readers of *Asian Business* who were asked to rate the business climate for women in 17 countries determined that Hong Kong was considered the most friendly business environment for women, followed by Singapore, the United States, and Malaysia. Other Asian countries, the Philippines, Taiwan, Thailand, China, Japan, and Indonesia, were all rated more friendly to women in business than were France and Germany (Bosrock, 1994).

Although some women in various countries may have received their first job opportunities from family or political connections, others advanced because of professional qualifications and job competence. Major problems women in the workforce have faced, such as child care and trying to combine a career and family, are common to all cultures. As more women are successful in managing multiple priorities and demands on their time, and as they demonstrate that they are equally effective in high positions in business and politics, it will be easier for women in all cultures to advance to positions of prestige, importance, and responsibility.

"Whatever women do, they must do twice as well as men to be thought half as good. Luckily, that is not difficult" (Charlotte Whitton, late mayor of Ottawa).

Work Attitudes

Attitudes toward work are culturally diverse. The term **work attitudes** refers to how people of a culture view work. **Work,** defined as mental or physical activities directed to socially productive accomplishments, in some societies is associated with economic values, status and class, and cultural values.

People in the United States value work and tend to subscribe to the **work ethic,** which means that hard work is applauded and rewarded, while failure to work is viewed negatively and with disdain. U.S. Americans admire people who work hard and are motivated to achieve; they have an aversion to idleness and prefer people of action to people of ideas. This concept of the United States as a work-ethic society is sometimes referred to as the Protestant ethic which suggests that a person's work (or "calling") comes from God and that people demonstrate their worth to the Almighty and to themselves through their work. Proverbs such as "Blessed is he who has found his work" and "Satan finds mischief for idle hands" express the idea that in the United States, work is virtuous as well as respectable (Ferraro, 1990). Reward systems in many firms are based on an employee's achievement and willingness to work beyond a 40-hour week. U.S. senior-level executives often work 56 hours a week, far more than in many European countries. They take only 14 days of vacation a year, far fewer than in some countries in Europe where people often close businesses for a month to go on vacation (Utroska, 1992). According to the Institut der Deutschen Wirtschaft, a consortium of economists, U.S. workers annually put in almost 300 more hours at work than their West German counterparts and 60 more hours than their Japanese peers. The report published in *Industrie Anzeiger* (Hans J. Heine, International Editor) gave these figures for 1995:

Country	Annual Working Hours
United States	1,896
Switzerland	1,838
Japan	1,832
Spain	1,772
United Kingdom	1,762
France	1,755
Italy	1,720
Eastern Germany	1,705
Western Germany	1,602

This attitude toward work and responsibility to one's job is ingrained from an early age in the United States. Parents teach their children about the American free enterprise system which is based on the premise that you are the master of your own destiny, that you can be anything you want to be if you are willing to try hard enough, and that you will be rewarded for hard work. In contrast, people in the Islamic countries place great importance on the will of Allah and believe that planning for the future would conflict with religious beliefs.

To people in the United States, the job is almost an identification badge. One's personal identity is associated with one's occupation. Evidence of this identification with the job is shown when making introductions. People tend to include the person's occupation or job title along with the name; for example, "I'd like to present Betty Freeman, owner of the Health Hut" or "This is Jay Hunt, president of Southern Express." Success is not only measured by the job title but by the perception of what one earns; the implication is that the high income has probably resulted from the person's willingness to work 12- and 14- hour days, seven days a week.

People in the United States are action oriented; they are often unable to relax because they feel guilty doing nothing. People from other cultures have observed that U.S. Americans even work at relaxing. Television commercials in the United States often depict as leisure, activities that persons in other cultures would consider manual labor such as gardening or washing the car. When they do take vacations, U.S. Americans are inclined to plan what they will do and where they will go so that the entire time is scheduled. Even those who participate in sports for recreation seem to try to make work out of it (Althen, 1988).

> A graduate student from India recounted his first experience at being invited to the home of a U.S. graduate student. When he arrived, his U.S. friend invited him into the house where he was dressing his son while his wife was sweeping the patio. His friend then asked him to help with grilling the chicken outdoors. As the Indian student narrated the story in his Intercultural Communication class, he expressed surprise that his friend and his wife did all their own work. In his country, he had never swept a floor, cooked a meal, or dressed his children.

Unlike people in many other countries, people in the United States consider spending hours visiting as a waste of time and may excuse themselves from a group because they say they need to get back to work. This apparent obsession with work is viewed with both amazement and amusement by persons in other countries.

In much of Europe, attitudes toward work seem to be more relaxed. Many businesses close during the month of August when people go on vacation. Most Europeans do not work on weekends or holidays, as they believe this is time that should be spent with family or engaging in personal activities. The French, in particular, value their vacation time and prefer not to work overtime. They enjoy the longest vacations of any country in the world; French law dictates that employees receive a minimum of five weeks of vacation a year. German companies appear to be moving in this direction as well. In spite of the extended free time, people of both France and Germany are very productive when they work. Australians, too, value free time; they say they work to get a vacation. Australians have the shortest working hours of any country in the world, and they enjoy taking frequent breaks throughout the day (Copeland & Griggs, 1985).

Although many people of the United States receive a two- or three-week vacation, the individual vacation time periods are staggered so that businesses will not be closed for an extended time. It is not unusual for upper level management workers to not take all of their vacation time each year. Because of these attitudes toward work, the culture of the United States is referred to as a "live to work" culture, in contrast to the cultures in countries such as Mexico which are "work to live" cultures.

The attitude of Japanese men toward work is very group oriented, and it plays a major role in their lives. They work Monday through Friday; 18-hour days are not unusual. Because of the long hours, relaxation does not include working around the house. Instead, they relax by watching TV, playing computer games, browsing the Internet, drinking, or joining their friends at the local bar. However, this attitude appears to be changing as they become more westernized.

Attitudes Toward Ethics

Ethical standards are guidelines established to convey what is perceived to be correct or incorrect behavior by most people in a society. According to Ferrell and Gardiner

(1991), ethical conduct "is something judged as proper or acceptable based on some standard of right and wrong" (p. 2). According to Borden (1991), being ethical means keeping your values in balance, and if you compromise your values, you are being unethical. What it comes down to, according to Rabbi Dosick (1993), is that you have to determine what is right and what is wrong. Though there are sometimes penalties for doing both right and wrong, you have to be able to live with yourself and sleep with yourself at night.

Truth, according to U.S. beliefs, is an important aspect of ethical behavior. People in the United States have been taught from childhood to always tell the truth. Parents even tell their children, "If you'll just tell me the truth, I won't punish you." So as adults, U.S. persons subscribe to the saying, "Always tell the truth; let your word be your bond, and let your honor be your word" (Dosick, 1993, p. 35).

> When Abraham Lincoln was a young boy, he was a clerk in a small dry-goods store. One day, after realizing that he had overcharged a customer, he walked two miles through the snow to return the overcharge of one penny (Dosick, 1993).

Personal ethics or moral standards may differ from societal ethics. Your own standards of what is right and wrong may be more stringent than those of your society as a whole. Problems may occur when the reverse is true: that is, when your ethical standards are lower than those considered acceptable by society. Of course, your ethical standards must meet the minimum level of behavior identified by law as acceptable.

Although many U.S. Americans are inclined to believe that their standards of business ethics are shared by other countries, in reality, standards of business ethics are not universal. For example, the Islamic standard of ethics is based on participating in religious ceremonies, adhering to codes of sexual behavior, and honoring one's parents. This definition or interpretation of ethical standards is not shared by U.S. Americans. Another dimension of business ethics relates to what is commonly referred to as using "backdoor connections" for conducting business; using such connections is common, for example, in South Africa and Nigeria as well as in the People's Republic of China. In fact, the Chinese use informal relationships in allocating resources and making decisions. Another ethical problem U.S. firms face when conducting business abroad is the unorthodox accounting and taxation practices used in some countries. In such countries as Brazil and Spain, keeping three sets of accounting books as a means of avoiding taxes is common. These practices violate not only the ethical standards of U.S. businesspersons, but violate the law in the United States as well. Another ethical problem encountered by U.S. firms doing business in other countries is the nonsanctity of legal contracts. To U.S. businesspersons, "a card laid is a card played." To Chinese, Koreans, and Japanese who emphasize long-term relationships, renegotiation is common. As a result, U.S. businesspeople are never sure when they have a final agreement. People of the United States also question the ethicality of certain activities such as taking a potential customer on a yachting trip or on a weekend gambling outing, clearly intended to influence buying decisions (Engholm & Rowland, 1996).

An increased concern for ethics has been seen in the United States because of the blatant misconduct of persons in government and industry. Religious leaders have been convicted of fraud, and Wall Street moguls have been found guilty of insider trading. Naisbitt and Aburdene (1990) forsee that all countries will have to give increased attention to values and ethics in their schools so that the next generation will be better prepared to make appropriate decisions involving ethical behavior.

Ethical standards should be addressed when conducting business with persons of other cultures especially those whose standards of ethical behavior differ markedly from our own. While we carry our frame of reference and value system with us when conducting business internationally, we should also be aware that *our* values may differ from those of other countries. For example in the United States, bribery and graft are illegal. In some of the Latin American countries, however, using gifts to assure success in sealing an agreement is an accepted way of conducting business. (Bribery is discussed in more detail in chapters 9 and 12).

Religious Influences

Religious influences have an impact on when and how business is conducted in international settings.

In some cultures, such as those of North and South America, Australia, and Europe, lifestyle and religion are separate. In much of northern Africa and southern Asia, no distinction is made between lifestyle and religion, since religion is a lifestyle. Businesspersons in these countries may seek the advice of religious leaders on business matters.

The United States has never had an official state church; religious observances rarely interfere with business. Although business is not conducted on such religious holidays as Christmas, no one feels obligated to participate in religious ceremonies or observe religious customs. Religion is a personal matter in the United States. Members of one family often hold different beliefs and belong to different denominations.

The United States subscribes to the doctrine of "separation of church and state." According to this doctrine, the government does not lend official support to any particular religion and may not interfere with a person's practicing any religion. About 24 percent of the population is Roman Catholic; the largest Protestant groups are Baptists, Methodists, and Lutherans (*Culturgram '98, U.S.A.*, 1997). Non-Christian groups include Jews and Muslims.

Some countries have officially recognized religions and participate in religious rituals that would affect business encounters. In Saudi Arabia, for example, Islam is the official religion. Muslims observe the ritual of stopping work five times a day to pray. Meetings with persons in Saudi Arabia should be sufficiently flexible to allow for this daily ritual which is a way of life for Muslims. Conducting business during the month of Ramadan (currently during February) would not be recommended as Muslims are required to fast from dawn to sunset. Because of the impact of religion on all aspects of life in Islamic countries, learning about religious rituals and beliefs prior to conducting business there is advisable. In contrast to Saudi Arabia, religion is not a significant part of life in China. While the ideology of communism in China endorses atheism, citizens may choose to believe in a religion or not. The majority of Chinese people practice a combination of Confucianism, Taoism, and Buddhism (Jandt, 1995).

A newly admitted patient became agitated about the arrangement of his hospital room. He kept saying that his bed should be on the opposite wall. The nurse explained that this would be impossible because the oxygen and other needed equipment had been installed on this side of the room and the wires were not long enough to reach the other side. When the nurse learned that the patient was Muslim and needed to face the east toward Mecca to say his prayers five times a day, she arranged for him to be moved to another room that met his needs (Dresser, 1996).

When working with people in countries that practice nonliterate religions (those that lack written precepts), an understanding of the logic of their beliefs is important. Some Native Hawaiians for example, believe in curses and spirits; this belief should be respected. Witchcraft is practiced in such countries as Zaire; conducting business with people of these cultures may involve changing the sales and marketing techniques that you would ordinarily use.

Religious beliefs and practices affect business in many countries. Although both the United States and Italy are primarily Christian countries, religious holidays are more numerous in Italy than in the United States. Sri Lanka, for example, has numerous holidays with a total of 27. Religious beliefs also affect consumption patterns; beef is not eaten by Hindus and pork is not eaten by Muslims and Orthodox Jews. When conducting business internationally, religion must be a consideration (Terpstra & David, 1991; Victor, 1992).

Individualism and Collectivism

Individualism refers to the attitude of valuing ourselves as separate individuals with responsibility for our own destinies and our own actions. Proponents of individualism believe that self-interest is an appropriate goal. **Collectivism** emphasizes common interests, conformity, cooperation, and interdependence (See Figure 3.1).

FIGURE 3.1 Individualism vs. Collectivism

Hofstede (1991) studied the IBM Corporation in 53 countries and determined the dimensions on which countries' business cultures differed. Using statistical analysis and theoretical reasoning, Hofstede developed five dimensions, which he labeled: Power Distance, Uncertainty Avoidance, Collectivism vs. Individualism, Femininity vs. Masculinity, and Virtue vs. Truth. The countries were then ranked according to their scores.

As shown in the following list, the United States ranks first in individualism, followed by Australia, Great Britain, Canada, and The Netherlands. Countries that ranked lowest on individualism included Colombia, Venezuela, Panama, Equador, and Guatemala (Hofstede, 1991, p. 53).

Score Rank	*Country or Region*	*Score Rank*	*Country or Region*
1	USA	28	Turkey
2	Australia	29	Uruguay
3	Great Britain	30	Greece
4/5	Canada	31	Philippines
4/5	Netherlands	32	Mexico
6	New Zealand	33/35	East Africa
7	Italy	33/35	Yugoslavia
8	Belgium	33/35	Portugal
9	Denmark	36	Malaysia
10/11	Sweden	37	Hong Kong
10/11	France	38	Chile
12	Ireland	39/41	West Africa
13	Norway	39/41	Singapore
14	Switzerland	39/41	Thailand
15	Germany F.R.	42	Salvador
16	South Africa	43	South Korea
17	Finland	44	Taiwan
18	Austria	45	Peru
19	Israel	46	Costa Rica
20	Spain	47/48	Pakistan
21	India	47/48	Indonesia
22/23	Japan	49	Colombia
22/23	Argentina	50	Venezuela
24	Iran	51	Panama
25	Jamaica	52	Equador
26/27	Brazil	53	Guatemala
26/27	Arab countries		

Source: From *Cultures and Organizations* (p. 53), by G. Hofstede, 1991, London: McGraw-Hill Book Company. Copyright ©1991. Reproduced with permission of McGraw-Hill.

People from the United States place great importance on individuality and self-reliance. Well-known phrases typically used by parents to convey this emphasis on self-reliance include "Do your own thing," "You made your bed, now lie in it," and "You'd better look out for yourself; no one else will." U.S. Americans have been conditioned from childhood to think for themselves, to express their ideas and opinions, and to make their own choices; they are taught to consider themselves as individuals who are responsible for their own actions as well as for their own destinies. Parents start training their children early in this way of thinking; they offer them choices of food, clothes, and toys and usually accommodate their preferences. When the choice does not work out, the child then experiences the results of the decision. The goal of parents is to form a self-reliant, responsible person by the age of 18. When children move out of the parents' home at that age and are completely self-supporting, parents feel successful. Children who still live with their parents past the age of 18 or 20 are viewed as immature and unable to live independently. The value U.S. Americans place on individualism, self-reliance, and independence is perceived by persons of different cultures as being self-centered with little consideration for other people (Althen, 1988). This emphasis on individuality carries over into college/university choices as well as job choices that may take children away from friends and family members. Although individualism and the value placed on the family as an important unit are often associated, evidence shows that this relationship may not always exist. Costa Ricans, for example, have individualistic tendencies but also value the extended family structure. Examining cultures within cultures is, therefore, important.

In other cultures such as the Japanese, emphasis is placed on the group approach rather than the individual approach to all aspects of life. The Chinese and Malaysians also value the group approach and the family. Their concern with following family traditions and with respecting the opinions of their parents is perceived as a sign of weakness and indecisiveness by U.S. Americans.

A brief description of selected cultural values of the six countries with which the United States conducts most of its international business follows.

CANADA

In Canada, women are accepted in business and government and are well represented. As in the United States, businesswomen feel free to invite businessmen to lunch or dinner; the one who extends the invitation usually pays. Women in Quebec are expected to dress conservatively for business meetings (Bosrock, 1995). The dominant religion in Canada is Catholicism, but people of British descent are mostly Protestant. Canada, like the United States, believes in the separation of church and state; however, religious organizations play a more visible role in politics in Canada than is seen in the United States. Canada is a work-oriented culture; both parents often work outside the home (*Culturgram '98, Canada*, 1997). Canada is a highly individualistic society; the country tied with The Netherlands for fourth place in Hofstede's ranking of individualistic countries.

GREAT BRITAIN

Although British women have made progress in the workplace, they have not fared as well as women in the United States and Canada. With the high visibility of Margaret Thatcher as Britain's first female prime minister from 1979 to 1990, anticipated gains in positions of leadership for businesswomen in Great Britain have not materialized. In 1994, British women made up 9 percent of the members of the House of Commons; in the United States, 11 percent of the House of Representatives seats and 8 percent of the Senate seats were held by women. According to 1992 figures, 19.5 percent of British barristers (lawyers) were women, while 23 percent of U.S. lawyers were women (Axtell, Briggs, Corcoran, & Lamb, 1997). Great Britain's state religion is the Church of England (Anglican Church) headed by the queen. Though it no longer has political power, the church has had much influence on Great Britain throughout its history. Other religions represented include Roman Catholic, Protestant (Presbyterian and Methodist), and Judaism (*Culturgram '98, England,* 1997). Great Britain is a very individualistic society; the country is ranked third in Hofstede's ranking of individualistic countries.

FRANCE

Though most urban French women work outside the home, few hold top business positions except in fashion, cosmetics, advertising, and art. Although many French men do not readily accept French women in business, women from other countries, especially those from Canada and the United States, are generally accepted (Axtell, et al., 1997). A businesswoman may feel free to invite a French man to lunch and pay the bill. The majority (90 percent) of the people of France are Roman Catholic; a small percentage are members of other Christian churches or are of the Jewish or Islamic faith (*Culturgram '98, France,* 1997). France is a moderately individualistic society; the country tied with Sweden for tenth place in Hofstede's ranking of individualistic countries.

GERMANY

Germany is a male-dominated society; few married women work outside the home. Women have received little acceptance in positions of power and responsibility in business. German women in 1995 held less than 5 percent of the managerial positions and only 25 percent of the positions in public administration. However, this appears to be changing somewhat; the younger generation is more open to the idea of women holding higher ranking positions. While sex discrimination is unlawful in Germany, cases are rarely pursued. A businesswoman should feel free to invite a German businessman to dinner and pay the bill without incident (Bosrock, 1995; Axtell, et al., 1997).

About 36 percent of the German people are Protestant and 35 percent are Roman Catholic. Although a number of other religions are active in Germany, almost one-fourth of the people have no official religious affiliation (*Culturgram '98, Germany,* 1997). In Hofstede's ranking of individualistic countries, Germany ranked fifteenth.

JAPAN

Women are highly visible in today's Japanese business world, comprising about 40 percent of the workforce. However, the majority hold lower-level staff positions rather than positions of power. Japanese women have made progress in the areas of government, advertising, publishing, and such technical fields as engineering. The possibility of their making significant advances to the higher levels of management in the near future is unlikely because traditionally the Japanese power structure has been male dominated (Axtell, et al., 1997). Practices similar to religions in Japan include Shintoism (87 percent) and Buddhism (73 percent); a majority of Japanese practice a combination of the two. Only about 1 percent of the Japanese are Christian. Japan is not an individualistic culture; in Hof-stede's ranking of individualistic societies, the country was tied with Argentina for twenty-second place. The Japanese traditionally place the welfare of the group over the welfare of the individual. They respect age and value ambition, education, hard work, loyalty, and politeness (Bosrock, 1994).

MEXICO

The role of women in Mexican society is changing. In the past, very few women entered business and politics. Now, however, Mexican women are holding more important positions in business and politics and are visible in the professions as dentists, doctors, lawyers, and teachers. Although Mexican men control Mexican society, it is the women who control the men. The traditional macho attitudes of Mexican men are more apparent among the lower classes than among upper-class males. Foreign businesswomen are not advised to invite Mexican businessmen to dinner since a man and woman dining alone suggests that they are romantically involved. The predominant religion (practiced by 89 percent of Mexicans) is Catholicism; small percentages are of Protestant and Jewish faiths. Although the Catholic Church has little political influence, it does play an important role in the Mexican culture. Mexico is not considered an individualistic culture; the country was ranked thirty-second in Hofstede's ranking of individualistic countries. However, Mexicans have a sense of individualism in certain areas. For example, they try very hard to distinguish themselves from other Mexicans as they are aware of how they are perceived personally (Bosrock, 1995). Mexicans also value the family and personal relationships.

Terms

- Attitudes
- Attribution
- Attribution training
- Collectivism
- Ethical standards

- Individualism
- Perception
- Semantics
- Uncertainty-reduction theory
- Values

- Work
- Work attitudes
- Work ethic

EXERCISE 3.1

Instructions: Circle T for true and F for false.

1. T F   Values are learned; they are not innate.
2. T F   In the United States, the family is a top priority.
3. T F   A characteristic valued by U.S. Americans is directness.
4. T F   People in Asian cultures value history.
5. T F   Semantic differences between cultures that speak the same language are rare.
6. T F   The word "yes" means the same in all languages.
7. T F   Women in management are treated similarly in all cultures.
8. T F   Japan has a well-enforced equal employment law preventing discrimination against women.
9. T F   The U.S. society is considered to have a strong work ethic.
10. T F   Ethical standards are culture specific.

Questions and Cases for Discussion

1. Explain how values are formed.
2. In what ways are the values of persons in the United States different from those of persons in other countries?
3. Explain how semantic differences can affect intercultural communication. Give some examples.
4. Explain what is meant by the term *attribution*.
5. How are attitudes toward women culturally different? In what countries are women and men treated equally in the workplace?
6. Explain the differences between work attitudes in the United States and other countries. Are your personal work attitudes typical of the U.S. culture or another culture?
7. How are attitudes toward ethics in the United States different from those in Latin America?
8. What role does religion play in conducting business in the United States and Saudi Arabia?
9. Explain *individualism*. Give examples of cultures that are primarily individualistic.
10. Explain *collectivism*. Give examples of cultures that are primarily collectivistic.

CASE 1

Ching Lee was transferred by his Asian firm to assume a managerial position in a large automobile production plant in the United States. In his first report to his supervisor, he expressed concern that U.S. workers were not giving him the proper respect. What behaviors by U.S. workers could have led Ching Lee to draw this conclusion?

CASE 2

A U.S. firm sent its senior-level manager, Laura Green, to negotiate a contract for a chain of fast-food restaurants in Saudi Arabia. What cultural attitudes and behaviors related to gender should she expect to encounter?

CASE 3

When Brandon Hunt was sent to Mexico to oversee a production facility for his company, he became concerned over what he perceived to be a lack of seriousness about work on the part of Mexican workers. Employees were frequently late for work, left early, or did not come in at all. When questioned, employees explained that they had to help members of their families with their problems. Explain the apparent differences in U.S. American and Mexican attitudes toward work.

CASE 4

When Disney opened its $4.4 billion Euro Disneyland outside Paris, concerns over the park's impact on French culture were expressed. To begin with, the French dedicate Sundays to family outings only. In addition, they are unaccustomed to snacking and eat promptly at 12:30, which creates bottlenecks at parks and restaurants. Disney learned that French employees objected to providing the friendly greetings and smiles expected of all amusement park workers. They then hired multilingual employees from across Europe since their goal was to attract people from all countries of Europe. A complaint of European investors was that rigid U.S. management style did not take into account the values and customs of the people it intended to attract. For example, Europeans often bring their own lunches and do not spend money at the park's gourmet restaurants and hotels. The park initially lost money after it opened in 1992. Discuss the course of action Disney could take to accommodate the values and customs of the people it hopes to attract.

Activities

1. Ask one person from each of the groups listed this question: "What is your attitude toward work?" Report their responses to the class.
   a. blue-collar worker
   b. business professional
   c. educator
   d. high school student
   e. college student
2. Clip an article from the local newspaper related to ethics in business; summarize the article for class members.
3. Ask a professor or student from another culture to speak to the class on attitudes toward women in his or her culture.
4. Prepare a list of the names of women in your state who have achieved high-ranking positions in either government or business. List the special qualifications these women possess that make them qualified for their positions. Prepare a similar list of women in high-ranking positions in another country of your choice.
5. Prepare a list of words (other than those mentioned in the chapter) that have different meanings in other areas of the United States or in other English-speaking countries.

References

Adler, N. J., & Israeli, D. N. (1994). Where in the world are the women executives? *Business Quarterly, 59*(1), 89.

Aburdene P., & Naisbitt, J. (1992). *Megatrends for women.* New York: Fawcett Columbine.

Althen, G. (1988). *American ways.* Yarmouth, ME: Intercultural Press, Inc.

Axtell, R. (1991). *The do's and taboos of international trade.* New York: John Wiley & Sons, Inc.

Axtell, R. E., Briggs, T., Corcoran, M., & Lamb, M. B. (1997). *Do's and taboos around the world for women in business.* New York: John Wiley & Sons, Inc.

Borden, G. A. (1991). *Cultural orientation.* Upper Saddle River, NJ: Prentice Hall.

Bosrock, M. M. (1994). *Put your best foot forward: Asia.* St. Paul, MN: International Education System.

Bosrock, M. M. (1995a). *Put your best foot forward: Europe.* St. Paul, MN: International Education System.

Bosrock, M. M. (1995b). *Put your best foot forward: Mexico/Canada.* St. Paul, MN: International Education System.

Copeland, L., & Griggs, L. (1985). *Going international.* New York: A Plume Book.

Culturgram '98. (1997). Provo, UT: Brigham Young University, Publications Division of the David M. Kennedy Center for International Studies.

Dosick, W. (1993). *The business bible.* New York: HarperCollins Publishers.

Dresser, N. (1996). *Multcultural manners.* New York: John Wiley & Sons, Inc.

Elashmawi, F., & Harris, P. R. (1993). *Multicultural Management.* Houston, TX: Gulf Publishing Company.

Engholm, C., & Rowland, D. (1996). *International excellence.* New York: Kodansha International.

Ferraro, G. P. (1990). *The cultural dimension of international business.* Upper Saddle River, NJ: Prentice Hall.

Gudykunst, W. B., & Ting-Toomey, S. (1988). *Culture and interpersonal communication.* Newbury Park, CA: Sage Publications.

Hofstede, G. (1991). *Cultures in organizations.* London: McGraw-Hill Book Company.

Jandt, F. E. (1995). *Intercultural communication.* Thousand Oaks, CA: Sage Publications.

Naisbitt, J., & Aburdene, P. (1990). *Megatrends 2000.* New York: William Morrow and Company, Inc.

Rossman, M.L. (1990). *The international businesswoman of the 1990s.* New York: Praeger.

Terpstra, V., & David, K. (1991). *The cultural environment of international business.* Cincinnati: South-Western.

Thiederman, S. (1991). *Bridging cultural barriers for corporate success.* New York: Lexington Books.

Utroska, D. R. (1992, November). Management in Europe: More than just etiquette. *Management Review,* 21–24.

Victor, D. A. (1992). *International business communication.* New York: HarperCollins Publishers.

Weaver, G. R. (1998). *Culture, communication, and conflict.* Needham Heights, MA: Simon & Schuster Publishing.

C H A P T E R

Cultural Shock

Objectives
Upon completion of this chapter, you will:

■ understand the nature of cultural shock and its relationship to success in overseas assignments.

■ be able to identify the typical stages of cultural shock.

■ learn ways to alleviate cultural shock including careful selection of persons for overseas assignments and predeparture training.

■ understand the role of cultural stress, social alienation, social class and poverty-wealth extremes, financial matters, and relationships in dealing with cultural shock.

■ understand how the extent to which persons in the host culture reveal their private selves may contribute to cultural shock.

Cultural shock (commonly called culture shock) is the trauma you experience when you move into a culture different from your home culture. Cultural shock is basically a communication problem that involves the frustrations accompanying a lack of understanding of the verbal and nonverbal communication of the host culture, its customs, and its value systems. Frustrations may include lack of food, unacceptable standards of cleanliness, different bathroom facilities (see Figure 4.1), and fear for personal safety.

A woman in her mid-fifties was attending an intensive Spanish language school in Mexico and developed all the typical signs of cultural shock. She finished her five-week course and went home to find a position teaching English as a second language. Her new position was in Albania. She reported to friends that she was happy she had experienced cultural shock in a non-job situation because when she started to feel the same things in Albania she was able to understand and work through the cultural differences. She enjoyed Albania so much she signed up for a second tour.

FIGURE 4.1

Cultural shock can result from bathrooms with different fixtures or arrangements.

In a survey of 188 students from two Mid-South universities who had traveled or lived abroad, the greatest degree of cultural shock was reported in the lack of modern conveniences and standards of cleanliness. Other types of cultural shock showing statistical significance included attitudes toward women, nonverbal communication, clothing/business dress, family and marriage practices, housing, climate, educational system, financial problems, and values and ethical standards (Chaney & Martin, 1993). The absence of conveniences (such as telephones that work, running water available 24 hours a day, or buses that run on time) which are taken for granted in the United States is an additional source of frustration. People with strong religious ties may feel spiritually adrift without a church of their faith. Without the bounty of U.S. shopping malls, supermarkets, and multiple television sets, depression may result. In addition to depression, people who experience cultural shock can become homesick, eat or drink compulsively, and even develop physical ailments.

Upon her arrival in La Paz, Bolivia, from Atlanta, Georgia, Katherine Montague asked directions to the ladies' room at the local university. Upon entering, she observed three males using urinals and made a hasty retreat. Her U.S. colleagues explained that all restrooms were unisex; Katherine decided to take a taxi to her hotel.

Cultural shock has received increased attention by researchers only in the past two decades. However, Jack London in his story, "In a Far Country," which was published in 1900, stressed that a visitor to another culture should be prepared to acquire new customs and abandon old ideals. He suggested that sojourners (people who visit or reside temporarily in another country) should find pleasure in the unfamiliar because those who could not fit into the new culture would either return home or "die" of both psychological and physical ailments. London's advice is still sound almost a hundred years later (Lewis & Jungman, 1986).

A special kind of cultural shock experienced by U.S. travelers has been identified by Engholm (1991). He terms it **AsiaShock.** Engholm identifies the five progressive stages of AsiaShock:

- Frustration with the culture which includes the language, the food, and an exasperation with local customs.
- Unwillingness to understand the rationale behind the local ways of doing things; people of the United States quickly label a cultural behavior as backward and inefficient without trying to understand the rational basis for the behavior.
- Ethnocentricity; people of the United States often label Asians as dishonest because they seem to say one thing and do another, failing to realize that Asians consider their behavior to be face-saving rather than dishonest.
- Racism, including the unflattering labeling of all Asians into such groups as *Japs* and *coolies.*
- Avoidance of the culture; people of the United States tend to form their own clubs at which they commiserate about the difficulty of doing business in Asia rather than intermingling with the people of the culture.

Source: From *When business east meets business west* (p. 307–310), by C. Engholm, 1991, New York: John Wiley & Sons, Inc. Reprinted with permission.

Cultural shock can be costly to a firm since it often results in the premature return of U.S. businesspeople working overseas. Ferraro (1990) quotes research that shows employees sent to work in foreign countries fail not because they lack technical or professional competence but because they lack the ability to understand and adapt to another culture's way of life. Estimates on early return of U.S. expatriate managers range from 45 to 85 percent (Ferraro, 1990). When companies implement measures to combat cultural shock such as conducting training programs for sojourners, the early return rate drops to less than 2 percent.

A family spent eight years in Saudi Arabia while the husband, an engineer, worked for Aramco. The youngest son had been born in Saudi Arabia. Upon moving back to the United States, the son who was 8 years old, went with his parents to buy a car. When the mother got in the car to drive home, the boy exclaimed, "But you can't drive a car, Mother!" He had never seen a woman drive in his entire life. Of course, his parents quickly explained in the United States driving customs and laws are different from those in Saudi Arabia.

Some companies have used short-term stays of two to three months to determine an employee's potential for tolerating the culture. Sometimes these short-term projects are designed to prepare the person for a longer stay later. On other occasions, these brief trips are simply ways to utilize the talents of technical professionals who would be unwilling to go in the first place if it meant disrupting the professional advancement of a career-oriented spouse. Short trips are also cost effective as the need to move the family is reduced or eliminated. Although the degree and type of cultural shock experienced by people who travel to another country for a short stay may be similar to the shock experienced by those who plan an extended visit, the strategies for coping during the short-term visit may differ.

Cultural shock and missing your way of life can cause you to give up free trips. A mid-level U.S. executive was in Taiwan for four weeks. The company policy was that if you were in the Far East for more than three weeks, you could take an all-expense paid trip to Hong Kong at the end of the third week. The executive chose to work through the weekend and the next week so he could finish early and go home.

Brislin (1981) identifies these five strategies used for coping with the new culture during short visits:

1. One strategy is *unacceptance* of the host culture; the traveler simply behaves as he or she would in the home culture. No effort is made to learn the language or the customs of the host culture.
2. A second strategy is known as *substitution*. The traveler learns the appropriate responses or behaviors in the host culture and substitutes these responses or behaviors for the ones he or she would ordinarily use in the home culture.
3. A third strategy is known as *addition*. The person adds the behavior of the host culture when in the presence of the nationals but maintains the home culture behavior when with others of the same culture.
4. A fourth strategy is known as *synthesis*. This strategy integrates or combines elements of the two cultures such as combining the dress of the United States and the Philippines.
5. The final strategy is referred to as *resynthesis*, the integration of ideas not found in either culture. An example of this strategy would be a U.S. traveler in China who chooses to eat neither American nor Chinese food but prefers Italian food.

Stages of Cultural Shock

Cultural shock generally goes through five stages: excitement or initial euphoria, crisis or disenchantment, adjustment, acceptance, and reentry.

The first stage is excitement and fascination with the new culture which can last only a few days or several months. During this time, everything is new and different; you are fascinated with the food and the people. Sometimes this stage is referred to as the "honeymoon" stage during which your enthusiasm for the new culture causes you to overlook minor problems such as having to drink bottled water and the absence of central heating or air conditioning.

During the second stage, the crisis or disenchantment period, the "honeymoon" is over; your excitement has turned to disappointment as you encounter more and more differences between your own culture and the new culture. Problems with transportation, unfamiliar foods, and people who do not speak English now seem overwhelming.

The practice of bargaining over the purchase price of everything, an exercise you origi-nally found amusing, is now a constant source of irritation. People at this stage often cope with the situation by making disparaging remarks about the culture; it is some-times referred to as the "fight-back" technique. Others deal with this stage by leaving, either physically or psychologically. Those who remain may withdraw from people in the culture, refuse to learn the language, and develop coping behaviors of excessive drinking or drug use. Some individuals actually deny differences and will speak in glow-ing terms of the new culture.

In the third stage, the adjustment phase, you begin to accept the new culture. You try new foods and make adjustments in behavior to accommodate the shopping lines and the long waits for public transportation. You begin to see the humor in situations and realize that a change in attitude toward the host culture will make the stay abroad more rewarding.

In the fourth phase, the acceptance or adaptation phase, you feel at home in the new culture, become involved in activities of the culture, cultivate friendships among the na-tionals, and feel comfortable in social situations with people from the host culture. You learn the language and may adopt the new culture's style of doing things. You even learn to enjoy some customs such as afternoon tea and the mid-day siesta that you will miss when you return to the home country.

The final phase is reentry shock which can be almost as traumatic as the initial ad-justment to a new culture, particularly after an extended stay abroad. **Reentry shock** is experienced upon returning to the home country and may follow the stages identified earlier: initial euphoria, crisis or disenchantment, adjustment, and acceptance or adap-tation. You would at first be happy to be back in your own country, then become disen-chanted as you realize that your friends are not really interested in hearing about your experiences abroad, your standard of living goes down, and you are unable to use such new skills as a foreign language or bargaining in the market. You then move into the ad-justment stage as you become familiar with new technology and view with appreciation such things as the abundance and variety of foods and clothing and the improved stan-dards of cleanliness. You finally move into the acceptance stage when you feel com-fortable with the mores of the home culture and find yourself returning to many of your earlier views and behaviors.

> A former student from the United Arab Emirants called his U.S. professor to ask for information on purchasing property on the North Carolina coast. He went on to explain that he was homesick for the United States and had decided to bring his family here every summer. After spending 15 years in the United States earn-ing his bachelor, MBA, and Ph.D. degrees with only occasional visits back to his home country, he was experiencing reentry shock. (He made the readjustment and did not buy the North Carolina property.)

Although reentry shock is typically shorter than the first four stages of cultural shock, expatriates who have made a good adjustment to the host culture may go through a rather long period of adjustment, lasting six months or more, when they are confronted with the changes that have taken place in their absence. Some of these changes are work related; expatriates may feel "demoted" when they return to middle-management positions without the bonuses, perks, and professional contacts they enjoyed abroad. In other situations, changes have taken place in the home country including politics and styles of clothing that require readjustment. In research conducted by Chaney and Martin (1993), the four types of reentry shock experienced by college students who had traveled abroad that were statistically significant were readjusting to lifestyle, change in social life, change in standard of living, and reestablishing friendships.

Some reentry problems are personal in nature. Many repatriates have changed; they have acquired a broadened view of the world and have undergone changes in values and attitudes. Personal problems may include unsuccessful attempts to renew personal and professional relationships as the realization sets in that their former friends do not share their enthusiasm for their overseas experiences and accomplishments. They must then make new friends who share this common experience. Children of repatriates encounter similar readjustment problems as their former friends have made new ones and they find that the education they received abroad is sufficiently different to cause problems when returning to schools in the United States.

Since reentry shock is a natural part of cultural shock, mulinational corporations must provide training for repatriates to assure that the transition to the home culture is a favorable experience. In the absence of such training, you can do much to counteract reentry shock by sharing your feelings (not your experiences) with sympathetic family members and friends, particularly those who have lived abroad. Correspond regularly with members of the home culture; ask questions concerning changes that are taking place. Subscribe to the home newspaper to stay abreast of current happenings. Keep in touch with professional organizations and other groups with which you may want to affiliate. Many repatriates have found that maintaining ties with the home culture cushions the shock associated with reentry (Dodd, 1987; Dodd & Montalvo, 1987; Khols, 1984; Klopf, 1991). Providing feedback on how employees are doing and developing them to their maximum potential will result in increased satisfaction with the assignment.

Alleviating Cultural Shock

Many multinational firms find that cultural shock can be alleviated by selecting employees for overseas assignments who possess certain personal and professional qualifications. Another method of easing cultural shock is to conduct training programs for employees prior to overseas deployment (Krapels, 1993). Providing feedback on how employees are doing and developing them to their maximum potential will result in increased satisfaction with the assignment.

SELECTION OF OVERSEAS PERSONNEL

Careful selection of persons for overseas assignments is important to enhance chances for a successful sojourn. Personal qualifications needed when working in an unfamiliar culture include adapatability, flexibility, empathy, and tolerance. Good interpersonal skills and a high self-esteem have also been found to be important.

The ability to react to different and often unpredictable situations with little apparent irritation shows a tolerance for ambiguity. Ambiguities are inherent in intercultural communication; many people, situations, rules, and attitudes make little sense. A lot of confusion results from being in another culture. Maintaining a high degree of tolerance and flexibility is essential. Some companies spend a lot of time at colleges recruiting because they are looking for candidates who already have such qualifications as language proficiency and overseas experience during which time the person has learned how to adapt to another culture. Many recruiters feel that tolerance can be developed but that adaptability is difficult to develop; they prefer, therefore, to hire persons who have already acquired this trait through living abroad (Geber, 1992; McEnery & DesHarnais, 1990). Adaptability screening reduces costly turnover. Harvey (1985) suggests the use of the following questions to determine a candidate's adapatability:

- Is the person cooperative, agreeable, and sensitive to others?
- Is the candidate open to the opinions of others?
- How does the person react to new situations and what effort does he or she make to understand and appreciate differences?
- Does the candidate understand his or her own culturally derived values?
- Is the candidate sensitive and aware of values of other cultures?
- How does the person react to criticism?
- How well does the candidate understand the U.S. government system?
- Will the candidate be able to make and develop contacts with counterparts in the foreign culture?
- Is the candidate patient when dealing with problem situations?
- Is the candidate resilient when faced with adverse situations?

By using such questions as these, interviewers are better able to determine a candidate's suitability for the overseas assignment as well as the person's motivation for wanting to work abroad.

The ability to see the environment from the perspective of the host nationals is an indication of empathy. Bennett's concept of empathy recommends replacing the Golden Rule (do unto others as you would have them do unto you) with the **Platinum Rule** (do unto others as they would have done unto them). You can still maintain your own cultural identity but be able to interpret the new culture through the eyes of the national (Broome, 1991).

Professional qualifications include a knowledge of business practices in the host culture and technical competence. Language skills are considered crucial by some companies. When the destination is the Far East, many companies believe some language training prior to departure is needed. When the use of English is pervasive in a country, proficiency in the host language may not be necessary. In any case, language knowledge seems to give an expatriate an extra chance of succeeding in the host culture. In addition to language knowledge, understanding the educational, political, economic, and social systems of a country is considered important (Tung, 1981).

PREDEPARTURE TRAINING FOR HOST COUNTRY

An effective approach to cross-cultural training is to first explore how people adjust to new cultures. Learning principles that affect the success of training programs for global managers can be broken down into three steps: observing and emulating behaviors of persons in the host culture; retaining what has been learned; and experimenting with the new behavior until it becomes comfortable. For example in the Philippines, social get-togethers are important in getting people of a company to feel comfortable together and to develop a camaraderie that will spill over into the workplace. These festive occasions which often include cooking together, singing, dancing, and story-telling, serve an important function in employer–employee relations. Attending and participating are important; those who do not participate are viewed as cold and aloof. U.S. managers who wish to be successful in the host culture, after observing such social events, would then sponsor similar social outings to demonstrate their desire to become part of the new culture (Black, Gregersen, & Mendenhall, 1992).

Because of the reported lack of intercultural training by U.S. multinational companies, acculturation problems have affected the overall success rate of businesspersons in foreign countries. Research conducted by Krapels (1993) involving 102 international businesspersons representing 35 international Mid-South companies determined that 46 percent of the firms participating offered some type of predeparture training; however, only one firm had a formal training program in place. Since early return rates drop significantly when training programs are implemented, many multinational firms are now experimenting with a variety of training programs. Some companies are trying to boost tolerance of another culture by including trainees from overseas locations in their U.S.-based training programs. Other firms conduct training sessions overseas and send U.S. managers to these courses to provide training in the host culture at the same time that some exposure to the culture occurs. Still other companies incorporate cross-cultural awareness into their regular management training courses.

Approaches to intercultural training may be grouped as follows:

- The **intellectual model** is also called the classroom model. Participants are given facts about the host country using a variety of instructional methods such as lectures, group discussions, and video tapes. This model, which is used most frequently, is based on the belief that cognitive understanding is necessary for performing effectively abroad. This training method is popular in the military as well as in business and educational institutions. Reasons for the popularity of the intellectual model are that staffing is relatively easy and participants are familiar with this approach. A limitation of this approach is the knowledge learned may not coincide with what is actually needed when a person lives abroad. In other words, the person has learned specific facts and generalizations about the culture that do not take into account everyday happenings the person experiences when living in the culture. The model teaches for knowledge; it does not develop problem-solving skills or attitudes of flexibility and is not experience based.
- The **area training model,** also called the simulation model, emphasizes affective goals, culture specific content, and experiential processes. This approach is centered on the trainee rather than the trainer, requires trainee involvement in the learning process, and emphasizes problem solving rather than the acquiring of information. Through field trips or such simulations as Bafa, Bafa, in which participants are divided into two cultures, Alpha and Beta, trainees learn the rules of their culture and interact with members of the other culture. Critics of this approach point out that since it is a simulation, training may still be dissimilar from the actual experience abroad. In addition, those who desire to have more knowledge about the culture as

would be the emphasis with the intellectual model would consider this a drawback of this approach.

- The **self-awareness model,** also called the human relations model, is based on the assumption that the trainee with self-understanding will adapt to the new culture better and will therefore be more effective in the overseas assignment. To accomplish desired outcomes, trainers use role play or may use the sensitivity or Training (T)-Group approach. The **sensitivity training** or **T-Group** movement, popular in the late 1960s and 1970s, has not received much attention in recent years. Using this approach involved training exercises in which people are told in a group setting by others why their behavior is inappropriate, i.e., they are perceived as arrogant, dogmatic, or judgmental. This training approach was controversial at best. Although some may have perceived the feedback as helpful, others were uncomfortable exploring their feelings and emotions and viewed it as threatening. Some critics of this approach point out that the American T-Group is based on U.S. values of directness, openness, and equality. Further, this approach does not give participants a framework of conceptual knowledge for analyzing future situations. In addition, cultural relativity and differences in values are not addressed.

- The **cultural awareness model** emphasizes cultural insight, and like the self-awareness model, stresses affective goals and an experiential process. In this approach, participants go from recognizing their own values to contrasting their values with those of other cultures using a variety of techniques including realistic role playing. This approach, though not as familiar to trainees as the intellectual approach, more nearly approximates interactions participants would experience in the new culture (Bennett, 1986).

- The **interaction approach** is based on participants' interacting with people in the host country, either nationals or U.S. persons who have been in the host country for an extended period of time (Harris & Moran, 1996).

- The **multidimensional approach** is based on the concept that using any single training approach is not as effective as using an approach which attempts to combine cognitive, affective, and behavioral aspects of training. Critics of this approach say that an integration is overly ambitious. However, advocates maintain that the integrated approach, balancing content with process, affective learning with cognitive, and culture specific with culture general, will better prepare participants for a successful overseas experience (Bennett, 1986).

Advances in communication technology are now being used in intercultural training. Global videoconferencing has been used by a major international firm to train employees and their families at more than 200 sites around the world. Global educational networks with various universities are being developed to train executives who are going abroad. Computers are being used to enhance training effectiveness. According to Harris and Moran (1996), computer-aided training or learning has immense potential for multicultural education because it cuts across traditional language barriers. Research indicates that such instruction not only encourages one-to-one learning, but can save 30 percent of the time of more traditional methods. Regardless of the type of training offered, companies realize that success is limited to the extent that there is no substitute for actually living with another culture.

PROVIDING FEEDBACK AND REWARDS

Global managers need feedback and rewards just as managers in the home culture do. The appraisal and reward system is different from the home system because people in overseas assignments have to be evaluated and rewarded in a way that takes into account the values of persons in the host culture and the expectations of the particular assignment. The evaluation criteria must be made clear. Areas typically included are leadership ability, interpersonal skills, negotiation skills, customer service, communication skills, and achievement of organizational objectives. For international managers, a key factor to be evaluated would often include profits, but in some countries, the main goal might be to build a presence in the country. In that case, making contracts and building close personal relationships with key officials in the host country would be important. Another consideration in appraising overseas managers is who should do the evaluating. Many companies use a rating team headed by a senior human resources management executive. Persons who may be involved in the appraisal process include on-site superiors, peer managers, subordinates, and clients. The team leader might be expected to prepare an appraisal on the global manager every six months (Black, Gregersen, & Mendenhall, 1992).

Reward systems for global managers include special allowances for housing/ utilities/furnishings, cost-of-living, hardship, education, home-leave, relocation, medical, car-and-driver, club memberships, and taxes. The main objective of whatever reward system is used is to attract and retain quality employees. Rewards are especially important in overseas assignments because employees need to be compensated for what they are leaving behind: favorite foods, recreation, family and friends, educational opportunities, and health care. In addition, reward systems used for global managers need to take into consideration the idea of equity, the ratio between what they contribute and what they receive. A manager in the host country who is supposed to be on the same level as the U.S. manager often sees a disparity between what the two contribute and receive; this situation can cause friction and add to feelings of inequity between expatriate managers and local managers. Additional feelings of dissatisfaction based on equity are experienced by managers/government employees from the same country but not the same company/government agency. One spouse of a U.S. expatriate complained that her husband's firm did everything "on the cheap," including housing allowances, bonuses, and home-leave airfares (economy class only) while their friends in other companies received higher housing allowances and bonuses and flew business class (Black, Gregersen, & Mendenhall, 1992).

DEVELOPING EMPLOYEES TO THEIR MAXIMUM POTENTIAL

In the past, insufficient attention has been given to reacclimating global managers, specifically in planning for the return of managers who have been in foreign posts for some time. As a result, many managers become dissatisfied with their positions upon their return to their U.S. firm and leave the company. In fact, estimates of the number of managers who leave the firm within a year following repatriation is 20 percent (Black, Gregersen, & Mendenhall, 1992). When one considers the firm's investment in the success of their global managers, the importance of focusing on repatriation becomes clear. Plans for successful repatriation adjustment should begin before the manager leaves the host country; the company should make clear the reason for the new assignment, what new skills and knowledge will be learned, and how the employee will contribute to the company's development upon his or her return. In addition, human resources department personnel should begin initial preparations for the manager's return at least six months prior to repatriation by providing home-country information and contacts. Other recommendations for successful repatriation include providing appropriate compensation for transition expenses, allowing sufficient time to move and get settled before reporting to work, assisting in the location of proper housing, and showing appreciation to the entire family for their contributions to the company during their overseas assignment (Black, Gregersen, & Mendenhall, 1992).

An American expatriate made this observation upon returning to his home in Dallas from an assignment in Caracas:

I was really looking forward to coming home, but now I don't feel like I belong. Before I left, I had a large corner office in my company; now I share an office with two other managers. Most people don't even know who I am. My wife isn't happy. In Caracas, our life was very social; we were invited to all the best parties. She had a cook, maid, seamstress, gardener, and nanny. Here she has no friends and no household help.

Aspects of Cultural Shock

Aspects of cultural shock include cultural stress, social alienation, social class and poverty-wealth extremes, financial matters, and relationships and family considerations. In addition, differences between the extent to which persons in the host and home cultures reveal their private selves may cause acculturation problems particularly in communication.

CULTURAL STRESS

Entering an unfamiliar culture is stressful; in fact, transitions of any type are both psychologically and physically stressful. The stress of getting ready for the move, of unpacking and getting settled upon arrival, and of adjusting to new foods can be so stressful that people become physically ill. Problems with housing, climate, services, or communication in another language bring additional stress.

Expatriates learn to utilize a variety of coping skills to alleviate stress. Unfortunately, some coping behaviors are negative. Taking drugs or drinking alcohol may provide a temporary superficial relief to the stressful situation but avoids dealing with the real source of stress. Another negative coping method, using food to alleviate stress, may create weight gain problems. Positive techniques include diversions such as taking up a hobby or learning a new skill, planning family events, sharing problems with friends and family members, and changing one's mental outlook. Physical coping mechanisms such as exercise and meditation are useful in alleviating stress, as are spiritual techniques such as volunteering to help others and religious worship.

Some companies have found that providing prospective expatriates with a mentor who has worked in the host country can help to reduce anxiety about adjustments that may be necessary in the new culture. Providing a second mentor located in the host country can reduce stress associated with learning acceptable behavior in the new culture and will help avoid serious business and social blunders.

To alleviate culture stress, prepare for the second culture by reading up on the country, studying the language, and becoming aware of customs and traditions in the culture. Maintaining a sense of humor is very important in dealing with cultural stress.

SOCIAL ALIENATION

An aspect of cultural shock that can have adverse effects upon the newcomer to a culture is social alienation and the feelings of loneliness that are associated with being isolated from friends and the home culture.

Feelings of alienation may be delayed somewhat since concern over such basic matters as housing, transportation, and work may buffer these feelings initially. As the months pass, however, you may feel more isolated as you experience numerous cultural differences such as what is considered an appropriate topic of social converstaion. The concern of people in the United States with fitness, exercise, and healthful eating are not shared by persons of many cultures and is, therefore, an inappropriate topic of conversation. You also may feel uncomfortable during political discussions because persons of other cultures cannot understand the logic behind such decisions as voting for a person for president who is inexperienced in the international arena rather than for a seasoned politician who is respected in the international community.

Making an effort to become familiar with the nuances of the culture and cultivating friendships with persons from the home culture as well as the host culture can alleviate feelings of alienation. Enrolling in language classes and including host nationals in social events can cushion the shock of the new culture and pave the way toward a better understanding and appreciation of the people and their culture.

SOCIAL CLASS AND POVERTY-WEALTH EXTREMES

In many developing countries, no "middle class" exists. Social classes and extremes in poverty and wealth are readily apparent.

The mention of social class in the United States is greeted with uncertain responses since many U.S. citizens prefer to believe that no social class exists in the United States. According to Fussell (1983), class distinctions do exist in the United States but are so complicated and subtle that visitors from other countries often miss the nuances and even the existence of a class structure. Therefore, the official propaganda of social equality is basically a myth. According to people in the lower stratum, class is related to the amount of money you have. People in the middle stratum acknowledge that money has something to do with it but believe that the kind of work you do and your education are almost as important. People in the top stratum believe that your tastes, values, style, and behavior indicate your class, regardless of your education, occupation, or money (Fussell, 1983). Since U.S. personnel are accustomed to perpetuating this "fable of equality," the obvious existence of social class in other societies may make U.S. Americans quite uncomfortable. In cultures with virtually no middle class, U.S. persons are usually forced into the upper class of the host culture and may, at least temporarily, feel quite ill at ease in a social role in which numerous servants are the norm and distinctions are made between acceptable and unacceptable friends.

The informality of U.S. Americans such as greeting strangers on the streets with "Hi!" and calling people they scarcely know by their first name, is a source of cultural shock for many visitors to the United States. In many cultures, starting a conversation with a stranger in a shop or on a bus is considered unacceptable; in the United States, this behavior is commonplace. Other sources of shock to foreigners is the discovery that not all U.S. Americans are wealthy and well educated—that we have large numbers of homeless persons and people who have not graduated from high school.

The poverty of the lower class in other cultures often makes U.S. Americans so uncomfortable that they feel compelled to help but may do so in socially unacceptable ways such as paying a gardener twice the usual rate simply because the person is poor. Mentors in the host culture can be very helpful in advising U.S. persons regarding acceptable ways of dealing with poverty–wealth extremes and with gaining an insight into the class structure of the culture (Althen, 1988).

FINANCIAL MATTERS

Because adapting to a new culture and reentering the home culture involves financial adjustments, companies should provide financial counseling both to expatriates and repatriates. Although the focus would be a little different, the primary consideration would be the same: optimum utilization of the financial resources available.

Financial counseling for expatriates would include such information as cost and availability of housing, banking practices (including exchange rates), use of credit cards and checks, and costs of schooling for employees with families. Since substantial salary increases are often related to an employee's willingness to relocate, these increases should be discussed in terms of real purchasing power. Expenses related to a higher standard of living which many expatriates enjoy would include hiring domestic help and investing in appropriate formal attire. Customs in purchasing such as bargaining in the market should be addressed as well as the additional marketing expenses which may include paying someone to guard your car while you shop, someone else to carry parcels, and another person to find fresh eggs or meat that are available only on the black market. Buying goods in grams rather than pounds is an additional purchasing considerations. Added expenses of securing goods such as the cost of tailor-made clothes in the absence of locally available appropriate clothing is another appropriate topic to discuss.

By providing counseling before home culture reentry, the company is acknowledging that financial problems will occur and is demonstrating a willingness to help with these problems. One financial problem relates to the loss of buying power; upon returning to the United States, the decrease can be about 30 percent in net disposable income (Clague & Krupp, 1980). The focus of financial counseling for repatriates would include costs involved in relocating in a stateside home, accompanying adjustments to a lower salary, and the loss of perquisites. Since the loss of elite status is often difficult to accept, counseling should include the positive side of the changes such as less money will be spent on clothes. To ease the transition financially, some companies provide a relocation pay supplement. Others grant annual leave in advance of the return to allow time for house hunting and related problems. Another expense that is receiving increased attention is the cost of providing counseling for family members, particularly children whose adolescence is delayed. Since repatriated children are usually retarded three to four years socially, counseling is often needed to help them work through this transition of readjusting to the home culture (Bird & Dunbar, 1991).

Relationships and Family Considerations

Problems with relationships such as the failure of the spouse and other family members to adapt to the new culture are a major factor in the early return of expatriates. Family and personal issues can be disruptive to acculturation, especially for families with children ages 3 to 5 and 14 to 16 (Harvey, 1985). The 3- to 5-year-olds often have emotional problems being uprooted from familiar surroundings; the 14- to 16- year-olds may have problems ranging from adapting socially to making adjustments to a different educational system. Adolescents in particular need social continuity and often feel resentment toward their parents for uprooting them. Care must be taken to prepare children for the move by discussing openly their anxieties and fears and by providing them with information concerning expected changes in their lives. Being separated from family members and friends in the United States may cause loneliness for all involved. In addition, the spouse is experiencing his or her own problems in adjusting to an alien work environment and is unable to provide the time and emotional support needed during this difficult period of adjustment. Two-career families in which one spouse (usually the wife) gives up a career to accompany the relocated spouse pose special adjustment problems. Job opportunities in the new culture may be nonexistent, and resentment and boredom may lead to family conflict. Adding unhappy children and an unhappy spouse to the stress of the new job in a foreign culture increases the probability of an early return to the home culture (Harvey, 1985).

Companies that provide training for employees prior to departure rarely include the family in such training. Since adjustment problems often involve the family, difficulties could be avoided in many cases by including family members in predeparture training.

Public and Private Self

People in various cultures differ with respect to how much of the inner self is shared with others. A method of considering a person's inner world is through the **Johari Window** which includes "panes" that represent the self that is known and unknown to oneself and the self that is known and unknown to others. The Johari Window (Luft, 1984), named for its creators, **Jo**seph and **Harri**ngton, is shown in Figure 4.2.

The first window pane is information that is shared; it includes what is known both to oneself and to others. This information may be limited to a few facts that the person chooses to share such as occupation or telephone number or it may include numerous facts and opinions that are shared with a large audience. The second pane represents what is known to others but not to oneself; it represents the person's blind area. This may include motives that others are able to discern but that the person cannot see. The third pane represents what is known to oneself but is unknown to others. Information that a person chooses to keep from others may range from a past indiscretion to aspects of one's family life such as marital status that the person does not wish to disclose. The

	Things I Know	Things I Don't Know
Things Others Know	Arena	Blind Spot
Things Others Don't Know	Hidden	Unknown

FIGURE 4.2

The Johari Window.

Source: From *Group processes: An introduction to group dynamics* by Joseph Light, Copyright ©1963, 1970, 1984, Palo Alto, CA: Mayfield Publishing Company. Used by permission.

fourth pane is that aspect of one's inner self that is unknown both to others and to oneself. This may be information that is embedded deeply in the person's subconscious to the extent that neither the person nor others know of its existence.

The major dimensions of the Johari Window (what is known to self and to others) can be translated into one's public self and private self. The public self may include information about a person's work, family, and interests or opinions on political and social issues. In some cultures such as the Japanese, the public self is relatively small while the private self is relatively large. People of the United States use a style of communication that includes a larger public self with the private self being relatively small. U.S. citizens readily express their opinions and reveal their attitudes and feelings to a larger extent than do persons from Asian cultures. U.S. Americans use a variety of communication channels including greater verbalization and greater use of nonverbal communication such as touch. They conceal less than the Japanese and communicate on a wide range of topics. The Japanese offer fewer opinions and feelings and have fewer physical contacts. People of the United States have less rigid boundaries between the public and private selves; they use more spontaneous forms of communication and fewer ritualized ones. Because of this larger public self, U.S. Americans are sometimes criticized by persons of other cultures as being too outgoing and friendly, too explicit, and too analytical (Barnlund, 1975).

Obstacles to effective communication may be overcome to some degree by becoming knowledgeable about the communication styles of other cultures and by compromising between the two styles. When communicating with the Japanese, for example, U.S. Americans should avoid prying questions, observe formalities and rituals, respect the use of silence, maintain harmony, and understand that evasiveness is a natural part of their communication process.

Cultural shock is a reality that must be addressed by firms doing business abroad. The subject must be openly explained and understood. By admitting the existence of cultural shock and explaining how it may affect individuals, the shock loses some of its intensity and adapting to the new culture is less traumatic.

The length of cultural shock/reentry shock will depend on such factors as personal resiliency, the length of the assignment, and the effort you put forth prior to departure to learn about the host culture.

Terms

- Area training model
- AsiaShock
- Cultural awareness model
- Cultural shock
- Intellectual model
- Interaction approach
- Johari Window
- Multidimensional approach
- Platinum Rule
- Reentry shock
- Self-awareness model
- Sensitivity training
- T-group

EXERCISE 4.1

Instructions: Circle the appropriate number to indicate the types and degree of cultural shock (either positive or negative) you experienced when entering a foreign culture.

Type of Cultural Shock	High Degree			Low Degree		None
1. Attitudes toward time	5	4	3	2	1	0
2. Attitudes toward women	5	4	3	2	1	0
3. Gestures, eye contact, and other nonverbal messages	5	4	3	2	1	0
4. Climate	5	4	3	2	1	0
5. Clothing/business dress	5	4	3	2	1	0
6. Customs, traditions, and beliefs	5	4	3	2	1	0
7. Educational system	5	4	3	2	1	0
8. Family and marriage practices	5	4	3	2	1	0
9. Financial problems	5	4	3	2	1	0
10. Food and diet	5	4	3	2	1	0
11. Housing	5	4	3	2	1	0
12. Lack of modern conveniences	5	4	3	2	1	0
13. Social class/poverty–wealth extremes	5	4	3	2	1	0
14. Social alienation (absence of people of same culture)	5	4	3	2	1	0
15. Standards of cleanliness	5	4	3	2	1	0
16. Transportation	5	4	3	2	1	0
17. Values and ethical standards	5	4	3	2	1	0
18. Work habits and practices	5	4	3	2	1	0

EXERCISE 4.2

Instructions: Circle T for true and F for false.

1. T F During the second stage of cultural shock, many sojourners develop such coping behaviors as drug and alcohol abuse.

2. T F Cultural shock can be alleviated by careful election of employees for overseas assignments.

3. T F The Platinum Rule states: "Do unto others before they do unto you."

4. T F The intellectual or classroom approach to intercultural training is basically fact-oriented training.

5. T F Cultural stress can have both psychological and physical consequences.

6. T F A source of shock to foreigners is the discovery that not all U.S. citizens are well educated.

7. T F A source of cultural shock for many U.S. persons living abroad is the financial burden of the required higher standard of living.

8. T F A major factor in the early return of expatriates is family problems.

9. T F The Johari Window represents how you see the world.

10. T F Children of repatriates experience less reentry shock than do adults.

Questions and Cases for Discussion

1. Explain what is meant by the term *cultural shock.*
2. Identify and discuss the stages of cultural shock.
3. How can multinational firms alleviate cultural shock?
4. Identify and describe the approaches to intercultural training offered by multinational firms.
5. Identify types of cultural stress that may confront persons who are living abroad.
6. Identify positive coping skills that may be used to alleviate stress.
7. How can social class and poverty–wealth extremes be sources of cultural shock for U.S. Americans in overseas assignments?
8. What types of financial adjustments may be associated with cultural shock?
9. Explain how the Johari Window is related to cultural shock.
10. What types of reentry problem are often encountered by persons returning to the home culture? How can reentry shock be alleviated?

CASE 1

Larry was sent to Japan to represent his company and wanted to make a good impression on his Japanese hosts. He immediately asked them to call him by his first name and told several humorous stories intended to break the ice. He brought along gifts containing his company's logo and asked about the state of the Japanese economy. Larry got the impression that things were not going well and that he may have behaved inappropriately. What advice would you give him?

CASE 2

Karl, his wife, and five-year-old son were completing a three-year assignment in Brazil and were scheduled to return to the United States in a month. Karl would return to work at the home office in Chicago. What should Karl and his family do to lessen the shock of returning to their home culture?

CASE 3

Frank's company was planning to enter the Mexican market and had sent him to meet with Juan, the manager of the firm with which they planned to establish a partnership. They agreed to meet for lunch at 2 p.m. at a restaurant in Mexico City. At 2:30 Frank, thinking he had misunderstood the time or place, was leaving when he encountered Juan who did not apologize for being late. Juan then ordered a special brandy for them and proceeded to talk about the local museums, churches, and other points of interest. Frank indicated that he did not have time to visit local sites and was anxious to discuss their proposed business partnership. When the brandy arrived, Frank declined saying he did not drink alcoholic beverages during the day. Each time Frank tried to turn the discussion to business, Juan immediately changed the subject to other topics including inquiring about Frank's family and personal life. At the end of the two-hour lunch, no business had been discussed. Frank returned to the United States the following day and reported to his supervisor the Mexican firm apparently had no interest in the proposed partnership. How could Frank have better prepared himself for the cultural shock he experienced?

CASE 4

Janice Davis, a marketing representative for a U.S. firm, was looking forward to her assignment in Japan since she had visited the country on one occasion. However, her anticipation quickly turned to frustration. Since all store signs were in Japanese, she didn't know where to buy even a broom. Directions and instructions for using appliances were in Japanese. How could Janice have better prepared herself for the cultural shock she experienced?

Activities

1. For persons who have traveled or lived in a foreign country for a time, discuss the degree of reentry shock experienced upon returning to the home country in the following areas:
   a. Reestablishing friendships
   b. Readjusting to lifestyle
   c. Readjusting to job
   d. Changes in social life
   e. Changes in standard of living
2. Assume that you have just been made manager of your company's plants in Egypt. Prepare a list of the types of cultural shock you would expect to encounter.
3. After a year in Kenya, you are being returned to your U.S. office. List the types of reentry shock you would expect to experience.

4. You are reviewing applications of persons in your firm who have expressed an interest in an overseas assignment. List the special qualifications you would look for in deciding which three to interview.
5. Conduct a library search to determine what training films or materials are available for predeparture intercultural training of businesspersons.

References

Althen, G. (1988). *American ways.* Yarmouth, ME: Intercultural Press, Inc.

Barnlund, D. C. (1975). *Public and private self in Japan and the United States.* Yarmouth, ME: Intercultural Press, Inc.

Bennett, J. M. (1986). Modes of crosscultural training: Conceptualizing cross-cultural training as education. *International Journal of Intercultural Relations, 10,* 117–134.

Bird, A., & Dunbar, R. (1991, Spring). Getting the job done over there: Improving expatriate productivity. *National Productivity Review,* 145–156.

Black, J. S., Gregersen, H. B., & Mendenhall, M. E. (1992). *Global assignments: Successfully expatriating and repatriating international managers.* San Francisco, CA: Jossey-Bass Publishers.

Brislin, R. W. (1981). *Cross-cultural encounters: Face-to-face interaction.* New York: Pergamon.

Broome, B. J. (1991). Building shared meaning: Implications of a relational approach to empathy for teaching intercultural communication. *Communication Education, 40*(7), 236–249.

Chaney, L. H., & Martin, J.S. (1993, October). *Cultural shock: An intercultural communication problem.* Paper presented at The Annual Convention of the Association for Business Communication, Montréal, Quebec, Canada.

Clague, L., & Krupp, N. B. (1980, Spring). International personnel: The repatriation problem. *The Bridge,* 11–14.

Dodd, C. H. (1987). *Dynamics of intercultural communication.* Dubuque, IA: Wm. C. Brown Publishers.

Dodd, C. H., & Montalvo, F. F. (Eds.). (1987). *Intercultural skills for multicultural societies.* Washington, DC: Sietar International, 70–80.

Engholm, C. (1991). *When business East meets business West.* New York: John Wiley & Sons, Inc.

Ferraro, G. P. (1990). *The cultural dimension of international business.* Upper Saddle River, NJ: Prentice Hall.

Fussell, P. (1983). *Class.* New York: Ballantine Books.

Geber, B. (1992, July). The care and breeding of global managers. *Training,* 33–37.

Harris, P. R., & Moran, R. T. (1996). *Managing cultural differences.* (4th ed.). Houston: Gulf Publishing Company.

Harvey, M. G. (1985, Spring). The executive family: An overlooked variable in international assignments. *Columbia Journal of World Business,* 84–92.

Khols, R. L. (1984). *Survival kit for overseas living.* Yarmouth, ME: Intecultural Press, Inc.

Klopf, D. W. (1991). *Intercultural encounters.* Englewood, CO: Morton Publishing Company.

Krapels, R. H. (1993). *Predeparture intercultural communication preparation provided international business managers and professionals and perceived characteristics of intercultural training needs.* Doctoral dissertation, Memphis State University. Memphis, TN.

Lewis, T. J., & Jungman, R. E. (Eds.). (1986). *On being foreign; culture shock in short fiction.* Yarmouth, ME: Intercultural Press.

Luft, J. (1984). *Group processes: An introduction to group dynamics.* Palo Alto, CA: Mayfield Publishing Company.

McEnery, J., & DesHarnais, G. (1990, April). Culture shock. *Training and Development Journal,* 43–47.

Tung, R. (1981, Spring). Selection and training of personnel for overseas assignments. *Columbia Journal of World Business,* 68–78.

CHAPTER 5

Language

Objectives
Upon completion of this chapter, you will:

■ understand how language affects intercultural business communication.

■ understand how language construction, thought, perceptions, and culture are linked.

■ understand the limits of using a second language.

■ be aware that language differences exist even when people speak the same language.

■ understand the importance of accurate translation and interpretation to intercultural communication.

■ understand how to use parables and proverbs as insights into the culture.

■ understand the concepts of the Sapir-Whorf and Bernstein hypotheses.

Successful communication with someone from another culture involves understanding a common language. Without this shared language, communication problems may occur when a third party, the translator or interpreter, attempts to convey both the verbal and nonverbal intent of your message. Although a shared language is important, only 20 percent of U.S. firms sending representatives to non-English speaking countries require their overseas representatives to speak the language of the country (Baker, 1984).

Although Chinese is the language spoken by the largest number of native speakers with English ranking second, English is considered the language of international business. However, you may fit in and be able to develop rapport if you are fluent in another's language. Because so many variations exist in the English language, messages are often misunderstood even when both parties speak this language with its many accents, dialects, and regional peculiarities. Unfamiliar accents may present barriers to effective communication.

People who speak English as a second language retain much of their foreign accent. Those for whom Spanish is a first language and English the second language, for example, often pronounce vowels as they are pronounced in the Spanish language. For

81

example, "e" is pronounced as "a" and "i" is pronounced as "e." They may also pronounce certain consonants as they would in Spanish such as "j" is pronounced as "h" (Hoolian for Julian). When the wrong syllable is accented (such as dév-eloped rather then de-véloped), understanding is difficult.

Language holds us together as groups, differentiates us into groups, and also controls the way we shape concepts, how we think, how we perceive, and how we judge others. When we understand how important and complex a culture's native language is, it is easier to see why in a country such as India, English is the official language. The Indian people do, however, use over 100 native languages or dialects for communication within their microcultures.

Women and men, at least in the United States, have different modes of discourse. Women engage in "rapport-talk" and men in "report-talk." Women seek connections and agreement and are more cooperative in discussions. Men tend to be more individualistic and controlling in their conversations. When women and men have conversations, the men talk and interrupt women more often and focus on their topics rather than listening to the women (Tannen, 1990). Many languages are spoken differently by the men and women of the culture. For example, in Japanese the women speak a softer intonation than do men.

The closest concepts to worldwide common languages are numbers and music. Unlike mathematicians, businesspeople must be sensitive to the nuances of a language. This is important to assure understanding when communicating with people whose first language differs from their own or even with those whose language is the same as their own. Language is only part of communication. How the language is used in relationship to nonverbal communication and the beliefs and values of the culture is also very important.

Sociolinguistics refers to the effects of social and cultural differences upon a language. People reveal class differences by their accent, phrasing, and word usage. According to Fussell (1983), U.S. Americans with good educational backgrounds and with relatively high incomes speak in a similar manner regardless of where they live in the country. People who use such terms as *ain't, reckon* (suppose), and *afeared* (afraid) are considered uneducated and/or from lower-class backgrounds.

How strongly group members feel about themselves and their membership in the group determines how members of a group will talk to people in other groups. If a group views itself as a vital *ethnolinguistic* group, (a group that views itself as culturally different from the main group and has developed its own language or dialect) they will be more likely to maintain their distinctive linguistics in a multilingual setting. The more important a language is viewed, the more important the group using the language is in terms of economic, social, and language status (Giles, Bourhis, & Taylor, 1977). Since people in other cultures also reveal their class level by their accent, pronunciation, and word usage, when selecting an interpreter be sure to determine if the person is experienced in the regional and sociolinguistic groups with whom you are dealing.

High- and Low-Context Language

The concept of high- and low-context language has been researched by Hall and Hall (1990). A **high-context language** transmits very little in the explicit message; instead, the nonverbal and cultural aspects of what is not said are very important. In high-context cultures reading between the lines in order to understand the intended meaning of the message is needed. The Japanese language and culture are an example of high-context communication. Bernstein (in Funakawa, 1997) calls the speech coding system of high-context languages **restricted code.** The spoken statement reflects the social relationship and the relationship's shared assumptions.

The United States, on the other hand, is an example of a language and culture of low-context communication. In a **low-context language** and culture, the message is explicit; it may be given in more than one way to ensure understanding by the receiver. In low-context languages, a person would state what is expected or wanted. High-context languages tend to be indirect and nonverbal whereas low-context languages tend to be direct and verbal. Since people of low-context cultures favor directness, they are likely to consider high-context communications as a waste of time. The speech system used in low-context cultures is **elaborated code.** In low-context cultures, a verbal elaboration is necessary due to fewer shared assumptions (Bernstein, in Funakawa, 1997).

Should there be perceived disagreement between the verbal and nonverbal message within either low- or high-context societies, the nonverbal signals are relied on versus what is actually said. However, in high-context cultures the nonverbal signals are much more subtle and elusive to the untrained senses. An example of high-context communication is the way the Japanese indicate *no.* The Japanese would say *yes* for *no* but would indicate whether *yes* is *yes* or really *no* by the context, tone, time taken to answer, and facial and body expressions. This use of high-context communication can be very confusing to the uninitiated, nonsensitive intercultural businessperson. In the United States, a low-context society, *no* means *no.* Group-oriented, collectivistic cultures tend to use high-context languages; individualistic cultures tend to use low-context languages.

Language Diversity

Achieving successful communication is difficult because of the diversity of dialects and accents within a language. In the United States more than 140 languages and dialects are currently spoken; about 11 percent of the population speak a native language other than English in the home (Tsunda, 1986).

The diversity between languages and within the same language is arbitrary. Words in themselves have no meaning; meanings were assigned at some point by people in a culture. For example, the word *business* in the United States connotes how we choose to make and exchange commodities. In other languages, people assign other sounds to mean *business* such as *shobai, bijinesu, shigoto, entreprise, comercio,* and *negocios.* In the English language, synonyms for *business* also exist such as *commerce, trade,* and *enterprise.*

The diversity of languages causes problems both for managers and applicants for jobs. What is the correct way to assess English-language skills of job applicants? Managers must ask themselves the question: How important is correct English-language skill in this position? Perhaps the ability to speak and write English well is not essential to job performance; on the other hand, it may be very important. Language qualifications for each position should be assessed separately.

Even when the language is the same as your native language, one must be careful. For example, Great Britain and Canada both speak English. However, many Canadians follow the British pronunciations and spellings. In some parts of Canada and the United States, people say the accents are nearly indistinguishable. Examples of pronunciation differences include "uh-GAIN" for "again," and "bean" for "been." And, of course, one-fifth of Canadians speak French as their primary language (Bosrock, 1995b).

Other problems caused by language diversity include foreigners who speak their native language on the job, a practice that is not viewed favorably by the nationals. Although the main reason foreigners may use their native language is that it is easier to express their ideas that way, this behavior is interpreted as an attempt to exclude nationals from the conversation and is considered extremely rude.

Slang and Other Informal Language

English in the United States is replete with slang, colloquialisms, acronyms, euphemisms, and jargon from numerous areas including the military, sports, computers, law, and engineering.

Slang includes idioms and other informal language. *Bottom line* and *back to square one* are examples of business slang.

Additional business expressions include (DeVries, 1994):

- asleep at the switch: inattentive
- back off: moderate one's stand or speed if driving
- blockbuster: great success
- cold turkey: abruptly, without warning
- cutthroat: harsh
- eat one's words: retract
- garbage: nonsense
- get off the ground: start successfully
- have someone's number: know the truth about someone
- kiss-off: dismissal
- miss the boat: lost opportunity
- piece of cake: something easy
- ring a bell: sound familiar
- two-bit: cheap, tacky
- red tape: many steps to completion
- bottom line: profits or loss
- ball park figure: an estimate

Colloquialisms are informal words or phrases often associated with certain regions of the country. Examples of colloquialisms include *y'all* (you all), *pop* (soda), and *ain't* (is/are not). **Acronyms** are words formed from the initial letters or groups of letters of words in a phrase and pronounced as one word. Examples of acronyms are *RAM* (random access memory), *BASIC* (beginner's all-purpose symbolic instruction code), *Fortran* (formula translation), and *OSHA (Occupational Safety and Health Administration)*. Initial abbreviations are pronounced as separate initials, such as *CEO* (corporate executive officer), *CAR* (computer-assisted retrieval), and *OJT* (on-job-training). **Euphemisms** are inoffensive expressions that are used in place of offensive words or words with negative connotations. Taboo words are dealt with through euphemisms. Examples of euphemisms are *to pass* or *pass away* (to die), *senior citizens* (old people), *customer service department* (complaint department), and *human relations* (personnel). **Jargon** is technical terminology used within specialized groups such as engineers, teenagers, and doctors. Examples of jargon include *on the ball* (on top of things), *oiled* (become suddenly wealthy), and *byte* (a string of binary digits) (Ferraro, 1990).

Informal language generally is begun by people in a subgroup of a community to differentiate themselves from the masses and determine who is a member of the "in group." Informal language should be used with caution in intercultural encounters because of potential miscommunication.

Forms of Verbal Interaction

Forms of verbal interaction include verbal dueling, repartee conversation, rituals, and self-disclosure.

Verbal dueling is like gamesmanship; the object is to see who can gain dominance in a friendly debate rather than imparting any needed information. The competitive conversations are generally meant in jest but are used in nonaggressive societies to release hostility. Often people who are also not familiar with verbal dueling may misunderstand the subtleties of the communication taking place. In the United States, urban black adolescent males have a form of insult contest called *playing the dozens*. The verbal dueling begins when one male insults a member of the opponent's family. The opponent can choose not to play; however, he will normally counter with an insult of his own. The verbal dueling continues until the males become bored or one is "victorious" (Ferraro, 1990). In Germany, France, and England, politics is an appropriate topic for verbal dueling. Verbal dueling may also take place when discussing sporting events such as which team is better or which team is going to win. In the business environment, verbal dueling may occur when a group is trying to decide on a new ad campaign and members of the group are polarized as to which campaign is best. Many times when companies are interviewing candidates for positions, verbal dueling will take place over who is the best candidate for the job.

Repartee conversation is a conversation in which the parties frequently take turns speaking, usually after the first few sentences. The speakers talk only for short periods of time, then listen while the other person speaks briefly. Repartee is a favorite form of interaction for people of the United States; they become very irritated when someone speaks for too long a period. In contrast, Africans and Arabs tend to speak for extended periods of time (Althen, 1988).

Excellent speech is important to the French and repartee is admired. The speaking skill is so important that for a foreigner to function effectively in France, he or she must speak French fluently (Hall & Hall, 1990).

Ritual conversation is culturally based and involves standard replies and comments for a given situation. In the United States, the interchanges are superficial; little meaning is attached to what is said. U.S. people are not actually interested in learning about others or in revealing their own emotions or personal information during such rituals as greeting others upon arriving at work. Latin Americans, on the other hand, will discuss health and other personal information for extended periods during ritual conversation. Arabs in ritual conversation will invoke Allah's goodwill; however, they avoid discussions of personal situations (Althen, 1988).

Self-disclosure is another form of interaction that involves telling other people about yourself so they may get to know you better. The amount of self-disclosure a person is willing to give another is culturally determined (Althen, 1988). Foreigners who need to know a person in order to do business with that person become very frustrated with the lack of personal information provided by people in the United States. If people in a culture feel the need to develop friendships prior to conducting business, doing business with U.S. persons can be very disconcerting since U.S. Americans are not viewed as being committed to forming friendships.

Linear and Nonlinear Language

Linear and nonlinear aspects of language involve cultural thought patterns; they indicate how people in a specific culture think and communicate (Tsunda, 1986).

Linear language has a beginning and an end, is logical, and object oriented. Linear languages such as English, look at time on a continuum of present, past, and future. This view has affected communication patterns and business practices in the United States; an example of such business practices is short-range planning.

Nonlinear language is circular, tradition oriented, and subjective. Nonlinear languages such as Chinese, look at time as cyclical and the seasons as an ever-repeating pattern. The nonlinear concepts are apparent in the long-range planning of the Chinese and Japanese and in the seasonal messages at the beginning of Japanese letters. The short term is unimportant in Asia. In the United States, for example, stockholders tend to sell their ownership in firms that are having short-term problems; Asians, on the other hand, look at the long-term position of the firm and hold onto the stock.

In intercultural business situations, people will respond in a dialogue based on their linear or nonlinear orientation. In the United States, linear explanations are given as answers to *why* questions. The Japanese, however, would give more details that do not need linear links. The Japanese would tell *what* happened and assume the *why* whereas U.S. people answer *why* and assume the *what*. For example, a U.S. manager might ask a Japanese worker why the production was stopped. The manager would expect a direct answer such as, "The parts are defective." The Japanese worker would answer nonlinearly with a very long detailed explanation including what the defects were and other related details. Miscommunication occurred because the Japanese answered with *what* was wrong instead of the *why* response expected by the U.S. manager (Tsunda, 1986).

Vocabulary Equivalence

Because language is influenced by various aspects of a culture, exact translations for all words in one language to a second language are not possible. For example in one language, the world *love* is used to mean love of another person, love of a pet, or love of an object while in a second language, different words are provided to distinguish between different types of love.

There are many vocabulary inequivalences including problems due to idiomatic equivalence, grammatical-syntactical equivalence, experiential equivalence, and conceptual equivalence (Jandt, 1995).

The English language is built on extremes, such as far and near, heavy and light, high and low, good and bad, wide and narrow, old and young, and long and short. These conceptual inequivalences can cause misunderstanding. The middle area between the extremes may or may not have words to describe it, forcing a person speaking English to use one of the polar ends. The Portuguese language has many words in the middle area between the extremes; however, when the Portuguese is translated to English only the extremes are available. Therefore, when the translation is read in English, it may not have a vocabulary equivalence and will not be asking or saying what was said in Portuguese. The Portuguese question, "Qual é a distancia a New York?" becomes "How far is it to New York?" However, what the Portuguese are actually asking for is the location in space of New York as opposed to the translation that stresses the far or near dichotomy of the English language (Stewart & Bennett, 1991).

An example of grammatical-syntactical equivalence is the following story.

A devout Catholic, David drove south from Minnesota to celebrate the papal visit to Mexico. Overcome with emotion upon seeing His Holiness, David ran through the streets of Mexico City shouting "¡Viva la papa! ¡Viva la papa!" David's newfound Mexican friend, while sharing in his excitement, thought it prudent to correct David's Spanish. "The Spanish word for 'pope' is el papa," the Mexican explained. "You're shouting 'Long Live the Potato'" (Bosrock, 1995b, p. 40).

FIGURE 5.1 Vocabulary Equivalence

In the United States, the word "love" is used to mean a strong preference for an object as well as physical or emotional "love."

Language misunderstandings related to vocabulary usage are numerous even between people who speak the same language. During his 1976 presidential campaign, for example, President Carter used the phrase *ethnic purity* to convey the message that our ethnic heritage and customs are important and should not be lost in the dominant culture. African Americans, however, interpreted it as a racist statement, and white South Africans interpreted it as support of their separatist policies. The individual cultural experiences of African Americans and white South Africans allowed for interpretations of the world *purity* that President Carter had not intended (Dodd, 1987). Translators must decide whether to translate a word or phrase based on its denotative, connotative, text normative, pragmatic, or formal equivalence.

World War II and the use of the atomic bomb may well have been the result of such a translation error. The Japanese government in response to the Potsdam ultimatum responded, "The government does not see much value in it. All we have to do is *mokusatsu* it." The Japanese had carefully chosen the word mokusatsu and intended it to mean no comment. The Western translators chose one of the word's other meanings which is to ignore or to treat with silent contempt (Jandt, 1995).

Homonyms, words that sound alike but have different meanings, can be troublesome when learning a new language. The Chinese language is particularly difficult in this regard because even though the word is pronounced the same, the voice tone and pitch can change the entire meaning of a word. Within a family of languages (such as the Romance languages) words with similar spellings and sometimes very similar pronunciations may have very different or very similar meanings. Assuming a similarity could be both costly and embarrassing during intercultural communication encounters (Ferraro, 1990).

Sound alike?

Chuck Blethen of Scottsdale, Arizona, recounts his experience when ordering in Spanish at a Madrid restaurant. "I ordered caballo. The waiter looked at me indignantly and said, 'Sir, we don't serve horse here.' I thought I was saying cebolla which means onion" (Schmit, Richards, & Swingle, 1993, p. 5e).

Experiential equivalence happens when there is no word in one language because the idea or object does not exist. Ideas such as *department store, mall shopping,* or *wind surfing* are words that do not always translate well.

Parables and Proverbs

A **parable** is a story told to convey a truth or moral lesson and a **proverb** is a saying that expresses a common truth. Parables and proverbs deal with truths simply and concretely and teach the listener a lesson.

Parables and proverbs can help to understand a culture and can help to determine if it is a group- or individual-oriented culture. Parables and proverbs may also help in understanding what is desired and undesired as well as what is considered correct or incorrect in the culture (Ferraro, 1990).

The U.S. proverb, "The squeaking wheel gets the grease," implies that the person who stands out and is the most vocal will be rewarded. The Japanese proverb, "The nail that sticks up gets knocked down," is an expression of their belief that the group is more important than the individual—the idea is that no one should stand out or be more important than anyone else.

Here are some other proverbs of selected cultures:

U.S. AMERICAN PROVERBS

"The early bird gets the worm."

"Waste not, want not."

"He who holds the gold makes the rules."

"An ounce of prevention is worth a pound of cure."

CHINESE PROVERBS

"Man who waits for roast duck to fly into mouth must wait very, very long time."

"He who sows hemp will reap hemp; he who sows beans will reap beans."

"Man who says it cannot be done should not interrupt man doing it."

"Give a man a fish and he will live for a day; give him a net and he will live for a lifetime."

GERMAN PROVERBS

"No one is either rich or poor who has not helped himself to be so."

"He who is afraid of doing too much always does too little."

"What's the use of running if you're not on the right road?"

JAPANESE PROVERBS

"Silence is golden."

"Still water runs deep."

"A wise man hears one and understands ten."

"A wise hawk hides his talons."

OTHER PROVERBS

"Words do not make flour." (Italian)

"He that wishes to eat the nut does not mind cracking the shell." (Polish)

"Why kill time when one can employ it?" (French)

"Wealth which comes in at the door unjustly, goes out at the windows." (Egyptian)

Parables and proverbs can provide important information concerning the nature of the culture such as whether or not it is basically an empathetic culture or an uncaring one.

Conversation Taboos

Conversation taboos are topics considered inappropriate for conversation with people in certain cultures or groups. Braganti and Devine (1992), Devine and

Braganti (1986, 1988), and Baldrige (1993) discuss the culturally preferred topics of conversation as well as those that are considered taboo. Meeting another person usually involves a certain amount of "small talk" before getting down to business so knowing what topics are considered appropriate and inappropriate is important. (Small talk as a business and social custom is discussed in more detail in chapter 9.)

In the United States, the most popular topic of small talk seems to be the weather or comments on some aspect of the physical surroundings such as the arrangement of the meeting room, some aspect of the building such as the landscaping or the building location. Topics that are included later in the encounter include favorite restaurants, television programs, cities or countries visited, one's job, recreational interests or hobbies, and news items. Topics people in the United States have been taught to avoid discussing include religion and politics even in family situations because they are too controversial. In the United States, family members often belong to different religions and political parties. The avoidance of such topics has caused people in other cultures to erroneously conclude that people in the United States are not intellectually capable of carrying on a conversation about anything more complex than weather and sports.

Some topics are considered too personal to discuss such as the state of one's health or the health of family members, how much things cost, a person's salary, and personal misfortunes. People in the United States have been taught never to ask another person questions related to sensitive areas such as age, weight, height, hair color, or sexual orientation or behavior.

Topics considered inappropriate in the United States are, however, considered appropriate in other cultures. People in Germany and Iran, for example, consider discussing and arguing about politics to be completely acceptable. The state of one's health and well-being and that of family members is an appropriate topic when people from Spanish-speaking countries meet for the first time. People from Saudi Arabia, on the other hand, would consider questions about the family inappropriate on an initial meeting.

General guidelines to follow when conversing with someone from another culture include (Baldrige, 1993):

- Avoid discussing politics or religion unless the other person initiates the discussion.
- Avoid highly personal questions including "What do you do?"
- Keep the conversation positive. Avoid asking questions that would imply criticism; phrase questions so they can be answered in a positive manner.
- Avoid telling ethnic jokes because of the possibility of offending someone.

A good rule to follow is to take your cue from the other person. Let the other person initiate the discussion, particularly with culture-sensitive topics. Be a good listener and stay informed on a wide variety of topics to expand your conversational repertoire.

Here are some appropriate and inappropriate topics of conversation in selected countries (Braganti & Devine, 1992; Devine & Braganti, 1986, 1988):

Country	Appropriate Topics	Topics to Avoid
Austria	professions, cars skiing, music	money, religion, divorce/separation
Germany	travel abroad, international politics, hobbies, soccer	World War II, questions about personal life
Great Britain	history, architecture, gardening	politics, money/prices, Falklands War
France	music, books, sports, the theater	prices of items, person's work, income, age
Mexico	family, social concerns	politics, debt, inflation problems, border violations
Japan	history, culture, art	World War II

Nature of Language

People who study the phonetic aspects of language and define language by the sounds speakers produce and listeners receive are known as **linguists.** People who study the meaning of words and where and how the words developed are known as **semanticists.** People who study how a language is governed, its grammatical forms, roots, and endings are known as **grammarians.** People who believe that language is a series of words arranged to produce harmonious sounds or to have a logical effect are known as **novelists** (Klopf, 1991).

   Syntactic rules govern how words are arranged in a sentence. Different languages choose variations. English, French, and Spanish mainly follow a subject/verb/object order. Japanese and Korean have the preferred order of subject/object/verb. Hebrew and Welsh follow verb/subject/object. The object does not come first in any language (Klopf, 1991).

   Different perceptual meanings are given depending upon our choice of word selection. **Denotative meanings** are definition meanings such as the name of a type of crab, the Japanese Spider Crab. **Connotative meanings** are the emotional meanings such as Alaskan King Crab. **Figurative meanings** are descriptive meanings such as *kicking the bucket* (Klopf, 1991).

   Verbal styles are different between languages (Klopf, 1991).

Translation Problems

When languages are translated, the intended meaning may be lost. Although these errors may seem hilarious, they are also costly. Translation is written and does not have the advantage of the nonverbal. Moreover, you are more likely to receive a literal translation than a literal interpretation.

Ethnic Group	*Verbal Style*
Japanese	• They converse without responding to what the other person says. Emphasis is on nonverbal communication so they do not listen. • They prefer less talkative persons and value silence. • They prefer as few words as possible. • They make excuses at the beginning of a talk for what they are about to say. They do not want apologies for what was already said. • The word "yes" has many different meanings.
Mexican	• They seem overly dramatic and emotional to U.S. persons. • They rise above and embellish facts; eloquence is admired. • They like to use diminutives, making the world smaller and more intimate. They add suffixes to words to minimize importance. • Mexicans appear to be less than truthful. Their rationale involves two types of reality—objective and interpersonal. Mexicans want to keep people happy for the moment. When asked directions if they don't know the answer, they will create directions to appear to be helpful.
Chinese	• They understate or convey meanings indirectly. They use vague terms and double negatives; even criticism is indirect. • Harmony is very important. During negotiations, the Chinese state their position in such a way that seems repetitious. They do not change their point of view without discussing it with the group. • They speak humbly and speak negatively of their supposedly meager skills and those of their subordinates and their family.
Arabian	• They encourage eloquence and "flowery" prose. They are verbose, repetitious, and shout when excited. • For dramatic effect, they punctuate remarks by pounding the table and making threatening gestures. • They view swearing, cursing, and the use of obscenities as offensive. • They like to talk about religion and politics but avoid talking about death, illness, and disasters. Emotional issues are avoided. • The first name is used immediately upon meeting but may be preceded by the title "Mr." or "Miss."
German	• In the German language, the verb often comes at the end of the sentence. In oral communication, Germans do not immediately get to the point. • Germans are honest and direct; they stick to the facts. They are low-context people; everything is spelled out. • Germans usually do not use first names unless they are close friends (of which they have few). • They do not engage in small talk; their conversations are serious on a wide variety of topics. Avoid conversations related to their private life.
U.S. American	• Some words are specific to an age group. • Men speak more, repeat more, and more often than women; women are more emotional and use such terms as "sweet," "darling," and "dreadful." • There are racial differences in verbal style. Black English includes rapping which is a narration to a musical beat. Shucking and jiving are terms used to conceal the true feelings of African Americans toward whites or authority figures by acting innocent or obedient with humility and deference.

Axtell (1991) identifies a number of U.S. translation problems: 1) General Motors automobile "Nova" in Spanish means "doesn't go"; 2) Pepsi-Cola's "Come Alive with Pepsi" when translated in Taiwanese is "Pepsi brings your ancestors back from the grave"; 3) Electrolux, a Swedish manufacturer, used "Nothing sucks like an Elecrolux," which failed because of the slang meaning of suck in the United States; and Bic pens were originally name Bich by their French manufacturer.

The word or concept may not have an exact duplicate in the other language. All languages do not have the same verb tenses and many verbs have multiple meanings. In English, for example, the verb "get" can mean to buy, borrow, steal, rent, or retrieve. When a language is the person's second language, slang, euphemisms, and cultural thinking patterns can cause problems.

Braniff Airlines promoted rendezvous lounges on its Brazilian routes. Rendezvous in Portuguese is a place to have sex.

For the 1994 World Cup, both McDonald's and Coca-Cola reprinted the Saudi Arabian flag including the verbage from the Koran on their paper bags and cans. Muslims were appalled that the Koran passage, "There is no God but Allah, and Mohammed is his Prophet," would be used to sell a product and be put on something that is thrown away.

President Kennedy giving a speech at the Berlin Wall said, "Ich bin ein Berliner," which when properly translated means, "I am a jelly doughnut."

One can ask a Russian who knows some English what the Russian word *drúk* means and the answer will be "friend." This is roughly true, but the precise social circumstances under which a Russian calls another person *drúk* are by no means the same as those under which we call someone a friend.

Bilingual dictionaries and easy word-by-word translations are inevitably misleading; the shortcut of asking what a form means must ultimately be supplemented by active participation in the life of the community that speaks the language. This, of course, is one of the major reasons why semantic analysis is so difficult (Hockett, 1967, p. 141).

Back translation is the concept of a written work translated to a second language, then having another person translate the work back to the first language to determine if the translations are equivalent.

One type of translation assistance is **Group Decision Support System** (GDSS), a software package that allows people to communicate by computer in a meeting utilizing language translation software which permits participants to comment on a topic at the same time, rank order the comments, and vote on the comments in their own language. People participate in their own language which will be translated into the other languages just as the others' communication would be translated into their own language. Words that do not translate directly are put in quotation marks to alert the reader to a possible translation problem. Pocket translators are also available to aid in learning and understanding another language.

Those who need oral interpretations or written translations in the United States can contact local universities for names of competent translators or consult the *Translation Services Directory,* published by the American Translators Association, 109 Croton Avenue, Ossining, New York 10562, or The American Association of Language Specialists in Washington, D.C. Rates for on-the-spot verbal translations are charged by the hour while written translations are charged by the word and the nature of the material being translated. AT&T has a Language Line Service (800-752-6096) to reach language professionals who interpret more than 140 languages; they are available 24 hours a day, 7 days a week.

Interpreter Use

An interpreter uses the oral or spoken word versus the written word. To be useful in a negotiation situation, an interpreter must be bilingual, bicultural, thoroughly familiar with the business culture of both sides, and able to use the correct meaning in all situations. However, what often happens is that interpreters are supplied by the host culture, are bilingual but not bicultural, and understand at least some business in their own culture and perhaps a little of the other side's business culture. Their loyalty is, of course, with their employer. When an interpreter is not bicultural, his or her thoughts, feelings, and hence translations, are formulated according to the interpreter's native language rather than the second language. When using an interpreter in international negotiations, a missed negative can turn an agreement into a disagreement. A poor translator can make the difference between the success or failure of the negotiation.

Many U.S. business travelers expect everyone to speak English and, therefore, do not feel compelled to get an interpreter. While people may speak English as a second language, they do not think the same as U.S. businesspeople unless they are bicultural. Because of this, it is very easy for an interpreter to misinterpret the English being used by the U.S. businessperson and to misstate facts when translating back to English. Unless the traveler is aware of the possibility of misinterpretation and asks additional questions, the traveler could leave with the wrong answer or conception.

When using an interpreter, review with him or her your notes, slides, presentation, or anything else you have brought with you before the meeting. The advantage of using bicultural interpreters is that you can ask them questions if you are not sure what to do next. A bicultural interpreter can also alert you to problems he or she may foresee. Interpreters should be allowed to use notes or a dictionary and be allowed sufficient time to clarify points. Try not to interrupt interpreters while they are translating. Use visuals to support presentations, but allow the bicultural interpreter to check them for anything that may be offensive to the other people. Remember to avoid sarcasm or innuendoes because they are very difficult to translate. Try to state concepts in more than one way to be sure the point you are making is understood.

The following tips will help you work with interpreters (Axtell, 1991; Bosrock, 1994):

- Get to know the interpreter in advance. Your phrasing, accent, pace, and idioms are all important to a good interpreter.
- Review technical terms in advance.
- Speak slowly and clearly.
- Don't be afraid to use gestures and show emotion.
- Watch the eyes; they are the key to comprehension.
- Insist that the interpreter translate in brief bursts, and not wait until the end of a long statement.
- Be careful of humor and jokes; it is difficult to export U.S. American humor.
- Use visual aids where possible. By combining the translator's words with visual messages, chances of effective communication are increased.
- Be especially careful with numbers; write out important numbers to ensure accurate communication.
- Confirm all important discussions in writing to avoid confusion and misunderstanding.
- Allow the interpreter to apologize for your inability to speak your counterpart's language.
- Ask your interpreter about meeting styles, small talk, and discuss major issues.
- Carefully place your interpreter remembering proper etiquette.
- Speak to your counterpart, not to the interpreter.
- Keep comments simple and direct.
- Get feedback through questions to be certain ideas are interpreted and understood correctly.
- Do not make statements you do not want your counterparts to hear, even if these points are not interpreted. Many counterparts can understand your language even if they are not speaking it.
- If the message is complex, meet with the interpreter prior to the meeting so the interpreter will have a clear understanding of what you are saying.
- Have a concluding session with the interpreters to see if they picked up all messages that will not translate.

Host Language

If you choose to use the language of the country you are visiting, the **host language,** be especially cautious. Be sure to speak clearly and slowly and eliminate jargon, idioms, and slang. When in doubt, ask questions. Avoid using expressions or gestures that could be misinterpreted. Find out if the meaning in the host language is modified by cadence, tone, or gestures.

Learning a business partner's language can help you learn how the person thinks. Learning a foreign language and living in another cultural community will affect your view of life. You will begin to think from the other person's perspective and will reevaluate your own cultural heritage. To live in another country, one must develop personal relations and function effectively. In order to function effectively, some fluency in the language will be important. A competency in a foreign language is time consuming, but is helped by the language families. The Romance languages (Spanish, French, Portuguese, and Italian) share Latin as their source and therefore have many **cognates** or words that sound the same and have the same meaning. However, you must be careful because not all words that appear to be cognates are.

As has been mentioned earlier, significant differences exist when both people speak the same language in the same country. Those living in the eastern United States are considered by many people in other parts of the country to be direct, rude, and to the point; Southerners are considered by many to be indirect, friendly, and more likely to skirt issues. When people speak the same language but are from different countries, additional problems are encountered. For example, the English spoken in the United States is quite different from the English spoken in Australia and Great Britain. The British use a very indirect style of verbalizing while people of the United States use a more direct style.

The best advice when using the host language is to maintain a pleasant disposition and a positive attitude toward the host language; avoid making comments that could be interpreted as criticism of their language.

The language people speak, the name of the countries, and what the citizens are called can be very confusing. The following list should make references easier (Bosrock, 1995a, p. 53).

COUNTRY	PEOPLE	LANGUAGE
• Austria	• Austrians	• German
• Belgium	• Belgians	
–Wallonia	–Waloons	–French
–Flanders	–Flemings	–Flemish/Dutch
• Canada	• Canadians	• English/French
• Denmark	• Danes	• Danish
• Finland	• Finns	• Finnish
• France	• French	• French
• Germany	• Germans	• German
• Greece	• Greeks	• Greek
• Ireland	• Irish	• English/Irish
• Italy	• Italians	• Italian
• Japan	• Japanese	• Japanese
• Luxembourg	• Luxembourgers	• Luxembourgish/French/German
• Mexico	• Mexicans	• Spanish
• Netherlands	• Dutch/Netherlanders	• Dutch
• Norway	• Norwegians	• Norwegian
• Portugal	• Portuguese	• Portuguese
• Spain	• Spanish/Spaniards	• Spanish
• Sweden	• Swedes	• Swedish
• Switzerland	• Swiss	• French/German/Italian/Romansch
• Turkey	• Turks	• Turkish
• United Kingdom	• British	• English
–England	–British/English	–English

–Scotland	–Scots	–English/Gaelic
–Wales	–Welsh	–English/Welsh
–Northern Ireland	–Northern Irish	–English

English is spoken as a native language, a semiofficial language, or is studied in the following countries (*U.S. News*, 1995).

NATIVE LANGUAGE

- North America
  - Canada, except Quebec
  - United States
- South America
  - Guyana
- Caribbean
  - Bahamas
  - Barbados
  - Grenada
  - Jamaica
  - Trinidad and Tobago
- Europe
  - Ireland
  - United Kingdom
- Pacific
  - Australia
  - New Zealand

SEMIOFFICIAL LANGUAGE

- Africa
  - Botswana
  - Cameroon
  - Ethiopia
  - Gambia
  - Ghana
  - Kenya
  - Lesotho
  - Liberia
  - Malawi
  - Mauritius
  - Namibia
  - Sierra Leone
  - South Africa
  - Sudan
  - Swaziland
  - Tanzania
  - Uganda
  - Zambia
  - Zimbabwe
- Asia, Pacific
  - Bangladesh
  - Fiji
  - India
  - Malaysia
  - Myanmar (Burma)
  - Pakistan
  - Philippines
  - Singapore
  - Sri Lanka
  - Tonga
  - Western Samoa
- Mideast
  - Israel
  - Malta

LANGUAGE STUDIED

- North America
  - Mexico
- Central America
- Caribbean
  - Costa Rica
  - Cuba
  - Dominican Republic
  - Honduras
- South America
  - Brazil
  - Colombia
  - Venezuela
- Europe
  - Austria
  - Belgium
  - Denmark
  - Finland
  - France
  - Germany
  - Greece
  - Iceland
  - Italy
  - Luxembourg
  - Netherlands
  - Norway
  - Portugal
  - Romania
  - Russian Federation
  - Sweden
  - Switzerland
- Africa
  - Algeria
  - Angola
  - Burkina Faso
  - Burundi

LANGUAGE STUDIED *(Continued)*

–Central African Republic	–Togo	–Afghanistan
–Chad	–Democratic Republic of Congo	–China
–Côte d'Ivoire	• Middle East	–Hong Kong
–Gabon	–Egypt	–Indonesia
–Guinea	–Jordan	–Japan
–Libya	–Saudi Arabia	–Nepal
–Madagascar	–Syria	–S. Korea
–Morocco	–Turkey	–Thailand
–Niger	–Yemen	
–Senegal	• Asia	

Thought

Thinking is universal; however, methods of classifying, categorizing, sorting, and storing information are very different.

Subjective interpretation is an interpretation placed on a message that is affected by the thought processes; it is influenced by personal judgment, state of mind, or temperament of the person. Subjective interpretation is learned through cultural contact. We perceive what is relevant to our physical and social survival and classify, categorize, sort, and store it for future use. What is important in one culture may not be important in another.

In the United States, people tend to think in a very functional, pragmatic way; they like procedural knowledge (how to get from point A to point B). Europeans, however, are more abstract; they like declarative knowledge which is descriptive. The Japanese have a different way of thinking; they like to work with precedents and rules rather than abstract probability (Borden, 1991).

Thoughts and views toward nature, for example, are culturally diverse. U.S. people view nature as something to conquer; however, Native Americans and many Asians view nature as something with which to coexist. Other cultures such as the Colombian mestizo, consider nature to be dangerous and have a fatalistic attitude toward it and their ability to control their destiny. A culture's perception of nature can be seen in their parables and proverbs, work ethic, and religion (Condon & Yousef, 1975).

A culture's way of thinking has adversely affected the culture's ability to make progress. People who worked with the Peace Corps, for example, found that introducing technology to a third world country could not be accomplished without a change in cultural attitudes toward technology (Condon & Yousef, 1975). Initial plans for people of the Russian states following the fall of communism in 1991 were to give them stock in businesses and housing. After generations of being told what to do, however, the people had a difficult time changing their way of thinking to include taking responsibility for themselves.

In our thought processes, we make associations between color and messages: i.e., in the United States *red* is associated with *stop; green* is associated with *go.* U.S. Americans associate white with purity but in China, white is associated with death. Additional information related to messages conveyed through the use of color will be presented in Chapter 6.

Language and Culture Interaction

Language can be both unifying and divisive. A common native language ties people together yet the presence of many different native languages in a small geographic area can cause problems. Culture and language both affect each other. We have the chicken and egg dilemma—which came first, the language or the culture? The use of language/culture in creating political, social, economic, and education processes is a consequence of favoring certain ideals over others. Understanding the culture without understanding the language is difficult.

Colonialism caused many areas of the world to lose or replace their native languages with the colonial language. Because the colonies spoke the colonizers' language, the colonizers treated them from an ethnocentric view. Many areas of the world that once were colonized are now trying to regain their native language in an effort to regain their ethnic identify (Ferraro, 1990).

Since most U.S. Americans are immigrants and have learned English, their native languages have died. Although many U.S. citizens may not speak the languages of their ancestors, many of the thought patterns have been passed from generation to generation such as how one shows affection for male and female friends, male and female family members, one's spouse and children, and an acquaintance. A person with a strong German background would be less likely to hug any of those group members in public; however, someone of Spanish or African descent would be much more likely to hug and show affection in public. Generally when people want to continue speaking their native language, it is because they are able to express their thoughts more clearly and maintain what is culturally comfortable.

English also changes from one region of the nation to another. All these differences cause unequal power relationships to develop between people from different social and power backgrounds. Because language determines your cognition and perception, if you are removed from your linguistic environment, you no longer have the conceptual framework to explain ideas and opinions. The Sapir-Whorf hypothesis, the Bernstein hypothesis, and argot offer additional insight into language and culture interaction (Samovar & Porter, 1991; Stewart & Bennett, 1991; Weaver, 1998).

SAPIR-WHORF HYPOTHESIS

The main idea of the **Sapir-Whorf Hypothesis** named for Edward Sapir and Benjamin Lee Whorf is that language functions as a way of shaping a person's experience and not just a device for reporting that experience. People adhere to the connections of their language to communicate effectively. Both structural and semantic aspects of a language are involved. The structural aspect includes phonetics and syntax. Although the syntax aspect of language is influenced by and influences perception and categorization, the semantic aspect of language deals with meaning.

The concept of linguistic determinism is often referred to as the Sapir-Whorf Hypothesis since the two men figured predominately in its development. **Linguistic determinism** is the assumption that a person's view of reality stems mainly from his or her language. Even though two languages may be similar, they cannot represent the same social reality; the worlds of the people who speak the two languages are different. So although languages often do have equivalencies in other languages, the social reality cannot be fully conveyed to a person who does not speak the language.

An example of the concept of linguistic determinism is the absence of a word for *snow* in Inuit, the language of the Inuit people. The language does, however, have numerous words for types of snow while other languages do not have the equivalent of *flaky snow* or *crusty snow,* for example. Since snow is important to the Inuit people, they need to be able to describe it precisely (Borden, 1991; Condon & Yousef, 1975; Dodd, 1987; Ferraro, 1990; Samovar & Porter, 1991).

ARGOT

Each language is suited to describing and dealing with the social realities peculiar to its culture. This concept is especially true of nondominant co-cultures. Since their values and lifestyles usually differ from those of the dominant culture, they develop a language all their own that sets them apart but also permits them to convey their unique social realities with others in the culture. The term for this co-cultural language code is **argot.** Argot is a vocabulary of a particular group; it is often regional. The primary difference between argot and a foreign language is the relationship between sounds and meanings. For example, in the Spanish language the word for house is *casa.* Although the sounds are different, what is being referred to is the same. In argot, it is the meanings that change while the sounds would stay the same.

U.S. co-cultures that use argot are numerous; they may be subdivided by culture (French, Chinese, Spanish, African Americans) or by behavior (prostitutes, gangs, drug users, prisoners, gays). African Americans have a distinctive language sometimes referred to as **Ebonics;** for example, they use such terms as *bad* (meaning the best), *haircut* (having been robbed or cheated), and *get down* (to show enthusiasm for a particular activity) when communicating with others in the African American community. Drug users use terms such as *pipe* (large vein), *hay* (marijuana), and *heat* (police) to communicate to others in the co-culture (Dodd, 1987; Samovar & Porter, 1991). England's Oxford English is not the same as U.S. English. To the British an elevator is a lift; a car hood is a bonnet; an international call is a trunk call. The concept of argot is important as it provides valuable information into the lifestyles and experiences of people in a co-culture as well as comprehension of the message.

Some African Americans speak a dialect called pidgin English or black dialect, Black **patois,** or ghettoese, some of which goes back to the days of slavery in the United States and communication between African Americans on various plantations. The five elements that describe African American communication are: 1) Assertiveness—speaker orientation toward one's own power, 2) Forthrightness—direct problem solving, 3) Ethical awareness—a belief in fairness and accountability, 4) Group identification—collectivism, and 5) Language—verbally inventive with call-response required (Pressley, 1987).

Within a society, there are two cultural qualities. The first is the **associative** (also called **gemeinschaft**—the smaller ethnic groups within the large abstractive **gesellschaft** society). The important point to understand is that these language variations develop because of a need within the cultural group. The new language is normally intelligent, sophisticated, spoken not written, and nonverbal elements are very important. Because of these qualities, the associated language tends to be a more intimate language. Because the associated language is more intimate, it is more difficult for abstractive language users to understand and translate. Everyone uses some associative language with loved ones and friends, e.g., terms of endearment and nicknames. This language is used within the associative cultural group and may be considered rude if used by someone outside the associative group. In order to be part of the large society, everyone must speak the language of the abstractive culture. The abstractive culture is more inclusive but less sensitive to emotions; the associative culture is less inclusive and more sensitive to emotions (Weaver, 1998).

BERNSTEIN HYPOTHESIS

The **Bernstein Hypothesis** explains how social structure affects language and is an extension of the Sapir-Whorf Hypothesis. Bernstein considers culture, subculture, social context, and social system to be part of social structure.

According to the Bernstein Hypothesis, speech emerges in one of two codes—restricted or elaborated. Communication transmission channels used in the **restricted code** would be oral, nonverbal, and paralinguistic. Restricted codes would include highly predictable messages; they are for those who know you and what you are talking about quite well. These codes are similar to argot in that the communication assumes a common interest or shared experience. Because of this shared experience and identity, elaborating on the verbal message is unnecessary. You may, for example, find that your best friend sometimes finishes your sentences or knows what you are going to say before you finish speaking because of shared experiences. **Elaborated codes** are used with strangers; they involve messages that are low in predictability. You would need to give very explicit information to ensure that the message is understood. The verbal channel is important in elaborated codes, while restricted codes make use of nonverbal and paralinguistic cues (Dodd, 1987).

Terms

- Acronyms
- Argot
- Associative
- Back translation
- Bernstein Hypothesis
- Cognates
- Colloquialism
- Connotative meanings
- Conversation taboos
- Denotative meanings
- Ebonics
- Elaborated codes
- Euphemisms
- Figurative meanings
- Geminschaft
- Gesellschaft
- Grammarians
- Group Decision Support Systems
- High-context language
- Homonyms
- Host language
- Jargon
- Linear language
- Linguistic determinism
- Linguists
- Low-context language
- Nonlinear language
- Novelists
- Parable
- Patois
- Proverb
- Repartee conversation
- Restricted codes
- Ritual conversation
- Sapir-Whorf Hypothesis
- Self-disclosure
- Semanticists
- Slang
- Sociolinguistics
- Subjective interpretation
- Syntactic rules
- Verbal Dueling

Instructions: Circle T for true and F for false.

1. T F   Nonverbal aspects are very important in low-context cultures.
2. T F   The Japanese language and culture are an example of high-context communication.
3. T F   The terms *sanitation engineer* and *garbage collector* are examples of colloquialisms.
4. T F   Politics is an appropriate topic for verbal dueling in Germany.
5. T F   Repartee involves taking turns speaking.
6. T F   People of the United States provide very little self-disclosure.
7. T F   Chinese is an example of a linear language.
8. T F   Conversation taboos in Mexico include politics and border violations.
9. T F   The concept of linguistic determinism is related to the Sapir-Whorf Hypothesis.
10. T F   The Bernstein Hypothesis involves restricted and elaborated codes.

Questions and Cases for Discussion

1. Explain how language differentiates us as groups.
2. Teenagers and other groups develop jargon and slang. Give examples of slang or jargon used by people with whom you associate.
3. The United States is a low-context country, and Japan is a high-context country. How would the Japanese react to a flamboyant U.S. salesperson?
4. Give examples of conversation taboos in your home or group of friends.
5. Why is a bicultural/bilingual interpreter better than a monocultural/bilingual interpreter?
6. In what employee positions would knowledge of a foreign language be more crucial for a company? Why?
7. Explain how ethnic groups in the United States participate in verbal dueling.
8. What does it mean to say two languages do not have vocabulary equivalence? To say the same language does not have vocabulary equivalence?
9. Explain what is meant by argot. Give examples from a culture with which you are familiar.
10. Explain the difference between restricted and elaborated codes in the Bernstein Hypothesis.
11. If thinking is universal, how does culture and language affect the way different groups of humans think?

CASE 1

In parts of the United States, particularly in Florida where there is a large Latin American population, the suggestion has been made that Spanish should be considered the first language and English the second language and that people whose native language is Spanish should be taught in Spanish with English taught as a second language. Based on the discussion of language in this chapter, what are the advantages and disadvantages of implementing such a system? How would your argument for or against this proposed change apply to similar situations in India, Canada, or the European Economic Community?

CASE 2

A U.S. production manager, Joe Sorrells, is sent to manage a manufacturing facility in Mexico. Upon arrival, his assistant production manager, Juan Lopez, suggests they go to the factory to meet the workers who have been awaiting his arrival. Joe declines Juan's offer and chooses instead to get right to work on determining why the quality and production rate of the Mexican plant are not equal to the U.S. plant. Juan stresses the importance of getting to know the workers first, but Joe lets Juan know he was sent to Mexico to straighten things out, not to form friendships with the local workers. Without further comment, Juan gets Joe the figures and records he requests. Joe instigated a number of changes and felt sure the plan he had prepared would improve quality and increase production. After a couple of months, no improvement has been made; Joe cannot understand why the workers seem to resist his plans. What went wrong?

CASE 3

You are responsible for hiring a sales manager whose territory will include South America. You have narrowed your search to two people. One is a citizen of Brazil who speaks Spanish and Portuguese but very little English. The second is a U.S. citizen who speaks English and a little Spanish. Your product line necessitates the sales manager hiring two additional people in South America, running a sales office with a receptionist/secretary, living in South America, and personally calling on customers in the different countries. Which of the two people would you choose? Give reasons for your choice.

CASE 4

You are in a meeting in a subsidiary of a German company in the United States. The meeting has two German citizens who are living in the United States and three U.S. citizens all of whom are employees. You have been discussing packaging of a new product, and suddenly the two Germans begin speaking in German rather than English. You wait for a couple of minutes, become irritated, and leave. Explain what is happening in this situation concerning the use of language.

Activities

1. Prepare a list of countries you have visited or countries in which you have worked. List one U.S. slang expression that would have a negative meaning in each country listed.
2. Quote a parable or proverb from one of the countries listed in Activity 1 and indicate how the parable or proverb characterizes some aspect of the culture.
3. List three conversation taboos in the United States and three taboos in one of the countries identified in Activity 1.
4. Write a paragraph about language problems you have encountered when communicating with students from other cultures. Include problems with tone, enunciation, pronunciation, slang, and so on.
5. Review a journal article or a chapter in a book related to use of interpreters. Prepare a one-page summary for submission to the instructor.
6. Since many books are translations from other languages, the Sapir-Whorf Hypothesis would say these translations may not preserve the exact meaning intended. This phrase paraphrased from the *Bible,* for example, has been translated numerous times: "It is easier for a camel to go through the eye of a needle than for a rich man to enter the kingdom of God" (Mark 10:23). (One other translation is: The eye of the

needle is a narrow doorway in an ancient wall.) Give other examples of exact translations that may make understanding a book difficult.

References

Althen, G. (1988). *American ways.* Yarmouth, ME: Intercultural Press, Inc.

Axtell, R. E. (1991). *The do's and taboos of international trade.* New York: John Wiley & Sons, Inc.

Baker, J. C. (1984). Foreign language and pre-departure training in U.S. multinational firms, *Personnel Administrator,* 63–72.

Baldrige, L. (1993). *Letitia Baldrige's new complete guide to executive manners.* New York: Rawson Associates.

Borden, G. A. (1991). *Cultural approach: An approach to understanding intercultural communication.* Upper Saddle River, NJ: Prentice Hall.

Bosrock, M. M. (1995). *Put your best foot forward—Europe.* St. Paul, MN: International Educational Systems.

Bosrock, M. M. (1995b). *Put your best foot forward—Mexico/Canada.* St. Paul, MN: International Educational Systems.

Bosrock, M. M. (1994). *Put your best foot forward—Asia.* St. Paul, MN: International Educational Systems.

Braganti, N. L., & Devine, E. (1992). *European customs and manners.* New York: Meadowbrook Press.

Condon, J. C., & Yousef, F. S. (1975). *Introduction to intercultural communication.* New York: Macmillan Publishing Company.

Devine, E., & Braganti, N. (1986). *The traveler's guide to Asian customs and manners.* New York: St. Martin's Press.

Devine, E., & Braganti, N. (1988). *The traveler's guide to Latin American customs and manners.* New York: St. Martin's Press.

DeVries, M. A. (1994). *Internationally yours.* Boston: Houghton Mifflin Co.

Dodd, C. H. (1987). *Dynamics of intercultural communication.* Dubuque, IA: Wm. C. Brown Publishers.

Ferraro, G. P. (1990). *The cultural dimension of international business.* Upper Saddle River, NJ: Prentice Hall.

Giles, H., Bourhis, R., & Taylor, D. M. (1977). Towards a theory of language in ethnic group relations. In H. Giles (Ed.), *Language, ethnicity and intergroup relations.* London: Academic Press.

Hall, E. T., & Hall, M. R. (1990). *Understanding cultural differences.* Yarmouth, ME: Intercultural Press, Inc.

Hockett, C. (1967). *A course in modern linguistics.* New York: Macmillan.

Jandt, F. E. (1995). *Intercultural communication.* Thousand Oaks, CA: Sage Publications.

Klopf, D. W. (1991). *Intercultural encounters.* Englewood, CO: Morton Publishing Company.

Pressley, G. (1987). Establishing a culture. In Jandt, F. E. (1995). *Intercultural communication.* Thousand Oaks, CA: Sage Publications.

Samovar, L. A., & Porter, R. E. (1991). *Intercultural communication: A reader.* Belmont, CA: Wadsworth Publishing Co.

Schmit, J., Richards, R., & Swingle, C. (1993, September 14). Travelers' bouts of foot-in-mouth disease. *USA Today.*

Stewart, E. C., & Bennett, M. J. (1991). *American cultural patterns.* Yarmouth, ME: Intercultural Press Inc.

Tannen, D. (1990). *You just don't understand: Women and men in conversation.* New York: Morrow.

Tsunda, Y. (1986). *Language inequality and distortion.* Philadelphia: John Benjamin Publishing Company.

U.S. News & World Report. (18 February 1995). In Jandt, F. E. (1995). *Intercultural Communication.* Thousand Oaks, CA: Sage Publications.

Weaver, G. R. (1998). American identity movements. Cross cultural confrontations. In Weaver, G. R. (Ed.) *Culture, communications, and conflict.* Upper Saddle River, NJ: Simon & Schuster Publishing.

Oral and Nonverbal Communication Patterns

Objectives
Upon completion of this chapter, you will:

■ be able to evaluate thought patterns and their relationship to intercultural business communication.

■ understand how paralanguage and metacommunication affect successful intercultural communication.

■ appreciate how attitudes toward time and use of space convey nonverbal messages in intercultural encounters.

■ understand the role that eye contact, smell, color, touch, and body language play in communicating nonverbally in cultural situations.

■ learn how silence is used to send nonverbal messages in various cultures.

Successful multicultural business encounters depend to a large extent on effective oral and nonverbal communication. Although much communication in the global arena is oral, the nonverbal aspects can contribute significantly to understanding and interpreting oral communication. **Nonverbal communication** refers to nonword messages such as gestures, facial expressions, interpersonal distance, touch, eye contact, smell, and silence.

Costly business blunders are often the result of a lack of knowledge of another culture's oral and nonverbal communication patterns. A knowledge of these aspects of intercultural communication is essential for conducting business in the international marketplace.

Thought Patterns

Patterns of thought or processes of reasoning and problem solving are not the same in all cultures and have an impact on oral communication.

Most people in the United States use the deductive method of reasoning to solve problems. The **deductive method** goes from broad categories or observations to specific examples to determine the facts and then the solution to the problem. The line of reasoning used by people in many other cultures, such as Asians, is typically the **inductive method.** People who use this approach start with facts or observations and go to generalizations (Samovar, Porter, & Stefani, 1998).

Thought patterns also include the pace or speed with which problems are solved or decisions made. Making quick decisions is a characteristic of an effective manager in the United States while this behavior would be viewed as impulsive by the Japanese. The slower method of problem solving is often a source of frustration for U.S. managers conducting business with the Japanese. Thought as an aspect of language is discussed in chapter 5.

Recognizing that people from other cultures may have different thought patterns is important to communicating and negotiating successfully in the global business environment.

Paralanguage/Metacommunication

Paralanguage is related to oral communication; it refers to the rate, pitch, and volume qualities of the voice, which interrupt or temporarily take the place of speech and affect the meaning of a message. Paralanguage includes such vocal qualifiers as: intensity (whether loud or soft), pitch (either high or low), extent (drawls and accents); vocal characterizers such as crying and laughing; and vocal segregates such as saying "uh" and "uh-huh" (Jandt, 1995). Paralanguage conveys emotions. Negative emotions of impatience, fear, and anger are easier to convey than the more positive emotions of satisfaction and admiration. An increased rate of speech could indicate anger or impatience; a decrease in rate could suggest lack of interest or a reflective attitude. An increased volume could also indicate anger; a lower volume is nonthreatening and sympathetic.

In the United States, people usually have no difficulty in distinguishing the speech of persons from specific regions of the country. Although the rate of speech and dialect may vary from region to region, they rarely cause major problems in the communication process.

Learning the nuances in speech that affect verbal messages will help when communicating with people of other cultures. Differences in volume of speech, for example, are culture specific as well as gender specific. Arabs, for example, speak loudly feeling this shows strength and sincerity. People from the Philippines, however, speak softly as they believe this is an indication of good breeding and education. Thais also speak softly, speaking loudly only when they are angry. When they first hear U.S. Americans speak, they think we are angry because of the loudness of our speech (Jandt, 1995). Males usually speak louder and in a lower pitch than females. Differences also exist in the rate at which people speak. U.S. Americans living in the northern states usually speak faster than those in the south; Italians and Arabs speak faster than do people of the United States. People who speak slowly sometimes have difficulty understanding the speech of those who speak rapidly. Accent is also an aspect of paralanguage. Some British are able to discern a person's educational background by his or her accent. In the United States, accent has been related to hiring decisions. In one U.S. research study, standard language speakers were given more supervisory positions while persons with accents were given more semiskilled positions (Jandt, 1995).

Metacommunication is the intentional or unintentional implied meaning of a message. Metacommunication, though not expressed in words, accompanies a message that is expressed in words. In both speaking and writing, people who receive messages are sensitive to not only the expressed message but the implied message as well. "You look nice today" could be interpreted as a compliment or that you usually do not look nice. Depending on context difference between cultures, the metacommunication can easily be misinterpreted. In Japan, if a company is interested in doing business with you, it will send a large contingent of people in order to show its interest; however, in the United States only one or two people would be sent. The Japanese would interpret this to mean that the U.S. company is not very interested in doing business with their firm.

Chronemics

Chronemics (attitudes toward time) vary from culture to culture. Two of the most important time systems that relate to international business are monochronic and polychronic time. Countries that follow **monochronic** time perform only one major activity at a time; countries that follow **polychronic** time work on several activities simultaneously.

The United States is a monochronic culture; other monochronic countries are Great Britain, Switzerland, and Germany. In monochronic cultures, time is spoken as something tangible; people use such terms as *wasting time* or *losing time.* In these cultures, it is considered rude to do two things at once such as reading a journal in a meeting.

Polychronic cultures include people of Latin America and the Mediterranean as well as Arabian people. These people are well adapted to doing several things at once and do not mind interruptions.

The following listing summarizes generalizations related to monochronic and polychronic time systems (Hall, 1966).

MONOCHRONIC PEOPLE	POLYCHRONIC PEOPLE
• Do one thing at a time	• Do many things at once
• Concentrate on the job	• Are highly distractible and subject to interruptions
• Take time commitments seriously	• Consider time commitments more casually
• Are committed to the job	• Are committed to people
• Show respect for private property; rarely borrow or lend	• Borrow and lend things often
• Are accustomed to short-term relationships	• Tend to build lifetime relationships

Being on time for work, business appointments and meetings, and social engagements is very important in the United States. Punctuality is considered a positive attribute that conveys the nonverbal message of being respectful of other persons.

Tardiness is interpreted as rudeness, a lack of consideration for others, or a lack of interest in the job or meeting. Being late also sends the nonverbal message that you are not well organized.

The length of time one has to wait to see another person also sends a message. In the United States, the length of the wait is associated with one's status and importance. The person perceived as high status would be seen immediately; the implied message is: "You are important; your time is just as valuable as mine." Generally in the United States, keeping a person with a business appointment waiting for five minutes is acceptable. Keeping a person waiting 15 minutes clearly implies that you consider yourself more important than your visitor. With a 20- to 30-minute wait, the message becomes stronger and implies contempt and/or annoyance; it also sends the message that the other person's time is not important (Fast, 1991). In time-conscious cultures, being aware of the subtextual implications associated with different lengths of waiting can be extremely important to avoid unintentionally demeaning or insulting a person with whom you wish to have a business relationship.

People of Germany and Switzerland are even more time conscious than are people from the United States. In fact, northern Europeans regard tardiness as a characteristic of an undisciplined person. Being on time is important to the people of Singapore and Hong Kong (except at banquets in Hong Kong—nobody arrives at the time stated on the invitation). Being punctual is also important in Malaysia and Indonesia, particularly when meeting with a person of superior status.

In Algeria, however, punctuality is not widely regarded. In Latin American countries, the "mañana" attitude (putting off until tomorrow what does not get done today) has been a source of frustration for time-sensitive U.S. executives when conducting business with people of that culture. Since their first obligations are to family and friends, Latin Americans would consider a request from a family member or friend to take precedence over a business meeting (Bosrock, 1997). People in the Arabic cultures also have a more casual attitude toward time; this attitude is related to their religious belief that God decides when things get accomplished (Engholm, 1991).

> The manager of a German bank offered to host a cocktail party for the South American delegation to a bankers' conference in Hamburg. Since the invitation stated that cocktails were at 7 p.m., the banker and his wife were ready to greet guests at 6:30 p.m. When no guests had arrived by 8:45 p.m., he asked his staff, "What kind of people have we invited?" The response: South Americans (Bosrock, 1997).

In southern Europe, people are also more casual about punctuality but position and relationship to the other party are considerations. In Spain, for example, specific but unwritten rules exist concerning who can be late and by how long in both social and business situations. The waiting also depends upon whether you want something from the other person or whether they want something from you. Arriving early is not recommended as this implies being too eager (Engholm & Rowland, 1996).

Consider these different attitudes toward time to work harmoniously with persons from other cultures. When conducting business with persons from cultures whose attitudes toward time differs from your own, it is advisable to verify whether the meeting time is, for example, Latin American time or U.S. time.

Proxemics

Communicating through the use of space is known as **proxemics.** The physical distance between people when they are interacting, as well as territorial space, is strongly influenced by culture.

Consideration should be given to interpersonal space when conversing with others. Hall (1966) reports that psychologists have identified four zones from which U.S. people interact: the intimate zone, the personal zone, the social zone, and the public zone. The **intimate zone,** less than 18 inches, is reserved for very close friends; it is entered by business colleagues briefly such as when shaking hands. The **personal zone,** from 18 inches to 4 feet, is used for giving instructions to others or working closely with another person The **social zone,** from 4 to 12 feet, is used for most business situations in which people interact more formally and impersonally such as during a business meeting. The **public distance,** over 12 feet, is the most formal zone; therefore, fewer interactions occur because of distance.

A psychology professor at a southern university gave his students an assignment to test *elevator proxemics,* the use of space in such crowded places as an elevator. They reported the usual U.S. behaviors of facing the front and watching the illuminated floor indicator, assuming the Fig Leaf Position (hands/purses/briefcases hanging down in front of the body), and positioning themselves in the corners or against the elevator walls. Then the professor added another assignment: students were to break the rules and get on the elevator, stand at the front facing the other occupants, and jump backward off the elevator just before the door closed. One of the elevator occupants was heard to whisper, "Call 911; we've got a real weirdo here" (Axtell, 1998).

People of the United States tend to need more space than do persons of certain cultures such as Greeks, Latin Americans, or Arabs. When interacting with persons of these cultures, U.S. Americans will back away because the person is standing too close. On the other hand, the Japanese stand farther away than do U.S. people when conversing. Negative nonverbal messages often conveyed by standing too close to a person who requires more space include being pushy or overbearing; standing too close may also be interpreted as unwelcome sexual advances.

People also communicate through space by the arrangement of desks and chairs. When U.S. people are conversing, they generally prefer the face-to-face arrangement of chairs placed at right angles to one another. People of other cultures such as the Chinese, prefer the side-by-side arrangement; this preference may be related to the custom of avoiding direct eye contact in that culture.

In the United States, nonverbal messages are sent by other aspects of the office environment. Private offices and offices with windows have more status than inside offices and large offices have more status than small ones. In addition to office size, higher ranking executives have their territory better protected than do lower-status employees; doors and secretaries are often used as barriers to access. Messages related to authority and position are also conveyed by the selection and arrangement of furniture. A large wooden desk and desk chairs with arms convey power and authority. Placing the desk and chair in front of a window or an arrangement of pictures on the wall creates a throne-like effect which adds to the sense of power (Chaney & Lyden, 1996). Office location also conveys the presence or absence of power and status. Offices on the fourth floor have more status than offices on the first floor. The top floors of office buildings are generally occupied by the top-level executives not only in the United States but in Germany as well. However, French top-level executives would occupy a position in the middle of an office area with subordinates located around them. The purpose of this arrangement is to help upper management stay informed of activities and to maintain control over the work area. The Japanese also do not consider private offices appropriate. In traditional Japanese firms only executives of the highest rank have private offices and they may also have desks in large work areas (Gudykunst & Ting-Toomey, 1988; Victor, 1992).

Oculesics

Some cultures place more emphasis on **oculesics** or oculemics (gaze and eye contact) than others. People in the United States, as well as those in Canada, Great Britain, and eastern Europe, favor direct eye contact. The eye contact, however is not steady; it is maintained for a second or two, then broken. Eye contact is considered a sign of respect and attentiveness in these countries. People who avoid eye contact may be considered insecure, untrustworthy, unfriendly, disrespectful, or inattentive.

> Students in a business communication class at a Mid-South university were asked to test the concept of gaze and eye contact in the United States by maintaining steady eye contact with a person in the car next to them when they stopped at a traffic light. Responses varied from obscene gestures to making faces to returning the gaze. Students concluded that U.S. persons are very uncomfortable with prolonged eye contact.

In other cultures, there is little direct eye contact. The Japanese direct their gaze below the chin; they are uncomfortable with maintaining direct eye contact throughout the conversation. People in China and Indonesia also lower the eyes as a sign of respect, feeling that prolonged eye contact shows bad manners. In the Middle East, on the other hand, the eye contact is so intense that it exceeds the comfort zone for most people in the United States. Prolonged eye contact with women, however, is considered inappropriate.

Thiederman (1991) summarized the cultural variations in eye contact as follows:

Very direct eye contact:	Middle Easterners
	Some Latin American groups
	The French
Moderate eye contact:	Mainstream Americans
	Northern Europeans
	The British
Minimal eye contact:	East Asians
	Southeast Asians
	East Indians
	Native Americans

Source: Adapted from Lexington Books, an imprint of Macmillan, Inc., from *Bridging Cultural Barriers for Corporate Success* by Sondra Thiederman. Copyright © 1991 by Sondra Thiederman.

Very direct eye contact can be misinterpreted as hostility, aggressiveness, or intrusiveness when the intended meaning was that of appearing interested. Minimal eye contact may be misinterpreted as lack of interest or understanding, dishonesty, fear, or shyness when the intended meaning was a desire to show respect or to avoid appearing intrusive.

The eyes can be very revealing during negotiations. The pupils of the eyes constrict or dilate in response to emotions. Well-trained negotiators will watch the pupils for signs that you are willing to make concessions (Borden, 1991). (See Figure 6.1.)

A prolonged gaze or stare in the United States is considered rude. In other cultures such as Japan, Korea, and Thailand, staring is also considered rude. In most cultures, men do not stare at women. In France and Italy, however, men can stare at women in public. In the United States, staring at a person is considered a sign of interest and may even be interpreted as sexually suggestive.

FIGURE 6.1 Hiding Eye Messages

Because people of the Middle East know they may give away how they feel with nonverbal eye messages, they may wear dark glasses to hide such messages.

Olfactics

Olfactics or smell as a means of nonverbal communication is important. A person's smell can have a positive or negative effect on the oral message. The way someone smells remains in our memory after the person has gone.

Most people of the United States respond negatively to what they consider bad odors such as body odor, breath odor, or clothes that emit unpleasant aromas such as perspiration. They place great importance on personal hygiene and consider it normal for people to remove body odors by bathing or showering daily and by brushing teeth to remove mouth odors (Althen, 1988). Advertisements on U.S. American television and in newspapers and magazines for underarm deodorants, perfumes, colognes, and mouthwash emphasize the importance U.S. Americans place on personal hygiene. In a television commercial that epitomizes the fixation U.S. Americans have concerning body odor, a young woman states: "If a guy smells, it's such a turnoff." People in the United States are not comfortable in discussing the topic, however, and generally will not tell another that his or her body odor is offensive; they will simply avoid being close to the person and will end the discourse as quickly as possible.

Other cultures have quite different concepts of natural odors; they consider them as normal and think attitudes of people in the United States are unnatural. Arabs are quite comfortable with natural odors and typically breathe on people when they talk. Smelling the natural body odors of one's friend is desirable; denying him/her this privilege is to act ashamed (Hall, 1966). Other cultures in which smell plays an important role include the Japanese and Samoans. Cultures that include little meat in the diet, such as the Chinese, say that people who consume a lot of meat, such as U.S. Americans, emit an offensive odor (Samovar & Porter, 1991).

> A medical doctor from Saudi Arabia was completing an internship in a hospital in the southern United States. Problems arose when patients refused to have the Saudi doctor examine them. Interviews with patients revealed two problems: he "smelled bad" and he breathed on the patients. The doctor's orientation had apparently failed to include the incongruence between Arabic and U.S. American olfactory perceptions and practices.

To maintain harmonious intercultural business relationships, remember these diverse attitudes toward smell and, if possible, adopt the hygiene practices of the country in which you are conducting business.

Haptics

Haptics or touch refers to communicating through the use of bodily contact. When used properly, touch can create feelings of warmth and trust; when used improperly, touch can betray trust and cause annoyance (Fast, 1991). Some cultures are very comfortable with bodily contact and others avoid it. People in the United States are taught that appropriate touch includes shaking hands but that in business situations giving hugs or other expressions of affection to supervisors and coworkers encourages familiarity that is generally considered inappropriate. Since touching may be interpreted as a form of sexual harassment, it is necessary to refrain from touching in business situations to avoid the appearance of impropriety.

Another consideration when using touch in the United States is a knowledge of the hierarchy involved. People of higher rank (the president of the company) may touch those of lower rank (office employees) but secretaries may not touch the president. Doctors may place a comforting arm around a patient, but patients may not touch doctors. Adults may touch children, but children should not touch adults unless they know them. Equals may touch each other. The general rule is that people who are older or of higher status may touch those who are younger or of lower status (Fast, 1991).

Several years ago when President Carter was mediating peace talks between Egypt and Israel, Anwar Sadat frequently placed his hand on President Carter's knee. While this subtextual message was intended as a gesture of warm friendship, the subtler message Sadat was conveying to the world was that he was President Carter's equal (Fast, 1991).

Axtell in *Gestures* (1998) has classified the following cultures as "touch" and "don't touch":

Don't Touch	Middle Ground	Touch
Japan	Australia	Latin American countries
United States	Estonia	Italy
Canada	France	Greece
England	China	Spain and Portugal
Scandinavia	Ireland	Some Asian countries
Other Northern European countries	India	Russia
	Middle East countries	

Source: Axtell, R. E. (1998). *Gestures.* Copyright © 1998 by John Wiley & Sons, Inc. Reprinted by permission of John Wiley & Sons, Inc.

In touch-oriented cultures such as those of Italy, Greece, Spain, and Portugal, both males and females may be seen walking along the street holding hands or arm-in-arm. In other cultures such as those in the Latin American countries, touching between men is considered quite acceptable (Figure 6.2).

A Mexican male will stand close to a male colleague and even hold him by the lapel or shoulder. Behavior between men in the Middle East is similar, but you would avoid touching the person with the left hand because the left hand is considered unclean and

FIGURE 6.2 Touch-oriented Culture

is reserved for personal hygiene. In other countries such as in the United States, touching between men may be construed as an indication of homosexuality.

An additional aspect of tactile communication concerns the location of the touch. In Thailand, it is offensive to touch the head as this part of the body is considered sacred. In fact, avoid touching all Asians on the head including small children. Even placing a hand on the back of an Asian worker's chair is considered inappropriate. While Muslims hug another person around the shoulders, in Korea young people do not touch the shoulders of their elders (Axtell, 1998). Tactile behavior is highly cultural; knowing when and how to touch in various cultures is important to conducting business globally.

Kinesics

Kinesics is the term used for communicating through various types of body movements including facial expressions, gestures, posture and stance, and other mannerisms that may accompany or replace oral messages.

FACIAL EXPRESSIONS

The face and eyes convey the most expressive types of body language. Research conducted by Leathers (1976) determined these 10 types of meaning can be communicated by facial expressions: happiness, surprise, fear, anger, sadness, disgust, contempt, interest, bewilderment, and determination. People of all cultures learn how to control facial expressions to mask emotions that are inappropriate in a specific setting such as crying when being reprimanded or yawning when listening to a boring presentation. In some countries such as China, people rarely show emotion. The Japanese may smile to cover a range of emotions including anger, happiness, or sadness while the smile to people in the United States means happiness. Asians will smile or laugh softly when they are embarrassed or to conceal any discomfort. Koreans rarely smile; they perceive people who smile a great deal as shallow (Samovar, Porter, & Stefani, 1998). The following proverb from the Korean culture illustrates the Asian attitude concerning the meaning of a smile: "The man who smiles a lot is not a real man" (Thiederman, 1991). People of Thailand, on the other hand, smile a great deal which may be why Thailand has been called "The

Land of Smiles" (Samovar, Porter, & Stefani, 1998). To interpret facial expressions correctly, you should take the communication context and the culture into account.

A study of a female communicating nonverbal messages—sadness, anger, surprise, and fear—involved respondents of Hispanic, Malaysian, African-American, and white American origins. In decoding the messages, the largest difference was between African Americans and white U.S. Americans (St. Martin, 1976).

Kochman's (1981, 1986) studies of African American and white U.S. Americans showed the "black mode" of conflict style as animated, interpersonal, and confrontational while the "white mode" was dispassionate, impersonal, and nonchallenging. Ting-Toomey (1986) found gender and race differences. Both black and white males preferred avoidance strategies when dealing with relational conflict. Black females were more verbal, were more emotionally and nonverbally expressive, and interrupted more often than white females.

GESTURES

Gestures are another important aspect of body language. Gestures can be emblems or symbols ("V" for victory), illustrators (police officer's hand held up to stop traffic), regulators (glancing at your watch to signal that you are in a hurry), or affect displays (one's face turns red with embarrassment).

Gestures are used to add emphasis or clarity to an oral message. Although the meaning of gestures depends upon the context, here are some general guides to interpreting the meaning of gestures in the United States (Axtell, 1998):

- Interest is expressed by maintaining eye contact with the speaker, smiling, and nodding the head.
- Open-mindedness is expressed by open hands and palms turned upward.
- Nervousness is sometimes shown by fidgeting, failing to give the speaker eye contact, or jingling keys or money in your pocket.
- Suspiciousness is indicated by glancing away or touching your nose, eyes, or ears.
- Defensiveness is indicated by crossing your arms over your chest, making fisted gestures, or crossing your legs.
- Lack of interest or boredom is indicated by glancing repeatedly at your watch or staring at the ceiling or floor or out the window when the person is speaking.

Source: Axtell, R. E. (1998). *Gestures.* Copyright © 1998 by John Wiley & Sons, Inc. Reprinted by permission of John Wiley & Sons, Inc.

Although regional differences exist, people in the United States typically use moderate gesturing. They rarely use gestures in which elbows go above the shoulder level as this is interpreted as being too emotional or even angry; one exception is waving hello or goodbye. Italians, Greeks, and some Latin Americans use vigorous gestures when speaking while Chinese and Japanese people tend to keep their hands and arms close to their bodies when speaking. Most cultures have standard gestures for such daily situations as greeting someone and saying goodbye; learn and respect such gestures when conversing with persons of another culture.

Here are some additional guidelines for gesturing in various cultures (Axtell, 1998):

- The "V" for victory gesture (Figure 6.3), holding two fingers upright with palm and fingers faced outward, is widely used in the United States and many other countries. In England, however, it has a crude connotation when used with the palm in.
- The vertical horns gesture (raised fist, index finger and little finger extended [Figure 6.4]), has a positive connotation associated with the University of Texas Longhorn football team. This gesture has an insulting connotation in Italy, but in Brazil and Venezuela, it is a sign for good luck. This symbol has various meanings in U.S. subcultures including serving as a satanic cult recognition sign signifying the devil's horns. The symbol should be used only when you are sure the other person understands its intended meaning.
- The thumbs up gesture (Figure 6.5) has been widely recognized as a positive signal meaning "everything is OK" or "good going." Although well known in North America and most of Europe, in Australia and West Africa it is seen as a rude gesture.
- The "OK" sign (Figure 6.6), with the thumb and forefinger joined to form a circle, is a positive gesture in the United States while in Brazil it is considered obscene. The gesture has yet another meaning in Japan—it is a symbol for money.

FIGURE 6.3 "V" for Victory Gesture

FIGURE 6.4 Vertical Horns Gesture

FIGURE 6.5 Thumbs Up Gesture

FIGURE 6.6 "OK" Gesture

An American engineer, sent to Germany by his U.S. company who had purchased a German firm, was working side by side with a German engineer on a piece of equipment. When the American engineer made a suggestion for improving the new machine, the German engineer followed the suggestion and asked his American counterpart whether or not he had done it correctly. The American replied by giving the U.S. American "OK" gesture, making a circle with the thumb and forefinger. The German engineer put down his tools and walked away, refusing further communication with the American engineer. The U.S. American later learned from one of the supervisors the significance of this gesture to a German: "You asshole" (Axtell, 1998).

- The beckoning gesture (Figure 6.7), fingers upturned, palm facing the body, is used by people in the United States for summoning a waiter; it is offensive to Filipinos as it is used to beckon animals and prostitutes. Vietnamese and Mexicans also find it offensive.
- The head nod in most countries means "yes," but in Bulgaria it means "no."

FIGURE 6.7 Beckoning Gesture

Since one culture's gestures may be misinterpreted by people in another culture, avoid using gestures when communicating in international business settings until you become knowledgeable about the meaning of such gestures.

POSTURE AND STANCE

Posture, the way someone stands, sits, or walks, can send positive or negative nonverbal messages. Posture can signal agreement or disagreement. For example, when people in a business meeting share a point of view, they are likely to mirror each other's posture. When a person disagrees with others in the group, his or her posture will also disagree with that of other group members. Posture can convey self-confidence, status, and interest. Confident people generally have a relaxed posture, yet stand erect and walk with assurance. Walking with stooped shoulders and a slow, hesitating gait projects such negative messages as lack of assurance and confidence. Walking rapidly and swinging the arms indicates that the person is goal oriented. A preoccupied walk, with hands clasped behind and head lowered, is thoughtful. Men who walk with hands on hips convey the message of wanting to get to their destination as quickly as possible (Fast, 1991). The posture of persons of higher status is usually more relaxed than that of their subordinates. Interest is demonstrated by leaning forward toward the person you are conversing with, while sitting back communicates a lack of interest. The posture of people in the United States tends to be casual; they sit in a relaxed manner and may slouch when they stand. This behavior in Germany would be considered rude.

President Ronald Reagan was well known for using posture to convey subtextual messages. In a 1985 article in *The New York Times,* a reporter described how President Reagan's posture revealed his emotions during an interview. He said that much of the time President Reagan settled back comfortably. When the issue of Star Wars was brought up, his posture changed; he leaned forward in his chair and became totally engaged. When the talk shifted to Soviet violations, however, he placed his back straight against the chair (Fast, 1991).

Posture when seated also varies with the culture. People in the United States often cross their legs while seated; women cross at the ankle and men cross with ankle on the knee (Figure 6.8). Crossing the leg with ankle on the knee would be considered inappropriate by most people in the Middle East. In the Arabic world, correct posture while seated is important; avoid showing the sole of your shoe or pointing your foot at someone as the lowest part of the body is considered unclean.

When communicating with persons of another culture, follow their lead; assume the posture they assume. Remember that in most cultures, standing when an older person or one of higher rank enters or leaves the room is considered a sign of respect.

An awareness of cultural differences in facial expressions, gestures, and posture is important to successful intercultural encounters. Body language can enhance the spoken message or detract from it. Even though we usually believe that actions speak louder than words, in intercultural interactions what the person says may give a clearer picture of the intended message than accompanying body language. However, if a gesture is used in the wrong context, it may be difficult for a foreigner to understand the intended message. The best advice is probably to keep gestures to a minimum when communicating with persons in other cultures; learn the words for "good" or "yes" in the local language rather than relying on gestures.

Chromatics

Chromatics or color can affect your mood, your emotions, and your impression of others. Certain colors have both negative and positive connotations. In the United States, for example, black is considered a sophisticated color, but it may also represent sadness. White is pure and peaceful, but in some cultures it is associated with mourning. Blue may represent peace and tranquility or sadness and depression, for example, "I feel blue."

FIGURE 6.8 Sitting Postures

Color may be used to symbolize such things as patriotism. People in the United States associate red, white, and blue (the colors in the flag) with patriotism. Cultural differences associated with colors include (Axtell, 1998; Ricks, 1993):

- Black is the color of mourning to many Europeans and U.S. Americans, but white is worn to funerals in Japan and many other nations.
- In the United States, white is typically worn by brides while in India, red or yellow is worn.
- Purple is sometimes associated with royalty, but it is the color of death in many Latin American countries.
- Red (especially red roses) is associated with romance in some cultures including the United States. Red is not an appropriate color for wrapping gifts in Japan. Dark red is the color of mourning along the Ivory Coast.
- Green is not used for wrapping packages in Egypt since green is the nationalist color (as red, white and blue are the nationalist colors in the United States). Men should avoid wearing a green hat in China as this signifies that their wife or sister is a prostitute.
- In many countries of the world, blue is considered a masculine color, but to people of France and the United Kingdom, red is more masculine. Blue, in Iran, is an undesirable color.
- While people of the United States consider pink to be the most feminine color, persons in most other countries think of yellow as the most feminine color.

United Airlines unknowingly got off on the wrong foot during its initial flights from Hong Kong. To commemorate the occasion, they handed out white carnations to the passengers. When they learned that to many Asians white flowers represent bad luck and even death, they changed to red carnations (Ricks, 1993).

Determining cultural meanings associated with various colors is advised to ensure that nonverbal messages associated with color are positive ones.

Silence

Silence is a form of nonverbal communication that may be interpreted in various ways depending upon the situation, the duration of the silence, and the culture. Interpretations of silence include agreement or disagreement, lack of interest, or contempt. Silence can also mean that the person is giving the topic some thought. Silence can be used to indicate displeasure in the United States and in other cultures (Samovar, Porter, & Stefani, 1998).

Other aspects of silence should also be considered: the duration, appropriateness, and relationship between people who are conversing. A prolonged silence following a question could be interpreted to mean that the person does not know the answer. Silence following an inappropriate statement such as the telling of a tasteless joke, would usually be interpreted as disapproval. Silence following a conversation with someone you know well could be interpreted as dissent or disapproval (Samovar, Porter, & Stefani, 1998).

People of the United States are rather uncomfortable with periods of silence except with people they know well. They will use fillers, such as comments on the weather, to avoid silence. In Italy, Greece, and Arabic countries, very little silence exists.

In some cultures, periods of silence are appropriate when communicating. People in east Asia consider silence an integral part of business and social discourse, not a failure to communicate. Silence in east Asia and Finland is associated with listening and learning; it protects your privacy and individualism and shows respect for the privacy and individualism of others. Silence in these cultures is viewed as restful and appropriate lulls in conversation (Lewis, 1996). The Japanese are quite comfortable with silence and use it as a bargaining tool when negotiating with persons from the United States. They know that U.S. Americans are not comfortable with long periods of silence and that the U.S. businessperson will offer a price concession just to get the discussion going again. Learn to remain silent when negotiating with the Japanese; they like periods of silence and do not like to be hurried. People who converse with no pauses are viewed as having given little thought to what they are saying and that their thinking lacks focus (Axtell, 1998). Breaking the silence may also give the impression that your proposal is flawed. Japanese proverbs such as "Those who know do not speak—those who speak do not know" emphasize the value of silence over words in that culture.

An appropriate caution would be to watch the behavior of the persons you are talking with and match their style. Allow pauses when speaking with Asians and avoid pauses when dealing with those from the Middle East.

Knowing cultural variations in the use of silence and other forms of nonverbal communication is helpful when conversing with persons in another culture.

A summary of guidelines related to various aspects of nonverbal communication for the six countries with which the United States conducts most of its international business follows.

CANADA

Punctuality is important to Canadians though not to the extent that it is to people of the United States. Being on time for business functions is expected; being 15 minutes late for evening social occasions is permitted. People stand farther apart in Canada than do persons of Latin America or the Far East. The standard space between people who are conversing is 2 feet; however, French Canadians often stand closer. Little touching is seen except between relatives and good friends. However, French Canadians commonly touch while conversing. Eye contact is important when conversing with someone. Gestures are similar to those used in the United States. Since some gestures may offend people of a certain cultural group, gesturing should be kept to a minimum. Pointing with the index finger is considered rude; the entire hand should be used to motion to someone. Beckoning is done with the fingers pointing up and motioning toward one's body with the palm inward. The U.S. American "thumbs down" gesture used to indicate "no" or that something is bad is offensive in Québec as is slapping an open hand over a closed fist. Appropriate seated posture for men includes legs crossed at the ankles, at the knees, or one ankle crossed on the other knee; appropriate seated posture for women is crossing legs at the ankle. (Axtell, 1998; Bosrock, 1995).

GREAT BRITAIN

Being punctual is very important to the British. Since the people of Great Britain are polite and reserved, they respect another's personal space and do not like for someone to get too close when conversing. The British do not always look at the person with whom they are conversing. Touching is avoided; avoid putting your arm around a colleague's shoulder or slapping him/her on the back. Many of the gestures used in the United States and Canada are used; however, the "V" for victory sign (typically with the palm out) is rude and offensive (meaning "up yours") when used with the palm inward. The accepted seated posture for men is crossing the legs at the knees rather than placing one ankle across the other knee; for women, crossing the legs at the ankle is the accepted seated posture (Axtell, 1998; *Culturgram '98,* 1997).

FRANCE

Punctuality is just as important in France as it is in the United States. Being on time is a sign of courtesy; however, arriving 15 minutes late for a party at someone's home is acceptable. The U.S. "OK" sign means "zero" or "worthless" to the French. Their gesture for "OK" is the "thumbs up" sign. The "V" for victory sign may be done with the palm faced outward or inward; both represent "peace" or "victory." Avoid slapping the open palm over a closed fist as this gesture is considered vulgar. Another gesture used is playing an imaginary flute to indicate that someone is talking too much or to signal that you question the truth of what is being said. Since good posture and decorum are virtues in France, one should sit upright with knees together or with legs crossed at the knee or ankle. Resting one's feet on tables or chairs is inappropriate. Other behaviors to be avoided include speaking loudly in public, chewing gum, and conversing with your hands in your pockets. (Axtell, 1998; Bosrock, 1995; *Culturgram '98,* 1997).

GERMANY

Being on time for all business and social engagements is perhaps more important in Germany than in any other country in the world. Being only two to three minutes late is insulting to German managers; an explanatory call is expected if you are delayed. Gestures/behaviors considered inappropriate in Germany include talking with your hands in your pockets and chewing gum in public. Pointing the index finger to the temple and making a twisting motion is an insult to another person; the meaning is "you are crazy." Rather than crossing the fingers to wish a person good luck, Germans make a fist folding the thumb in and pounding lightly on a surface. The gesture for waving goodbye is extending the hand upward, palm out, and waving the fingers up and down rather than side to side, which means "no." When trying to get someone's attention, for example, a waiter, raise the hand, palm out, with only the index finger extended; do not wave. Posture is important; people should cross their legs with one knee over the other; feet should not be placed on furniture (Axtell, 1998; Bosrock, 1995; *Culturgram '98,* 1997).

JAPAN

Punctuality is valued. Being late to a business meeting is considered rude, but being late for social occasions is acceptable. Because the Japanese are a "do not touch" culture, avoid standing close, patting a person on the back, or any prolonged physical contact. Prolonged eye contact should also be avoided. The U.S. "OK" gesture may signify "money" in Japan. The gesture for beckoning someone is placing an arm out, palm down, and making a scratching motion with the fingers. Chewing gum or yawning in public are impolite; standing with your hands in your pockets is inappropriate. Also avoid shouting or raising your voice in anger; the Japanese are a polite, gracious people and show great restraint. The correct seated posture includes having both feet on the floor and arms placed on chair armrests or in the lap. Slouching, leaning back in a tilted chair, or placing your feet on a table are inappropriate. Crossing the legs at the knees or ankles is acceptable; placing an ankle over a knee, however, is improper (Axtell, 1998; *Culturgram '98, Japan*, 1997; Morrison, Conaway, & Borden, 1994).

MEXICO

Punctuality is not highly regarded in Mexico; 30 minutes past the scheduled meeting time is considered punctual by Mexican standards. Foreigners, however, are expected to be on time for business meetings. For social engagements, being 30 minutes to an hour later than the time stated on the invitation is expected. Time may be stated as *la hora americana* meaning that punctuality is expected; *la hora mexicana* implies a more relaxed time frame. People of Mexico usually stand close together while conversing and sometimes touch the other person's clothing, shoulders, or arm. Avoid the temptation to step back; this indicates that you are unfriendly. Increased touching should be viewed positively as it usually indicates the development of a good relationship. Hand and arm gestures are often used during a conversation. Most people of Mexico are familiar with U.S. gestures; however, the "V" for victory sign when made with the nose in the wedge of the V and mouth covered with the palm, is a very rude gesture. The U.S. gesture for "thumbs down" is vulgar in Mexico; the "thumbs up" gesture means approval. Waving the hand from side to side with the index finger pointed up and palm facing forward means "no." Avoid standing with your hands on your hips as this implies that you are angry. Standing with your hands in your pockets is considered rude (Axtell, 1998; Bosrock, 1995; *Culturgram '98*, 1997).

Terms

- Chromatics
- Chronemics
- Deductive method
- Haptics
- Inductive method
- Intimate zone
- Kinesics
- Metacommunication
- Monochronic
- Nonverbal communication
- Oculesics
- Olfactics
- Paralanguage
- Personal zone
- Polychronic
- Proxemics
- Public distance
- Social zone

EXERCISE 6.1

Instructions: Match the facial expression to the meaning portrayed.

1. Disgust
2. Contempt
3. Sadness
4. Interest
5. Surprise
6. Anger
7. Happiness
8. Determination

EXERCISE 6.2

Instructions: Circle T if the statement is true or F if false.

1. T F   Asians typically use the deductive method of reasoning to solve problems.
2. T F   People in the United States speak faster than Italians and Arabs.
3. T F   Latin Americans need more space than people of the United States.
4. T F   Punctuality is not widely regarded in Algeria.
5. T F   Private offices are generally reserved for top-level executives in all cultures.
6. T F   When conversing with the Japanese, it is best to keep steady eye contact throughout the dialogue.
7. T F   People of all cultures respond negatively to body and breath odor.
8. T F   More bodily contact occurs between Western men than between Arabian men.
9. T F   Touching the head of a Thai is forbidden.
10. T F   Smiling is interpreted as happiness in all cultures.

EXERCISE 6.3

Instructions: Match the following terms with their definition.

___ 1. Space   A. Chromatics
___ 2. Body language   B. Chronemics
___ 3. Smell   C. Deductive approach
___ 4. Gaze/eye contact   D. Haptics
___ 5. Implied meaning of message   E. Inductive approach
___ 6. Goes from facts to generalizations   F. Kinesics
___ 7. Time   G. Metacommunication
___ 8. Color   H. Oculesics
___ 9. Volume, pitch, and rate that affects message meaning   I. Olfactics
___ 10. Touch   J. Paralanguage
                                                       K. Proxemics

Questions and Cases for Discussion

1. Explain how thought patterns and problem solving differ in the United States and other cultures.
2. Discuss differences in paralanguage and metacommunication of people in various cultures.
3. Explain how attitudes toward time vary from culture to culture.

4. Discuss differences in space needs of persons in the United States, Japan, Greece, and Latin America.
5. Identify cultures that favor direct eye contact and those that avoid eye contact.
6. Give examples to show how olfactics is an important aspect of intercultural nonverbal communication.
7. Identify cultures that are comfortable with bodily contact and those that avoid bodily contact. Give examples of appropriate and inappropriate bodily contact in the United States.
8. Discuss cultural differences in body language of people in the United States, Japan, China, Italy, Greece, and Latin America.
9. Explain how the use of color communicates nonverbal messages.
10. Identify cultures that are comfortable with silence and those that are not. Discuss possible meanings of silence in various situations.

CASE 1

Barbara works for a subsidiary of a German corporation in the United States. Her job involves ordering products from Germany and following up on the status of deliveries. Barbara does not speak, read, or write German; however, this is not a problem as Barbara's contact Anna speaks, reads, and writes English. Normally all of Barbara's telexes, letters, and faxes are written in English from Anna. Lately the German factory has been having difficulty, and Barbara has been sending telexes to Anna with inquiries about the product delays. In her last telex, Barbara asks why the Germans cannot get their materials shipped on time. Barbara's answer comes back in German. Discuss what nonverbal communication was being conveyed in the situation and how you would change the behavior to be more positive.

CASE 2

A U.S. company has sent a representative to negotiate a contract with a Japanese firm. The U.S. representative arrives at the appointed time for this meeting and is shown to the meeting room where six representatives from the Japanese firm meet with him. During his presentation, the Japanese move their heads in an up and down motion; however, they say very little. The presentation was given in English as the representative had been told the Japanese understood English. When the representative asked if there were any questions, everyone nodded politely; however, no one said a word. After a few minutes, the representative asked if they were ready to sign the contracts. One of the Japanese said, "It is very difficult for us to sign." At this point the representative said, "Should I leave the contract with you?" The Japanese said, "Yes." The U.S. representative returned to the United States expecting the Japanese to return the contract which did not happen. Explain what the Japanese were really saying by nodding their heads and using the word "difficult."

CASE 3

On his first trip to Mexico, Harry, a U.S. manager interested in negotiating a contract for his firm with a Mexican firm, was invited to a dinner party by his Mexican counterpart. Since the invitation indicated that cocktails would begin at 7 p.m., Harry arrived promptly at that time. His host seemed surprised, and no one else had arrived. People began arriving about 8 p.m.; Harry knew he had read the invitation correctly but felt he had gotten off to a bad start. What advice would you have given Harry?

CASE 4

Fred, the manager of a large U.S. bookstore, hired Ching Wu, a newcomer from China, as one of his clerks. In an attempt to get to know Ching Wu better, Fred invited her to join him for coffee. Throughout their conversation, he noticed that Ching Wu always looked down at the floor and never gave him eye contact. He interpreted this as a lack of respect. Discuss the nonverbal communication differences in this situation.

Activities

1. Write a paragraph describing an incident from your own experience involving oral and/or nonverbal miscommunication with someone from another culture. Suggest a plausible explanation for the miscommunication.
2. Prepare a short skit to illustrate nonverbal communication blunders that a person from the United States might make in a country of your choice.
3. Demonstrate a gesture (such as thumbs up or the U.S. "OK" sign) and ask class members to explain its meaning in a specific country.
4. Demonstrate the amount of space considered acceptable when interacting with persons in Latin America, the United States, and Egypt.
5. Demonstrate the amount of eye contact considered appropriate in the United States, Japan, and the Middle East.

References

Althen, G. (1988). *American ways.* Yarmouth, ME: Intercultural Press, Inc.

Axtell, R. E. (1998). *Gestures.* New York: John Wiley & Sons, Inc.

Borden, G. A. (1991). *Cultural orientation: An approach to understanding intercultural communication.* Upper Saddle River, NJ: Prentice Hall.

Bosrock, M. M. (1995). *Put your best foot forward: Europe.* St. Paul, MN: International Educational Systems.

Bosrock, M. M. (1997). *Put your best foot forward: South America.* St. Paul, MN: International Educational Systems.

Chaney, L. H., & Lyden, J. A. (1996, April). Impression management: The office environment. *Supervision, 57*(4), 3–5.

Culturgram '98. (1997). Provo, UT: Brigham Young University, Publications Division of the David M. Kennedy Center for International Studies.

Engholm, C. (1991). *When business east meets business west.* New York: John Wiley & Sons, Inc.

Engholm, C., & Rowland, D. (1996). *International excellence.* New York: Kodansha International.

Fast, J. (1991). *Body language in the workplace.* New York: Penguin Books.

Gudykunst, W. B., & Ting-Toomey, S. (1988). *Culture and interpersonal communication.* Newbury Park, CA: Sage Publications.

Hall, E. T. (1966). *The hidden dimension.* Garden City, NY: Doubleday, 107–122.

Jandt, F. E. (1995). *Intercultural communication.* Thousand Oaks, CA: Sage.

Kochman, T. (1981). *Black & white styles in conflict.* Chicago, IL: University of Chicago Press.

Kochman, T. (1986). Black verbal dueling strategies in interethnic communication. *International and Intercultural Communication Annual, 10,* 136–157.

Leathers, D. (1976). *Nonverbal communication systems.* Boston: Allyn & Bacon.

Lewis, R. D. (1996). *When cultures collide: Managing successfully across cultures.* London: Nicholas Brealey Publishing.

Morrison, T., Conaway, W. A., & Borden, G. A. (1994). *Kiss, bow, or shake hands.* Holbrook, MA: Bob Adams, Inc.

Ricks, D. A. (1993). *Blunders in international business.* Cambridge, MA: Blackwell Publishers.

Samovar, L. A., & Porter, R. E. (1991). *Intercultural communication: A reader.* Belmont, CA: Wadsworth Publishing Company.

Samovar, L. A., Porter, R. E., & Stefani, L. A. (1998). *Communication between cultures* (3rd ed.). Belmont, CA: Wadsworth Publishing Company.

St. Martin, G. M. (1976). Intercultural differential decoding of nonverbal affective communication. *International and Intercultural Communication Annual, 3,* 44–57.

Thiederman, S. (1991). *Bridging cultural barriers for corporate success.* New York: Lexington Books.

Victor, D. A. (1992). *International business communication.* New York: HarperCollins Publishers.

CHAPTER 7

Written Communication Patterns

Objectives
Upon completion of this chapter, you will:

■ know the guidelines for writing international messages in English.

■ be familiar with letter formats commonly used by U.S. business firms and how they differ from formats used in other countries.

■ understand how facsimiles are commonly used for communicating between U.S. firms and those in other countries.

■ understand how writing tone and style vary from culture to culture.

■ understand cultural differences in other types of written communication such as the résumé and related job-search documents.

Many U.S. companies correspond with foreign corporations; it is important, therefore, to be aware of differences in the format, tone, and style of written communication. Research results show that 97 percent of outgoing international correspondence is sent in English with about 1 percent each in Spanish, French, and German. Percentages for incoming international messages are similar: 96 percent are in English with the remaining 4 percent divided between French, German, and Spanish (Green & Scott, 1992). Since English is used for most international written messages, making these messages as clear as possible is important. Understanding the business communication practices of the culture you are writing to will help you to communicate effectively.

International English

International English is English for businesspeople that either deal with other cultures whose native language is not English or for whom English may be a second language; it is limited to the 3,000 to 4,000 most common English words. Two excellent references are P. H. Collin, M. Lowi, and C. Weiland's, *Beginner's Dictionary of American English Usage*, 1991, and *International English Usage*, 1987. In order to utilize international English, three cultural factors are important: an understanding of business communication in the other culture and/or residence in the other culture, an idea of how business communication is taught in the other culture, and a knowledge that content errors are more difficult than language errors for another culture to discern.

Content errors are **lexical errors** and refer to errors in meaning. **Syntactic errors** are errors in the order of the words in a sentence. A native speaker of a language will discover the syntactic errors in a sentence much easier than the lexical errors.

EXAMPLES OF LEXICAL ERRORS:

We *baste* (based) this opinion on our many years of experience.
Thank you for your *patients* (patience).
The device *omits* (emits) a high-pitched signal when it is receiving.
We realize that your office will be closed on this *wholey* (holy) day.
It is *there* (their) material.
We *expect* (accept) the invitation to dinner.

Business communication is not necessarily taught in other countries as it is in the United States. The course may not contain any information on the theory of communication and what happens between the sender and receiver. Many of the business communication courses being taught in a country that desires to do more business with the United States will simply be translation courses.

Guidelines for "internationalizing" the English language have been developed to enable both native and non-native speakers of the language to write messages clearly to decrease the possibility of misunderstanding between people of different cultures. The following guidelines adapted from those developed by Riddle and Lanham (1984–85) are important for situations in which both cultures speak English as well as for situations in which English may be a second language for one or both of the communicators.

- Use the 3,000 to 4,000 most common English words. Uncommon words such as *onus* for burden and *flux* for continual change should be avoided.
- Use only the most common meaning of words or words that have singular rather than multiple meanings. The word *high* has 20 meanings; the word *expensive* has one.
- Select action-specific verbs and words with few or similar alternate meanings. Use *cook* breakfast rather than *make* breakfast; use *take* a taxi rather than *get* a taxi.
- Avoid redundancies (*interoffice memorandum*), sports terms (*ballpark figure*), and words that draw mental pictures (*red tape*).

- Avoid using words in other than their most common way such as making verbs out of nouns (*impacting* the economy and *faxing* a message).
- Be aware of words with a unique meaning in some cultures; the word *check* outside the United States generally means a financial instrument and is often spelled *chèque*.
- Be aware of alternate spellings in countries that use the same language; for example, *theatre/theater, organisation/organization, colour/color,* and *judgement/judgment.*
- Avoid creating or using new words; avoid slang.
- Avoid two-word verbs such as to *pick up;* use *lift.*
- Use the formal tone and maximum punctuation to assure clarity; avoid the use of first names in letter salutations. If you know the other country's salutation and closing, use them. End with a closing sentence that is thoughtful.
- Conform carefully to rules of grammar; be particularly careful of misplaced modifiers, dangling participles, and incomplete sentences.
- Use more short, simple sentences than you would ordinarily use; avoid compound and compound-complex sentences.
- Clarify the meaning of words that have more than one meaning.
- Adapt the tone of the letter to the reader if the cultural background of the reader is known; for example, use unconditional apologies if that is expected in the reader's culture.
- Try to capture the flavor of the language when writing to someone whose cultural background you know. Letters to people whose native language is Spanish, for example, would contain more flowery language (full of highly ornate language) and would be longer than U.S. letters.
- Avoid acronyms (ASAP, RSVP), **emoticons** (: -o), and "shorthand" (U for you and 4 representing for) in writing letters, faxes, or e-mail messages.
- If photocopies to other members of the organization are appropriate, be sure to send them a copy or ask who should receive copies.

Remember that numbers are written differently in some countries; for example, 7,000 may be written 7.000 or 7000. Money designations are also written differently across the globe.

Writing Tone and Style

The tone and writing style of correspondents from foreign countries are usually more formal and traditional than U.S. companies typically use. When the tone and style differ greatly from that used by the recipient, the intended positive message may be negatively received.

Authors of business communication textbooks in the United States recommend the use of the direct approach for beginning good-news and direct request/inquiries, and neutral messages and the indirect approach for bad-news messages. The direct approach means simply that you begin with the goods news or other pleasant ideas in the good-news message, the request or inquiry in request/inquiry messages, and the most important idea in neutral messages. When using the indirect approach, beginning with a buffer is recommended. A **buffer** is a paragraph that tells what the letter is about, is pleasant, but says neither *yes* nor *no.*

In the United States, we also teach using a "you-approach" or "reader orientation"; however, in a collectivistic country, you would want to use an inclusive approach such as "we" or "our" to avoid making the reader lose face or be singled out. In a collectivistic culture, it is improper for one person to be addressed because the whole team will be responsible for the outcome.

Women writing to men internationally will have to be very careful about the tone and word choice. Women have to make an exceptionally good impression if they are to be taken seriously. Flattering statements when written to a man must be carefully worded so they cannot be interpreted as flirtatious. Compliments should be given from the company or the department rather than from the woman directly. Many countries do not consider women as serious businesspeople and would feel a woman was too assertive if she used firm and direct words. Direct words such as *expect* or *require* should be softened to *would appreciate* (DeVries, 1994).

Although Germans use the buffer occasionally, they are usually more direct with negative news. Latin Americans do not use buffers; they avoid the negative news completely, feeling it is discourteous to bring bad news. For that reason, U.S. Americans must be able to read between the lines of letters from Latin American businesspeople. The Japanese begin letters on a warm, personal note which is an inappropriate way of beginning a U.S. letter. The Japanese try to present negative news in a positive manner, a quality that has sometimes caused a U.S. counterpart to feel that the person was deceitful.

> The Japanese will begin a letter regardless of the type of news with a statement about the season: "It is spring, and the cherry blossoms smile to the blue sky."
> Islamic people will use the phrase, "God willing" (*Inshallah* in Arabic).

A way to show respect is to include common phrases of the country that help to make the recipient feel comfortable. Most nations consider politeness to be a very important quality in business encounters. A compliment showing knowledge of the cultural heritage of the country is also appreciated.

> U.S. businesspeople tend to be very direct in discussing business and do not want to waste anyone's time. However, showing politeness and a little small talk is considered the proper way of doing business in most countries in the world.
> Also, what U.S. persons view as a request can appear to be boasting, obnoxious, or arrogant in another culture because of the way the request is phrased.

In the United States, ending negative messages on a positive note is important while the French do not consider this important. Beginnings and endings of French business letters are very formal, but endings tend to be somewhat flowery: "Sir, please accept the expression of my best feelings"; the French organize some types of business letters differently. They recommend apologizing for mistakes and expressing regret for any inconvenience caused. U.S. business letter writers, on the other hand, avoid apologies and simply state objectively the reason for the action taken. Endings of German letters tend to be formal (Kilpatrick, 1984; Varner, 1987, 1988).

An awareness of the differences between the format, tone, and style of written communication can go far in building goodwill between cultures. If you receive a letter in which you are addressed "Dear Prof. Dr. Judith C. Simon," you need to be able to read past the unimportant style or tone differences and look for the meaning in the letter. The overuse of politeness is very common for many cultures and should not distract U.S. readers. However, as a writer, keep these cultural differences in mind to avoid sounding harsh and insensitive to the reader.

> British writers assume less shared knowledge than the Finnish writer does (Lampi, 1992). Politeness strategies differed when a group of Dutch businesspeople were using their native language or using English. The type and frequency of use of politeness changed when a second language was used (Geluyckens & van Rillaer, 1996).

The length of U.S. letters tend to be shorter than letters written in other cultures. As a sign of friendship, it would be wise for U.S. businesspeople to change the tone of their letters when writing to businesspeople in another culture. The **parochialism** or ethnocentrism that so many U.S. people display in their writing to other cultures can easily be tempered with a knowledge of the person to whom they are writing.

Letter Formats

Letter formats used by other countries often differ from styles used by U.S. businesses. Some countries still use the indented letter style with closed punctuation. The preferred styles in the United States are the blocked (all lines beginning at the left margin) and modified blocked (date and closing beginning at the center and paragraphs blocked). Writing styles use either standard punctuation (colon after the salutation or comma after the closing) or open punctuation (no punctuation after either the salutation or closing).

The French tend to use the indented style for business letters. The French place the name of the originating city before the date (Norvège, le 15 décembre 2---). (Use the overstrike function, symbol function, or multinational insert function of your word processing software to type special marks used in other languages).

The format of the inside address may vary. In the United States, the title and full name are placed on the first line; street number and name on the second line; and city, state, and zip code on the last line. The format used in Germany puts the title (Herr, Frau, or Fräulein) on the first line; full name on the second line; street name followed by the street number on the third line; and zip code, city, and state on the last line. The street number also follows the name of the street in Mexico and South America.

While U.S. letters always place the date before the inside address, the French sometimes place the date after the inside address. In their letters, the inside address is typed on the right side with the zip code preceding the name of the city (74010 PARIS); in U.S. letters, the inside address is on the left. The punctuation style used in their letters differs from that used in U.S. correspondence; the salutation is followed by a comma rather than a colon or no punctuation which is used in standard and open punctuation styles of U.S. letters. The complimentary close is rather formal in French business letters; the writer's title precedes the writer's name. Care should be taken to format the inside address and the envelope address exactly as it is shown on the incoming correspondence.

Guidelines for addressing the envelope if you do not have an address to copy is:
Mr./Mrs./Ms./or appropriate title plus first then last name
Street number followed by street name
Zip code information is placed sometimes before and sometimes after the city
The country name is typed in full capital letters. Whether the country and city are at the beginning or at the end of the address is affected by the collectivistic or individualistic nature of the society.

Examples:

Mr. Hans-Dieter Duden	JAPAN, Tokyo	Mr. John R. Smith
Bosch Gmbh	Hachioji-shi	2350 Walnut Grove
1600 Bretton Due	47-25 Nanyodai	Memphis, TN 38152
GERMANY	Nakamura Yoko	USA

Dates are written differently also. While people in the United States would use January 5, 2---, in many other countries the date would be written 5th of January 2--- or 5 January 2---.

U.S. business letters are single-spaced, but in many other countries, they may be either single- or double-spaced. In U.S. letters, the name of the writer is typed four lines below the complimentary close with the title placed on the next line. In German letters, the company name is placed below the complimentary close; the writer signs the letter, but the writer's name and position are not typed in the signature block. In Japan and China, the surname is always placed before the given name (such as Smith Jack rather than Jack Smith).

Depending on how international the Japanese, Chinese, or Far Eastern businessperson is, they may switch the names to make you comfortable.

Example: Wu Chei will change his name to Chei Wu (surname last) to please you.

Salutations and closings are more formal in many other countries. Salutations for German letters would be the English equivalent of Very Honored Mrs. Jones and in Latin American countries, My Esteemed Dr. Green. Complimentary closings would often be the English equivalent of Very respectfully yours (Kilpatrick, 1984; Varner, 1987, 1988).

DIPLOMATIC TITLES
Written Forms of Address and Salutations

Title and Address Form	Salutation
Ambassador His/Her Excellency (name) The Ambassador of (country)	Excellency: (or) Dear Mr./Madame Ambassador:
Chargé d'Affaires The Honorable (name) Chargé d' Affaires of (country)	Dear Sir/Madame:
Minister The Honorable (name) The Minister of (country)	Dear Sir/Madame: Dear Mr./Madame Minister:
Consul General The Honorable (name) Consul General of (country)	Dear Mr./Ms. (name):
Consul The Honorable (name) Consul of (country)	Dear Mr./Ms. (name):

(Bosrock, 1995, p. 54)

Samples of Japanese, French, Spanish, and Chinese letters that have been translated into English from the native language are shown in Figures 7.1 through 7.4. Samples of a British and U.S. letter are shown in Figures 7.5 and 7.6.

The Japanese have a traditional format beginning with the salutation followed by a comment about the season or weather.

Examples of seasonal greetings:

January—	I feel my body frozen as severe cold days continue. Full scale "Winter Shogun" has arrived. (An analogy between Shogun and nature is used.)
February—	Hope you are coping with the last phase of the cold season. Cold winter still remains strong.
March—	Spring has just begun on the calendar, but the cold wind reminds us winter is not over yet. Glad to smell the soil covered by snow for a long winter.
April—	Buds of cherry tree are getting large. Spring has arrived and every field is covered by hundreds of flowers.
May—	Wind blowing over the field feels like a beginning of the summer. Flapping wind kite in the sky looks great.
June—	Rice paddy fields are ready to be planted. Continuous rain ended, and it is a beautiful day.
July—	It was the hottest day of the year. It is a season of summer festivals, and people having fun.
August—	Indian summer is still around this week. Keeping a lot of summer memories in my heart.
September—	Hope you are in good health with the cool weather. The sun is still strong and casting shadow reminds me the summer season is not over.
October—	It is autumn, when the sky is blue and people have an appetite. The smell of Matsutake reminds me of fall.
November—	The tree on the boulevard is bare of leaves. All mountains are burning with crimson foliage.
December—	Frost is on the ground and breath is white. The year is almost over.

(Tsuji, 1998)

Next will follow a kind remark about a gift, kindness, or patronage. They then include the main message and close with best wishes for the receiver's health or prosperity (Haneda & Shima, 1982). Japanese who are doing business internationally are adjusting and changing the way they write. They are using a shorter seasonal greeting and writing the business message sooner. Studies show that Japanese businesspeople are using both deductive and inductive writing patterns (Kubota, 1997).

AZ409
April 7, 2---

Showa Machine Works Ltd.
Attention of Sales Department

5-1 Moriyama Maguro
Moriyamaku, Nagoya 463
Asumi Trading Co., Ltd.

President: Nobuaki Iwai

Allow us to open
with all reverence to you:

The season for cherry blossoms is here with us and everybody is beginning to feel refreshed. We sincerely congratulate you on becoming more prosperous in your business.

We have an inquiry from a foreign customer and shall be very happy to have your best price and technical literature for the item mentioned below:

Wire Drawing Machine
6 units for Taiwan

Specifications:
1. Finished sizes: 0.04 mm to 0.10 mm
2. Spooler: Single
3. Speed: Min. 1500 meters/min.
4. Type of spooler: Expanding arbor
5. Capstan: Must be covered with ceramic
6. Dimension of spool:
   Flange diam.   215 mm
   Barrel diam.   163 mm
   Bore diam.   97 mm
   Traverse   200 mm

The above are all the information available for this inquiry. We ask you to recommend a machine that can meet these specifications.

We shall be very pleased if you will study the inquiry and let us have your reply as soon as possible. We solicit your favor.

Let us close with
great respect to you.

FIGURE 7.1 Japanese Letter

In the letter from France, notice the "we" attitude and manner of indirect apology; note also the way of explaining the situation and the format: typing the surname in all capital letters. The date, salutation, and closing also differ from the U.S. letter.

Similarities and differences between the Spanish letter and the U.S. letter include the date, salutation, and closing.

The following letter from China is shown as it was received; notice how the syntactic errors develop when people are not writing in their native language. Also notice that the writer has used the U.S. format in deference to another culture.

As shown in Figure 7.5, the British do not use a period after Mr, Mrs, Ms, or Dr. The British are very conscious of forms of titles and addresses and expect others to use them appropriately (Janner, 1977). The British class system is becoming less rigid; how you address someone is less formal than a few years ago. However if you do not know someone well, you need to use his or her title and surname. When writing about someone in a letter, you would include after the name, the abbreviations for military and civil orders and decorations, highest degree or diploma, professional memberships, and professions. In the typed signature line, include in parentheses the title you prefer to use such as Ms. The British are also fond of humor or sarcasm (Scott, 1998).

In the example of a U.S. letter that conveys bad news (Figure 7.6), notice the use of a buffer in the first paragraph which does not suggest a negative message. In the second

---

FIGURE 7.2 Letter from France

Marie Portafaix
7, Avenue Felix
75541 Paris

Mr. Pierre DESBORDE
Professor d'économie politique
IUT BB Commercial Techniques
Doyen Gosse Place
38000 GRENOBLE

MTP/GM/05.22

Paris, 25 September 2---

Sir,

We are in receipt of your letter and have given our best attention to your request.

We are unhappy to inform you, we are not able to give your proposition a favorable report.

As a matter of fact we are grateful for the interest and your support, but we must consider essential publications hereafter for the media.

We want to renew our regrets and thank you for your belief. Sir, be assured our sentiments are the best.

Public Relations Director
Marie Thérèse PORTAFAIX

8 June 2---

Zapatería Elegánte, S. A.
May 5 Avenue
Caracas, Venezuela

Esteemed clients and friends:

Permit us to communicate to you that the fabric of the shoes of Miss Modalo that were ordered has been discontinued. Therefore much to our regret we will not be able to serve you in this situation.

We always want to fill your catalog requests, and if you find another model from the enclosed catalog that you like we would be very glad to send them.

We regret your loss and hope to be able to serve you on another occasion as you deserve.

Very cordially yours,

CIA. LATIN AMERICANA, S.A.

José Mendoza Lopez
General Manager

FAL/age

FIGURE 7.3 Spanish Letter

paragraph the bad news is placed in a dependent clause to deemphasize it. The letter ends with an action close, avoiding any reference to the bad news. The letter style is blocked with standard punctuation.

Facsimiles (Faxes)

Multinational businesses in the United States have found that the facsimile (fax) machine is more dependable than the mail service in many countries. However, in some countries the telephone system is also poorly managed which means the fax machine may not be better than the mail. Poor service of both mail and phone systems occurs during the stormy seasons that a number of countries experience. In addition, many countries lack regular mail and telephone service in their remote areas. However, through telecommunication satellites, telephone service is becoming more dependable than the mail in many locations around the globe.

April 5, 2---

Prof. L. S. St. Clair
71 South Perkins Extd.
Memphis, TN 38117-3211

Dear Prof. St. Clair:

I've received your letter of Jan. 30 and your report passed on to me by Dr. Jones of CSU, Long Beach. Thank you deeply for your kindness to let me have it. I have perused it and found it very creative and enlightening. I especially admire your servant and ingenious analysis. I fully support your suggestion to establish course in intercultural business communication. Never has it been so important to globalize business communication education as it is today. It is time now to join our effort in this important area.

I made a report on the development of BC in the U.S. at a convention in Chicago last month.

You are welcome to visit China and help us with the development of business communication in China.

Sincerely,

Feng Xiang Chun
Vice President

FIGURE 7.4 Letter Written in English by Chinese Writer

The fax should be written as you would write a letter. If you are sending production schedules, budgets, or other types of written information, then a cover letter or transmittal sheet should be used so that the operator knows to whom the fax is directed, from whom the material originates, and how many total pages are included. Figure 7.7 is an example of a fax.

Electronic Mail (E-Mail)

When using electronic mail internationally, you should use the same writing techniques you would use for a letter. However, since the format is a memorandum with TO:, FROM:, DATE:, and SUBJECT: already stated, you would not use an inside address.

Proper e-mail courtesy includes addressing the receiver by name in the opening sentence (i.e., Mr. Slovinsky, thank you for sending me the figures I requested). Avoid

23 October 2---

Mr Stevens J. Martin, Jr.
AOC Incorporated
1627 Byhalia Road
Collierville, TN 38067

Dear Mr Martin:

I have pleasure in submitting our quotation as follows:

A.   Cost incurred to date.
    1.   Design. All designs presented to date and working
        drawings to entire booth to enable USA contractor to build.
                £1500.00
    2.   Model. Production, packing and shipment.
                £1100.00
B.   Refurbishment of existing display.
                £9425.00

I hope the above meets with your approval and should you have any queries,
please do not hesitate to contact Alan Roast at Walker Roast.

It is essential that our contractors are instructed to proceed today to meet the
shipping deadline. I apologise for putting pressure on this decision but time is now
of the essence.

Yours sincerely,

Edward Bales

FIGURE 7.5 British Letter

addressing the person by his or her first name unless permission has been granted to use the first name. The electronic mailbox should be checked at least once a day and responses should be prompt, preferably within 24 hours. Messages should be concise and brief; most messages should be kept to a maximum of two screens. Devising an electronic "signature" is recommended since, unlike a letter, it is not on company letterhead (Sabath, 1998).

Major cities around the world are connected by the Internet and have e-mail available. E-mail is a very convenient way of sending documents, and many times the printout will be clearer than when using a facsimile machine. Telephone lines are a problem in some countries, and the cost may be much higher than in the United States. (See chapter 8 for a discussion of e-mail etiquette.)

September 15, 2---

Mr. Larry Green
2871 Goodlett Street
Memphis, TN 38817

Dear Mr. Green:

A beautiful driveway not only enhances the beauty of a home, but it also increases a home's value.

Although the driveway we installed at your home six years ago is no longer under warranty, we will be glad to send one of our service representatives to inspect your driveway and give you a free estimate on repairing or replacing it.

Please call 767-6334 to arrange a time for one of our representatives to evaluate the condition of your driveway.

Sincerely,

Thomas L. Johnson

pl

FIGURE 7.6 U.S. Letter

FIGURE 7.7 Korean Fax

To: Jim Cain, President
Cainable Vegetables

From: Wu H. Chu

I received your fax message delightly. How is your business doing? I really think that our election was better for all business in Korea. If you can make a videotape of Ray Manner' farm, that would be great. Videotape, Blueprints together you can send me by airmail *not by ship,* regardlessly special or regular with the bill I would appreciate it very much. In designing of my vegetable farm I am take your experienced advice in good consideration. Thank you. I will look for your advices more.

Résumé and Job-Search Information

Globalization has definitely expanded the information people need if they intend to get a position in a country other than their own. Europeans have always lived with differences and adjusted as they crossed national boundaries. In the United States and other parts of the world, a person looking for a position could use the job-search method they were taught in school. The following is a description of job-search information needed to find a position in the United States, Great Britain, France, Germany, and Spain.

UNITED STATES

According to research by Harcourt, Krizan, and Merrier (1991), U.S. hiring officials prefer the résumé to be one to two pages long. Important résumé items include personal information (name, address, and telephone number), job objective (to give the reader an idea of what type of work you would like and your plans for advancement), educational background (universities attended), and work experience (current position, company name and location, job title, dates employed, responsibilities, and accomplishments). Most hiring officials prefer that you include three or four references (names of people who could verify your work experience, educational achievements, and character). Information about your family, age, religion, ethnicity, or gender should not be included nor should you include a photograph. The résumé is accompanied by an application (cover) letter.

In the United States, good sources of job opportunities are the Sunday edition of major newspapers in cities where you are interested in working. The *Wall Street Journal* on Tuesdays has a special employment section and also produces a newspaper, *The Employment Weekly* which is a collection of all employment advertising for the previous week in all U.S. regions. In larger cities, public and private employment agencies are also good at assisting people in finding positions.

GREAT BRITAIN

The résumé for professional business persons in Great Britain is one to two pages in length, is typed, and generally does not have a photograph attached. The résumé will contain a professional objective, name, address, phone number, professional experience, education, hobbies and other activities, and references. Military service is not listed and family and other personal information is omitted. The résumé is sent with an application letter that is typed and formal. The letter would include your reasons for wanting the position and a request for an interview.

The universities in Great Britain offer career advisory services for their graduates. Check the ads in the following journals: *The Guardian* and *The Daily Telegraph* on Thursday, *The Guardian* and *The Daily Telegraph* on Tuesday for management positions, *The Daily Telegraph* on Wednesday and the *Sunday Times* for commercial and technical positions, and the *Financial Times* on Wednesday and Thursday for finance-related positions (Tixier, 1992).

FRANCE

In France, the vita is much like the U.S. résumé. An application (cover) letter is included. The résumé or vita should list your full name, address, and age. In addition your telephone number, photograph, and family information are included. You would include a job objective, education, and experience as in the U.S. résumé. In addition, include information about your hobbies and the foreign languages in which you are proficient.

In France, it is very difficult for someone directly from the university to get a position without experience. Connections are very important in obtaining the first position. Graduates of the Grande Écoles, business, and engineering schools would have an advantage over others as graduates of these institutions are considered the intellectual elite. Age is a factor in hiring; 40 is considered old. French laws do not prevent age discrimination.

Two daily newspapers that are a good source of available positions are *Le Cosigaro* and *Le Monde*. The magazine *L'Exprès* is also a source of potential jobs (Desborde, 1993).

GERMANY

The Germans expect applicants to be well educated for their positions and to have experience. The résumé is a complete dossier of the candidate. A length of 20 to 30 pages is not unusual. Included would be positions the candidate has held, photocopies of diplomas and degrees the candidate has earned, letters of recommendation from teachers, verification of previous employment, a recent photograph, and a statement of computer skills. Other information would include the names and profession of the candidate's parents; names of brothers, sisters, spouse, and children; religious affiliation, and financial obligations. In addition to the diplomas and degrees, transcripts would be provided to certify all course work completed. Professional activities, including publications and personal references, would also be given. The résumé would begin with a typed letter of application that is one to two pages in length. The style should be very conservative and formal.

In Germany, college students often enter into a contract with a company while in college. The two large journals where employment ads are placed are the: *Frankfurter Allgemeine Zeitung* and *Süddeutsche Zeitung* (Tixier, 1992).

SPAIN

The résumé is a maximum of two pages. It is in typed letter form and is a chronology of experience, military service, and education. Including information on the family, profession of parents, clubs and associations, and a picture is not unusual. A professional objective is mentioned. Many positions are gained through personal referral rather than through school placement or advertisements. Journals that have position advertisements include *El Pais* and *La Vanguardia* (Tixier, 1992).

Books and government documents can help prevent a faux pas (social blunder or error in etiquette). The Department of State's *Background Notes* by country, Brigham Young University's *Culturgram* series, The Department of Commerce's *Overseas Business Reports*, *The World Factbook*, and *The Statesman's Year-Book* are good sources for specific information on various cultures.

Terms

• Buffer	• International English	• Parochialism
• Emoticons	• Lexical errors	• Syntactic errors

EXERCISE 7.1

Instructions: Circle the T for true and F for false.

1. T F Native speakers of a language will discover lexical errors easier than the syntactic errors.
2. T F The writing style of U.S. letters is more formal than most foreign correspondence.
3. T F The use of a buffer in bad-news messages is typical of the writing style of Latin Americans.
4. T F The Japanese try to present negative news in a positive manner.
5. T F Ending messages on a positive note is important in both French and U.S. letters.
6. T F The indented letter style for business letters is used by the French.
7. T F Salutations of German letters are more formal than in the United States.
8. T F The Japanese traditionally begin letters with comments about the season or weather.
9. T F Résumés submitted to a German firm would typically be longer than those submitted to a U.S. firm.
10. T F Spanish résumés are typically in letter form.

Questions and Cases for Discussion

1. Explain how the format of business letters differs in U.S. correspondence and in Latin American countries.
2. How does the tone and writing style of Japanese letters differ from those in the United States?
3. In order to utilize international English, what cultural factors do you have to understand?
4. Explain the difference between lexical and syntactic errors.
5. Explain why people from two cultures that speak the same language may have difficulty communicating.
6. Define a buffer and how it is used.
7. Which countries expect the reader "to read between the lines" for meaning?
8. What in the German culture might explain the very long and detailed résumé that is required when job hunting in Germany?
9. What items are currently included in résumés in the United States?
10. Explain the major differences between résumés in the United States and other cultures.

CASE 1

You work in the personnel division of a multinational organization. You have been asked to provide a list of potential candidates for a management position in the corporation's German office. Because of their laws, you want a German national for the position. How would you go about obtaining résumés to review?

CASE 2

If you are dealing with a foreign corporation in which no one speaks English as a native or second language, what may be necessary in order for your corporation and the foreign corporation to work together? How does a U.S. corporation react when the other corporation does not speak its language? If the corporation has the flexibility to deal with another company in which someone speaks its language versus one in which no one does, which company would receive the order?

CASE 3

A U.S. executive was working with a convention booth builder in England. The English would not give a date of completion for the booth or a shipping date to the United States and were not working on the booth. Every week for about six weeks, the U.S. executive would call and inquire about the state of the booth. One day the executive called and was given the usual litany of excuses so he gave the English an ultimatum. The next week the ultimatum was not acted upon, and the U.S. executive informed the company he would have a trucking company pick up and ship the booth to the United States. Twice the trucking company went to pick up the booth and was told by the English company that they were not authorized to pick up the booth. The U.S. executive finally had to hire the advertising firm in England that had originally hired the booth manufacturer to intervene and get the booth shipped. When the booth arrived in the United States, it had not been packed properly and required additional work. What cultural differences were involved in this situation? How could the executive have handled the situation differently?

CASE 4

A British National was sent to the United States to work in a subsidiary. He was an engineer in a management position in charge of building a new factory for the corporation. He was initially offered intercultural training; however, he felt comfortable since both countries spoke the same language and declined the training. The British engineer later complained to the home office that he was not getting the cooperation he needed. The home office hired an intercultural trainer to go to his office to review his correspondence and sit in on some of his meetings. The intercultural trainer discovered that the U.S. employees did not understand his communications. The engineer was interjecting British humor and sarcasm in both his oral communication and e-mail messages. The U.S. subordinates did not know when he was serious about a problem and when they were to ignore his statements. What are some examples of humor U.S. persons use with foreigners that they expect them to understand?

Activities

1. Examine the Latin or Germanic roots of simple and difficult words in the English language.
2. Take a passage from a journal or textbook in another language and compare it, in terms of sentence and paragraph length, to a passage from a journal or textbook written in English.
3. Modify a bad-news letter so it will be effective for a reader who is Japanese, French, Spanish, or German.
4. Search the want ads of the local newspaper; bring to class a job announcement of a position with a multinational corporation, a position involving overseas travel, or a position located in a foreign country.
5. Prepare a résumé to be sent to a multinational company applying for an overseas assignment in a country of your choice.
6. Write a letter of application to accompany the résumé prepared in activity 5.

7. Write a letter in English to someone who speaks English as a second language following the International English Guidelines.
8. Find the errors in Figure 7.4 and explain why these particular errors may have happened.
9. Read the following two facsimiles and determine the reader's probable reaction. What choice of words could have been improved upon? The first fax is from the U.S. corporate office to Taiwan; the second is from Taiwan to the U.S. corporate office.

TO: XYZ
ATTN: WU
FROM: BOB SMITH
DATE: SEPT. 4, 2---

RECEIVED THE HUGGER PACKAGE TODAY AND WAS VERY DISAPPOINTED. FIRST I WANT TO SAY I SUSPECT YOU MAY NOT HAVE SEEN THE PARTS BEFORE THEY WERE SENT. IT LOOKED LIKE EVERYTHING WAS JUST THROWN INTO A BOX AND A COUPLE OF THIN PIECES OF POLYFOAM LAID ON TOP. NOTHING WAS PROTECTIVE WRAPPED. THE HUGGER HOUSING IS SO BEAT UP IT LOOK LIKE SOMETHING OUT OF THE JUNK PILE.

THE HANGER BRACKETS WERE JUST THROWN INTO THE BOTTOM OF THE BOX WITH NO PROTECTION AT ALL. MOST OF THE SCREWS FOR THE TOP OF THE BALL WERE SCATTERED THROUGHOUT THE BOX AND NOT ASSEMBLED TO THE BRACKETS.

I'M AFRAID WE WILL NOT BE ABLE TO USE THE HANGER BRACKET ASSEMBLIES TO FIELD TEST THE HUGGER BECAUSE THE BALL HOLD DOWN SCREWS INTERFERE WITH THE TOP OF THE BALL. THE FIT IS SO TIGHT THAT THE BALL WILL NOT ROTATE AND CENTER IN THE SOCKET. WHAT WE REALLY NEED IS FOR THE THREE SCREWS TO CLEAR THE BALL BY APPROX. 1/32 INCH (ABOVE THE BALL) AFTER THE SCREWS HAVE BEEN ASSEMBLED TO THE BRACKET.

YOU MAY HAVE TO ADJUST THE VERTICAL LOCATION OF THE SCREW FROM THE DRAWING DIMENSION TO MAKE SURE THE SCREWS JUST CLEAR THE BALL.

PLEASE ADVISE WHEN YOU CAN SEND NEW BRACKET ASSEMBLIES SO WE CAN GET ON WITH THE TESTING. ALSO PLS HAVE YOUR PEOPLE PROTECTIVE WRAP EVERYTHING.

THANKS

BOB SMITH

TO: XYZ   DATE 9/7/2---

ATTN: MR. BOB SMITH

FROM: XYT

RE: 52″ HUGGER PARTS

At first, we have to apologize to you for not having good package of samples. With thin polyfoam for package is easily to break out when air freight. Besides say sorry to you, we will improve the protection of samples.

1. New hanger housing was made by hand. Without mold, it needs some time. Can we just make one set?
2. Hanger bracket ball—When we revised it per drawing, we found when hanger bracket is setted on ceiling plate. The fit is too tight that the ball will not rotate and center in the socket. We will ask vendor to make proper correction to improve these problem.
3. The distance above the ball and three screws needs 1/32 inch. Will also revise it.
4. Blade iron after our shaking test. It results over 60,000 times. How about your testing result?
5. After we complete correction hanger bracket and ball, will send samples to you again. We will improve our protective wrap of samples.

Best Regards,

WU

10. Have an international student write a letter for you in English but with their native language style, tone, and format. Compare the letter to the style, tone, and format of U.S. letters.

References

Bosrock, M. M. (1995). *Put your best foot forward: Europe.* St. Paul, MN: International Education Systems.

Collin, P. H., Lowi, M., & Weiland, C. (1991). *Beginner's dictionary of American English usage.* Lincolnwood, IL: National Textbook Co.

Desborde, R. (1993, July 23). Personal interview.

DeVries, M. A. (1994). *Internationally yours: Writing and communicating successfully in today's global marketplace.* Boston: Houghton Mifflin.

Geluyckens, R., & van Rillaer, G. (1996, March). *Face-threatening acts in international business communication: A quantitative investigation into business writing.* Paper read at the 22nd and 23rd LAUD Symposium, The cultural context in communication across languages, Duisburg, Germany.

Green, D. J., & Scott, J. C. (1992). International business correspondence: Practices and perspectives of major U.S. companies with related implications for business education. *NABTE Review, 19,* 39–43.

Haneda, S., & Shima H. (1982). Japanese communication behavior as reflected in letter writing. *Journal of Business Communication, 19*(1), 21–32.

Harcourt, J., Krizan, A. C., & Merrier, P. (1991, April). Teaching résumé content: Hiring officials' preferences versus college recruiters' preferences. *Business Education Forum,* 13–17.

Janner, G. (1977). *The businessman's guide to letter writing and to the law on letters* (2nd ed.). London: Business Books.

Kilpatrick, R. H. (1984). International business communication practices. The *Journal of Business Communication, 21*(4), 40–42.

Kubota, R. (1997). A reevaluation of the uniqueness of Japanese written discourse. *Written Communication, 14*(4), 460–481.

Lampi, M. (1992). Rhetorical strategies in "Chairman's Statement" sections in the annual reports of Finnish and British companies: Report on a pilot study. In P. Nuolijarvi & L. Tiittula (Eds.), *Talous ja Kieli 1[Language and Economics1]* (pp. 127–143). Helsinki School of Economics and Business Administration. Helsingin kauppakorkeakoulun julkaisuja D–169. Helsinki.

Riddle, D. I., & Lanham, Z. D. (1984–85, Winter). Internationalizing written business English: 20 propositions for native English speakers. *The Journal of Language for International Business, 1,* 1–11.

Sabath, A. M. (1998). *Business etiquette: 101 ways to conduct business with charm and savvy.* Franklin Lakes, NJ: Career Press.

Scott, J. C. (1998). Dear ???: Understanding British forms of address. *Business Communication Quarterly, 61*(3), 50–61.

Tixier, M. (1992). *Travailler en Europe.* Paris: Editions Liaisons.

Tsuji, M. (27 October 1998). Personal interview.

Varner, I. I. (1987). Internationalizing business communication courses. *The Bulletin of the Association for Business Communication, 1*(4), 7–11.

Varner, I. I. (1988). A comparison of American and French business correspondence. *The Journal of Business Communication, 25*(4), 55–65.

C H A P T E R

Global Etiquette

Objectives
Upon completion of this chapter, you will:

■ understand cultural differences in making introductions as well as customs related to business card exchange.

■ understand how position and status affect cultural interaction.

■ be familiar with rules of etiquette that apply to communicating by telephone and electronically with persons of other cultures.

■ understand how cultural differences in dining practices may affect intercultural communication.

■ be familiar with cultural nuances of tipping.

■ understand how practices of giving gifts vary from culture to culture and the role of gift giving in establishing favorable intercultural relations.

■ learn the importance of travel etiquette in conveying a positive image of one's firm and one's country.

When conducting business abroad or in the United States with someone of another culture, a knowledge of certain rules of business and social etiquette is important. **Etiquette** refers to manners and behavior considered acceptable in social and business situations. **Protocol** refers to customs and regulations dealing with diplomatic etiquette and courtesies expected in official dealings (such as negotiations) with persons in various cultures. Protocol will be discussed in greater detail in chapters 10 and 11.

> President Clinton, during his first state dinner abroad on a visit to Korea, confused his translator and embarrassed South Korean officials when he stepped to the microphone to give his dinner speech and invited a translator to stand between himself and President Kim Young Sam. Since in South Korea it is an insult for anyone to stand between two heads of state, President Clinton had committed a serious faux pas. (Kim, 1993).

Proper social behavior includes learning cultural variations in making introductions, exchanging business cards, recognizing position and status, communicating interculturally, dining practices, tipping etiquette, giving gifts, and traveling.

Introductions

Being sensitive to cultural variations when making introductions will ensure that your first encounter with a person from another country will leave a positive impression. First impressions are made only once but are remembered for a long time.

The procedure for making introductions varies from culture to culture. First names are used almost immediately by people from the United States and Great Britain, but introductions are more formal in some other cultures. Titles are used when introducing people in Germany and Italy; they often indicate the person's profession or educational level. Germans always address each other as "Herr Guenther" or "Frau Kurr" in and out of the office, reserving first names for close friends and family.

Remember that in some cultures such as the Chinese, the surname comes first and the given name last. Ching Lo Chang would be addressed as Mr. Ching.

President Clinton, in a meeting in Korea, addressed South Korean President Kim Young Sam's wife, Mrs. Sohn Myong-suk, as Mrs. Kim. He should have addressed her as Mrs. Sohn since in Korea it is the custom for women to maintain their maiden name when they marry (Kim, 1993).

Men and women from Latin American countries will often add their mother's maiden name to their surname so you would use the next to the last name when addressing them. Thus, Evelyn Rodrigues Castillo would be addressed as Señorita Rodrigues. When women marry, they drop their mother's surname and add their husband's father's surname. When in doubt ask what name is to be used. Because of such widely diverse customs in the use of titles, it is wise to research the customs of the particular culture involved (Devine & Braganti, 1988).

Introductions are accompanied by a handshake, an embrace, or a bow depending upon the culture. Handshakes may vary from the soft handshake of the British to the firm handshake of U.S. persons. Hugging or embracing when being introduced is considered inappropriate in business situations in the United States but is common in many South American countries. The bow, common in China and Japan, is uncommon in many other cultures. Additional information on greeting customs, including handshakes, is included in chapter 9.

Business Card Exchange

An important aspect of business protocol is knowing the proper procedure for exchanging business cards. Since all business contacts require a business card, the admonition of a well-known credit card company, "Don't leave home without it," applies.

Although most U.S. businesspeople carry business cards, they do not always exchange them when meeting unless there is a reason to contact the person later. Rank,

FIGURE 8.1

Business card presentation in Japan is completed by presenting your card with both hands, positioned so that the person can read it, and bowing.

title, and profession are taken quite seriously in some cultures, so it is important to include your position and titles or degrees in addition to your company name on your card. Include foreign headquarters as appropriate as well as your fax number and perhaps e-mail address. Avoid colored type and paper. Be conservative by choosing white paper with black ink.

Presentation of the card varies with the culture. The practice in the United States of glancing at the business card and promptly putting it in the pocket is considered rude in countries like Japan. The Japanese examine the business card carefully and make some comment while accepting it. During meetings, place the business cards of others attending in front of you on the conference table to properly refer to names, ranks, and titles. Use both hands when presenting your card in Japan or South Korea; position the card so that the person can read it (Axtell, 1993; Baldrige, 1993). (See Figure 8.1.)

In non-English-speaking countries, have the information on your card printed in English on one side and in the local language on the other side. An exchange of business cards is an expected part of all business introductions and most personal ones in Europe. Other parts of the world in which an exchange of business cards is the norm include the Middle East, the Pacific, Asia, and the Caribbean. In most of southeast Asia, Africa, and the Middle East (with the exception of Israel), avoid presenting the card with your left hand as the left hand is reserved for taking care of bodily functions (Axtell, 1993).

Position and Status

Position and status may have an impact on the success of intercultural communication encounters. No standard definition of social class exists that applies to all countries because people in different cultures have their own way of identifying the classes. Some cultures believe that people should occupy their proper places and that some are entitled to more respect than others. Most people of the United States show limited respect for rank and authority while many other cultures are very conscious of position and power.

Although the United States is not considered a nation of classes, distinctions in position and status do exist. Because class distinctions in the United States are subtle, visitors from other cultures may not be able to spot the existence of a class structure and may believe the official propaganda of social equality. Visitors to New York, Washington, D.C., and other cities, however, may see both the homeless and more affluent persons in public places. Although a system of inherited titles and ranks does not exist in the United States, certain factors distinguish between the top class, the upper middle class, the mid-middle class, and the lower middle class. As was discussed in chapter 3, money is one factor associated with class. Further distinctions are made between those whose money is inherited but who are not currently employed and those who have inherited money and are employed. Style, taste, and awareness are equally important. Social class is also associated with educational opportunities and a person's occupation or profession (Fussell, 1983).

Status is associated with education in a number of cultures. Educational titles are used in introductions as a sign of respect and acknowledgment of the person's educational achievement. In Germany and Italy, executives and other professionals are proud of titles preceding their names as they often reflect their education or profession. People with a college degree are entitled to be called Doctor (*Dottore* in Italian); the same rule applies to architects and lawyers. In Germany, the U.S. equivalent of president or managing director of a company is called *Herr Direktor;* a medical doctor, if a woman, is called *Frau Doktor* and a female engineer is addressed as *Frau Ingenieur.* In Mexico, a lawyer is addressed as *Licenciado,* a title that is considered very important. In Great Britain, special protocol exists for addressing royalty, peers, clergy, and others. The managing director in a British firm is usually the top official and equivalent to a U.S. corporate president (U.S. corporate vice presidents do not carry much clout abroad.) (Axtell, 1990). In some cultures such as India, a very rigid class system exists with the society divided into castes. The particular **caste** a person belongs to is determined at birth; each caste system has its status, rights, and duties. Although discrimination based on caste has been outlawed, in many areas particularly rural ones, it is still a major influence on life in India. In India's rigid caste system, interaction between members of different castes is often limited as in the case of India's untouchables (Samovar & Porter, 1988).

Cultural differences also exist concerning the status of women in a society. Women in some cultures play a less prominent role in business than do men. The Arabs are becoming more accustomed to women executives, and they are beginning to accept women executives from other countries. U.S. women doing business with the Arabs should understand this difference in cultural attitude and should make a special effort to conduct themselves appropriately including dressing very modestly. In some Middle Eastern countries, men may refuse to work with women; women executives in Latin America may not receive the same respect given men executives. Women in the United States are being given increased opportunities for business travel, management positions in overseas operations, and transfers to overseas assignments. In her book, *The International Businesswoman of the 1990s,* Rossman (1990) predicts that the progress U.S. women have made will set a precedent for change overseas since the United States is often a catalyst for international change.

In some cultures such as the Chinese, people are very aware of age and hierarchy. Age is viewed as an indication of seniority. In addition to the Asian culture, the Arabian world has a great respect for age. Advanced years represent wisdom and respect. Age takes precedence over rank, but rank is still important. In the Japanese society, knowing the rank of the people with whom you come in contact is important. The middle-level manger in a large company outranks a department head from a smaller company.

The higher the rank of the person you are introduced to, the lower you bow. The person of lower rank bows first and lowest. Status is also shown by who goes first when entering a room or an elevator. Those of lower rank wait for those of higher rank to precede them. If you are the foreign guest, you may be expected to enter a room ahead of others so if you are motioned to enter the room, do so quickly. When the Chinese or Japanese enter a room, they generally enter in protocol order with the highest ranking person entering first. They will also assume that the first member of your negotiating team to enter the room is the head of your group and has the higher rank. Sitting in rank order from highest to lowest during a meeting is helpful (Axtell, 1998).

Proper Etiquette When Communicating Electronically

Aspects of protocol related to successful intercultural communication include telephone manners and cyberspace etiquette sometimes referred to as **netiquette** (network etiquette).

Many intercultural encounters are via the telephone. When talking on the telephone, the initial impression is formed mainly by vocal quality (70 percent) rather than on the words spoken (30 percent). Thus, opinions are formed more on how something is said and the voice tone rather than on what the person actually says (Mitchell, 1996).

Good telephone manners include answering the phone promptly (first or second ring), identifying yourself properly by giving your department and your name, and being courteous at all times including the frequent use of "please" and "thank you." Successful telephone communication involves recognizing and avoiding behaviors that typically irritate others. Being put on hold has been identified as the single most irritating behavior. When the telephone call is to another country, being put on hold can go beyond irritation. Other negative behaviors that should be avoided include mouth noises, not paying attention, and having a negative or rude attitude. A positive behavior appreciated by callers is "the voice with a smile." Callers also appreciate a cheerful attitude.

When voice mail is used, be brief but complete when leaving a message. Include your name, company, the date, and the time of the message. Give your phone number slowly and include a brief summary of what the call concerns.

Since more companies are communicating by e-mail, certain rules of etiquette should be observed. E-mail is more informal than a letter or memorandum and is inappropriate for conveying certain types of messages. Negative information such as a person's failure to get a promotion or personal information such as announcing the birth of a baby are not appropriate uses of e-mail. Proper netiquette avoids the following:

- **shouting**—typing the message in all capital letters;
- **dissing**—speaking ill of someone;
- **flaming**—sending vicious, insulting messages;
- **spamming**—mass mailings of commercial advertisements or material cross-posted to numerous newsgroups (Segaloff, 1998).

In addition to these suggestions, avoid the use of humor and sarcasm. Additional suggestions were included in chapter 7.

Since one's firm may be liable for information leaked into cyberspace, employees should be very careful about the messages they send. A good rule to follow—if you would not want your message posted on the company bulletin board, do not send it via e-mail. Pressing the "delete" key after sending a message does not mean that it cannot be tracked to you (Sabath, 1998).

Care should be taken in deciding how a message should be sent. E-mail has the advantage of having low preparation and fast delivery time as well as being personal and convenient for the receiver. The disadvantage is lack of confidentiality and, of course, the lack of nonverbal interaction (Kenton & Valentine, 1997). Of course, not all countries use e-mail as frequently as people in the United States. In South American countries, nonprofit and commercial groups are joining the *superautopista de información* or information superhighway despite the high cost. Equipment often costs as much as 40 percent more than in the United States (Bosrock, 1997).

The use of fax messages is increasing as a quick method of communication between countries. The basic guidelines for writing a fax are included in chapter 7; points of etiquette regarding their transmission follow:

- Call ahead to confirm the fax number and to alert the person that you are sending a message (in case the fax machine shares a line with a person's telephone). The message should follow within 15 minutes.
- Certain documents should not be faxed—documents of more than 10 to 12 pages, personal or confidential information, and negative news.
- Avoid using the fax when impressions are important. Résumés and proposals submitted on fax paper will not get the same attention as those submitted on good quality, linen finish paper (Glassman, 1998).

Dining Practices

Cultural dining practices vary widely. In many parts of the world, the main meal is at noon while in the United States the main meal is in the evening. In Mexico, lunchtime is from 2 p.m. to 4 p.m. and is the main meal of the day. However, in places near the United States–Mexican border, local businesses conform more to the U.S. lunchtime of noon to 2 p.m. The dinner hour also varies. In the United States, the dinner hour varies from 5 p.m. to 7 p.m. but in such countries as Spain, it may be as late as 10 p.m. In some cultures, business meals are eaten in private homes while in other cultures they are usually eaten at restaurants. When entertaining visitors from other countries, be considerate and ask them whether they prefer the main meal at noon or in the evening and take them to restaurants where they would have a choice of a light or heavy meal (Devine & Braganti, 1988).

Cultural variations exist in the number of courses typically served as well as when the salad is served. A formal luncheon usually consists of two to three courses, and a formal dinner consists of three to seven courses. In some countries including those in Latin America, even informal meals typically have numerous courses. In Italy and France, salads are often served after the main course rather than before.

Dining practices are viewed differently in various cultures. A U.S. dining practice that seems unusual to people of other cultures is the serving of a glass of iced water at most restaurants. Other countries that serve water do so without ice or serve bottled mineral water. Another dining practice that is viewed with astonishment is the habit of offering coffee at the beginning of a meal; serving coffee at the end of the meal is common in most cultures. The popularity of decaffeinated coffee in the United States has not yet spread to other countries so visitors are often surprised by a waiter's question of "Will you have regular coffee or decaf?" Another U.S. custom that sometimes amazes people from other cultures is designating certain sections in restaurants as smoking and nonsmoking. A practice that makes little sense in other cultures is the U.S. custom of conducting business at breakfast. The French especially do not like breakfast meetings; they prefer a leisurely breakfast with time to read the paper in the morning. The French do conduct business over lunch; however, the meal may last two hours or more. Another U.S. business custom questioned by people in other cultures is the lengthy cocktail "hour" before dinner. Italians have commented that the endless rounds of cocktails before ordering a meal is exhausting and may result in discussions that make little sense (Baldrige, 1993).

The manner of eating is also diverse. The **U.S. eating style** uses the "zigzag" technique: cutting the meat with the knife held in the right hand and the fork in the left, then placing the knife on the plate, shifting the fork to the right hand, and eating. Diners using the **Continental eating style** place the fork in the left hand and knife in the right; they use the knife to push food onto the back of the fork, then move the food into the mouth with the tines of the fork down. Asians use chopsticks especially for eating rice but may use a spoon for soup. They appreciate foreigners' attempting to use chopsticks and are often willing to demonstrate correct usage. (See Figure 8.2.)

Other cultural variations in dining also exist. Tahitian food is eaten with the fingers. In the Middle East, be prepared to eat with your fingers if your host does but use the right hand only. In Bolivia, you are expected to clean your plate; Egyptians, however, consider it impolite to eat everything on your plate (Axtell, 1993).

A dining practice in France that seems unusual to those in other cultures is the custom of bringing pet dogs into restaurants where the waiter takes the dog into the kitchen to be fed a treat. Dogs in most cultures are not allowed in public eating establishments. They may, however, be on the menu in such Asian countries as South Korea.

FIGURE 8.2 Cultural Variations in Eating Style

A wealthy American couple was touring Asia accompanied by their pet poodle. They decided to dine one evening at a nice looking restaurant where, as it turned out, restaurant employees could speak no English. Since the tourists could not speak the local language, they ordered from the menu by pointing to certain items. They also tried to order food for their poodle. After several attempts using a type of sign language, the waiter seemed to understand. He pointed to the dog, then pointed to the kitchen. The couple, thinking this meant that the dog could eat in the kitchen but not the dining room, nodded their agreement. After a lengthy wait, the waiter proudly entered and lifted the lid of one of the serving platters to display a well-cooked poodle (Ricks, 1993, pp. 8–9).

Dining in Japan, especially in Japanese homes, requires sitting in a kneeling position on a tatami mat. Men keep their knees 3 or 4 inches apart; women keep their knees together. Being able to lower yourself to this position and rise from it gracefully requires practice. If you have frequent contact with the Japanese, practicing this art would be warranted (Axtell, 1993).

Tipping

People communicate nonverbally by their tipping practices; those who are basically miserly and those who are generous will reveal these traits by their tipping behavior. Although it is difficult to establish definite rules for tipping, generally when service has been good or when service people go out of their way to do a favor, a tip is merited. If the service is very bad, you are not expected to leave a tip but should report the situation to the manager. "Insult tipping" (leaving a few coins) shows a lack of respect and is inappropriate regardless of how poor the service.

Trends in tipping appear to have changed in the last few years. Although a tip of 15 percent of the bill was considered to be a generous tip in fine restaurants, 20 percent is now closer to the norm when the service is excellent.

Traveling in the United States involves numerous situations in which tipping is expected. When traveling, have a supply of $1 and $5 bills in your pocket for tipping the cab driver, the bellhop, and other service personnel who may carry your luggage, summon a cab, or perform other services such as delivering food or small appliances to your hotel room. Travel tipping needs to be included in anticipated travel expenses; tipping service personnel at a resort or luxury hotel may add an additional 25 percent to your bill.

Tipping in a nontipping culture can offend or insult the people of that culture. However, letters of thanks to people who have been especially helpful, including hotel managers, are very much appreciated. Tipping in Japan is frowned upon. People in this culture consider helping you with your luggage as a gesture of hospitality and would be offended if you tipped them. If a hotel employee has performed an extra service that you wish to reward, place the yen in an envelope since the Japanese would consider openly receiving money as embarrassing or as "losing face."

In many places such as Europe, a service charge is added to your restaurant and hotel bill; you are usually not expected to leave an additional tip. In the absence of a service charge, leave the usual 15 to 20 percent that you would leave in the United

States. Observing cultural differences in tipping can communicate nonverbally that you have researched the country and that you consider local customs to be important (Axtell, 1993).

Gift Giving

Each country has its seasons and occasions for giving gifts. Gift giving in some cultures is an art and is considered an integral part of building intercultural professional and social relationships. The careful selection and wrapping of a gift and presenting it at the proper time with panache (style) conveys to others your social sensitivity and good manners.

Business gifts in the United States are very modest in price; the rule to follow (because of tax regulations) is to limit the price to $25 or less. Business gifts are sometimes given to members of your staff on such occasions as birthdays and Christmas. In addition, secretaries are generally treated to flowers and/or lunch on Secretaries' Day. Remember that business gifts to staff members should be personal; an electric pencil sharpener would be inappropriate. However, they should not be too personal—cologne or lingerie to a member of the opposite gender could be misinterpreted. Gift certificates to the person's favorite restaurant or specialty shop would be in good taste. Subordinates wait for their supervisors to set the tone on gift giving. If you are new in an office, ask what tradition is usually followed in exchanging gifts. Several years ago when the office Christmas party was popular, colleagues often exchanged gifts as part of the occasion. The practice of exchanging gifts among colleagues, even token gifts (the office grab bag), seems to have been discontinued in many firms in favor of contributing the amount of money you would spend on such gifts to a local food bank or pooling the amount to give gifts of food or money to members of the custodial staff.

In the United States, gifts are opened in front of the giver. The gift is admired, and appreciation is expressed verbally. The oral expression of thanks is followed by a written note of appreciation unless the gift is small and is used as an advertisement (e.g., a paperweight with the company logo). Business gifts to the office or department, such as a basket of fruit or box of candy, are opened immediately and shared by all. (The manager's taking the gift home to share with his or her family is considered to be in poor taste.) The manager would write a note of thanks to the company that sent the gift and convey expressions of appreciation from staff members.

Although flowers make appropriate gifts, learn cultural taboos related to color, variety, and number. Red roses are associated with romance in some cultures. In some countries such as China, white is the color of mourning, and gladioli are often used in funeral sprays; thus, a gift of white gladioli would be inappropriate. In most European countries, avoid a gift of carnations which are for cemeteries only. Chrysanthemums would be inappropriate in both Japan and Italy; they are associated with funerals and mourning. Although flowers are not expected by a Mexican host, they are appreciated; but avoid sending yellow, red, or white flowers as these colors have negative connotations for some Mexican people. In some cultures the number of flowers given has a special significance (Barnum & Wolniansky, 1989). Armenians give an uneven number of flowers on happy occasions; even numbers of flowers are associated with death. For the Chinese, four is the most negative number (it sounds like their word for death) so gifts of four flowers—or four of anything else—should be avoided (Dresser, 1996). Since in

Thailand and Hong Kong, three is a lucky number, give gifts in threes in these countries (Bosrock, 1994). A flower shop in the host country would be the best place to get information concerning local customs about giving flowers.

> Exhibitors at a trade show could not understand why Chinese visitors were not stopping by their booth. Workers were wearing green hats and were using them as giveaways as well. They later learned that for many Chinese, green hats are associated with infidelity; the Chinese expression "He wears a green hat" indicates that a man's wife has been cheating on him. When they discarded the green hats and gave out T-shirts and coffee mugs instead, they had a number of Chinese visitors (Dresser, 1996).

Gift giving is very much a part of conducting business in countries as Japan. Japan's major gift giving times are Ochugen (July 15) and Oseibo (December). Companies give gifts to their customers as an expression of appreciation for past and future business. They also reward their employees at these times with large bonuses. U.S. companies that have ongoing business relationships with the Japanese should remember their associates with a gift at both of these times. Since Japan is one of the United States' largest trading partners, knowing the nuances associated with Japanese gift giving is considered an important aspect of protocol with people in that culture.

The Japanese are a gracious people for whom gift giving seems to be an art. The wrapping of the gift and the manner of presenting it are just as important as the gift itself. Gifts are beautifully wrapped but without the ornate bows and other decorations typically used on gifts in the United States. The color of the wrapping should be consistent with the occasion: red, gold, and white for happy events; black and purple or black and white for other occasions. The Japanese do not open a gift in front of the giver so you should avoid opening your gift in their presence. Also avoid giving a gift when someone else is present. In the Arabian countries, on the other hand, you must present a gift when others are present so it will not be interpreted as a bribe. Do not surprise your Japanese host with a gift as it might cause the person to lose face. Let your host know ahead of time by mentioning, for example, that you have found a special commemorative coin to add to his collection. Favorite gifts with the Japanese are imported liquor, consummables of high quality, and designer-made products with such names as Gucci, Tiffany & Co., or Mark Cross. Musical tapes and CDs are also good choices. Avoid giving gifts manufactured elsewhere in Asia as this would be an insult.

> A Japanese-American, whose firm conducted business in Japan, told how he once averted a near disaster in United States–Japanese relations. His company selected and addressed 500 Christmas cards to its Japanese joint-venture partner. The cards were red (in Japan, funeral notices are red). The Japanese-American manager stopped the mail just in time. He said, "We almost sent 500 funeral cards to our Japanese partner!" (Engholm, 1991, p. 228)

These additional guidelines for gift giving in Asian countries should be observed because of the importance placed on this aspect of developing and maintaining harmonious business relationships:

- Take time to research the perfect gift; it could be related to the Asian counterpart's profession or hobby. Adding an item to a person's collection is much appreciated. Remember to buy gifts in the United States; avoid anything made in an Asian country.
- Always wrap gifts (no bows) and include an appropriate card. While wrapping the gift in red paper (the color of luck) is appropriate, using red ink when addressing the card or writing the accompanying note is not; in China using red ink would indicate a desire to sever a relationship forever.
- Be aware of superstitions and taboos related to gifts. Avoid any gift depicting white wolves since the wolf is symbolic of cruelty and greed. Also avoid a gift of straw sandals or a clock in China.
- Recognize the significance of numbers in gift giving: three is a lucky number in Thailand; eight and nine are lucky in Hong Kong (the word for *eight* sounds like prosperity; the word for *nine* is a homonym for eternity).
- Expect a gift to be declined out of politeness at least once in some Asian countries; they will then accept. You are expected to decline once, then accept with thanks (Engholm, 1991). Since gift giving is very important in the Japanese culture, asking advice from a Japanese colleague or from someone who has lived in Japan is recommended (Axtell, 1993; Yager, 1991).

Knowing when to present the business gift is also important. In Korea, business gifts are usually given at the beginning of formal negotiations. In Germany, however, business gifts are seldom exchanged at the beginning of negotiations but may be given at their conclusion. In Latin American countries, present gifts only at the conclusion of negotiations.

Other gift-giving practices and guidelines in various cultures include the following:

1. When dining in a person's home in western Europe, present your gift when you arrive so that it does not appear to be intended as payment for the meal.
2. Avoid giving gifts to the French until a personal relationship has been developed. Avoid gifts of perfume or wine; those are their specialties.
3. Gifts to Germans should not be wrapped in black, brown, or white.
4. Avoid gifts of a clock in the People's Republic of China as the clock is considered a symbol of bad luck.
5. A striped tie is not an appropriate gift to a British man; it may represent a British regiment other than his own.
6. Avoid gifts of a knife or handkerchief to persons in Latin America. The knife is interpreted as a desire to cut off the relationship; the handkerchief is associated with tears.
7. Avoid gifts of liquor or wine for an Arab. Since alcohol is illegal in Islamic cultures, the gift would be confiscated by customs.
8. Since the cow is sacred in India, do not give any gifts made of cowhide.
9. In Islamic countries, exercise restraint in admiring personal possessions; you will probably find yourself the recipient of the object you have admired (Axtell, 1993; Stewart, 1997).

When people of the United States select business gifts for people in other countries, they should remember that the gifts should be made in the United States, be utilitarian, and have conversational value. Good choices include things that are representative of the United States such as Native American art or jewelry; videotapes of U.S. movies; United States-made sports equipment; or food that is unique to the United States such as candy, nuts, and California wines. Avoid gag gifts; people of some other cultures do not appreciate them (Stewart, 1997).

Travel Etiquette

Travel etiquette begins with a pleasant, positive attitude and a sense of adventure especially when it comes to international travel. People who approach international travel with eager anticipation, who look forward to meeting new people, seeing new places, and experiencing a new culture seem to have more favorable experiences than those who approach travel with a sense of foreboding. In other words, people seem to get what they expect.

Since most international travel is by airplane, etiquette in this section will concentrate on air travel and will cover such topics as dressing and packing for the trip, proper behavior on the plane, and handling problem situations.

Travel dress is important because the people you meet, including ticket agents, will be strangers who will judge you first on your appearance. Being well dressed makes a favorable impression on others and in many cultures is associated with competency and respect. You are a representative of your company and your country; dressing professionally sends the message that you care about the impression you make on your compatriots and on persons of other cultures. Another benefit of being well dressed (wearing a suit or executive casual) when traveling is that you often get better service from airline personnel and from hotel employees upon your arrival. Women may wish to wear their business blouse and jacket with coordinating slacks then carry a skirt in the carry-on luggage and change in the plane lavatory just before landing. This is especially important when a presentation is scheduled for that same day or when you are being met at the airport by a business colleague from the host country.

Christopher Patterson, an MBA graduate student at a Mid-South university, was invited for an interview in St. Louis for a much coveted managerial position with an international air transport firm. Because his usual classroom attire was a T-shirt, torn jeans, and a baseball cap worn backwards, his communication professor gave him this advice: "Dress professionally on the flight; you never know who you'll meet." He followed this advice on the flight over, felt very confident after the interview with three of the company's top-level executives, but relaxed and reverted to his classroom attire on the return trip. To his surprise, one of the three executives who had interviewed him was on the flight. The executive with a shocked look said, "Well, I almost didn't recognize you. You don't look like the same person we interviewed." Christopher reported to the professor on his return: "You were right; I blew it." As it turned out, he did blow it—he didn't get the job.

When packing for a trip, keep in mind that conservative business attire is usually preferred in other countries. This means dark suits for both men and women, classic leather shoes, and good quality accessories. One's luggage should also be of good quality to create a positive impression. All belongings should be packed in the luggage; carrying personal belongings in shopping bags does not convey a professional image. Checking large suitcases and limiting carry-on luggage to the size and number specified by the airline is important. Women should remember that they are responsible for their own luggage including lifting a suitcase to the overhead bin of the airplane. Luggage with wheels is a good investment. With multiple bags, a porter or a cart may be used.

Travel etiquette also involves courteous treatment of airline personnel. When flights are late or canceled, travelers should remain calm and be polite to travel clerks who are anxious to get them to their destinations. Passengers who are courteous when they are inconvenienced often receive better treatment, including free food and lodging, than those who are rude and insensitive. Flight attendants should also be treated with respect. While they are not tipped, flight attendants should be thanked at the end of the trip along with the captain/co-captain.

> A passenger standing in line at an airline ticket counter listened to a person yelling and screaming at the ticket agent. After the mad, rude customer left, the passenger complimented the ticket agent on his patience, attitude, and calm demeanor. The clerk replied: "Thank you for your kind words, but don't worry; it's all right." The passenger asked, "How can it be all right?" The clerk answered: "It's all right because, you see, that man is going to Cleveland, but his luggage is going to Singapore" (Dosick, 1993).

Proper behavior during the flight is especially important because of the close quarters. Complete strangers are forced into another person's intimate space. Therefore, airline passengers should be especially considerate of those around them and careful that their behavior does not offend anyone. Because of the limited space, passengers should refrain from wearing strong fragrances. They should respect the preferences of those seated next to them related to conversations. Those who do not wish to talk can take out a book or papers to work on to discourage a conversation. Putting one's seat back in a reclining position when traveling coach without first asking permission of the person seated behind you is very insensitive. Because of the limited space, it is difficult for the person seated behind you to exit, to eat or drink, or to work with the seat in front of them in a reclining position. Passengers should also remember to stay out of the aisles as much as possible and limit their time on the telephone and in the bathroom. If they are traveling with their family, they should make sure that their children do not engage in such activities as kicking the seatback of the person in front of them or standing up in the seat and staring at the person behind them.

Sometimes problem situations arise because other passengers do not know or practice proper etiquette. When confronted with an incessant talker, one might say, "I would like to talk more, but I must finish this report." To the person in coach who reclines his seat, you might respond, "Would you please pull your seat forward while I am eating." Asking the flight attendant to make this request is also appropriate. If you are seated next to a crying baby or a loud, obnoxious person, ask the flight attendant for another seat assignment.

A summary of rules for business and social etiquette for the six countries with which the United States conducts most of its international trade follows.

CANADA

Social and business etiquette in Canada is quite similar to that of the United States, but Canadians are more conservative than people of the United States. As in the United States, shaking hands when meeting and upon departure is the usual form of greeting. Most business entertaining is done in restaurants, and tipping is about the same as in the United States. Because of the strong French influence in certain parts of Canada, French cuisine is offered in many restaurants. If invited to someone's home, you would want to take flowers (but not white lilies as they are associated with funerals) to the hostess (Axtell, 1993).

GREAT BRITAIN

A soft handshake accompanied by "How do you do?" is the common greeting in Great Britain. Avoid the typical U.S. greeting of "Hi" (too informal) and avoid saying "Have a nice day" when departing (the British interpret it as a command). As in the United States, first names are often used after knowing the person only a short time. When dining in Great Britain, you may wish to try some of their specialties: crumpets, steak and kidney pie, or Scotch eggs which are deep-fried hardboiled eggs with a coating of sausage and breadcrumbs. Pubs and restaurants, rather than private homes, are used for most business entertaining. If invited to dine in a British home, a gift of flowers (except for white lilies) would be an appropriate gift for the hostess (Axtell, 1993; Braganti & Devine, 1992).

FRANCE

A light handshake when you greet someone or when you say goodbye is the usual acknowledgment in France. Use last names unless you know the person quite well. Remember that dining can be rather lengthy as the French enjoy lively discussions while they eat. Try some French specialties: their pastries, wine and cheese, and special dishes such as quiche Lorraine (pastry filled with bacon, eggs, and cheese), crêpes (thin sweet pancakes), and pâté de foie gras (goose liver). If you try it, be prepared to finish it; the French expect you to eat everything on your plate. As in many European countries, a service charge of 10 to 15 percent is usually added to checks. The proper gift when invited to a French home for dinner—which is rare—is a box of candy or an odd number of flowers (except chrysanthemums which suggest death or red roses which suggest romance). Business gifts are not expected, but gifts with aesthetic appeal such as art work and books, are considered appropriate (Axtell, 1993; Braganti & Devine, 1992).

GERMANY

When greeting people in Germany, remember to use last names and a firm handshake. Status is recognized; men allow people of higher status or older women to precede them when entering a door or elevator. When dining in a restaurant, a service charge of 10 to 15 percent is generally added to the check so you do not need to leave an extra tip. Try some German specialties: beers, sausages, and potato pancakes. As in France, eating everything on your plate is considered polite. Gifts to your German host should be something simple and rather inexpensive as Germans consider expensive gifts to be in bad taste. When invited to a German home, bring the hostess a gift of flowers (an odd number except 13 and no red roses) (Braganti & Devine, 1992).

JAPAN

In Japan, the usual form of greeting is a bow rather than a handshake; however, many Japanese who regularly associate with persons of other cultures may use both a bow and a handshake. Follow the lead of your Japanese host. The exchange of business cards is common so be sure you have a good supply. These should be printed on one side in English and the other side in Japanese. Remember to address your Japanese host by his last name; only family members and close friends use the first name. Most business entertaining is done in Japanese restaurants. Some Japanese specialties include sake (rice wine) and sashimi (sliced raw fish). Do not tip in restaurants; the waiter will return the money if you do. Although being invited to a Japanese home is not the norm, if invited remember to remove your shoes at the entrance of the home. A box of candy, rather than flowers, is an appropriate gift for the hostess. Since social and business etiquettes are very different in Japan, do a thorough study of the culture and their customs before you go (Axtell, 1993; Devine & Braganti, 1986).

A world traveler from Switzerland describes how he temporarily lost his fondness for eating fish while dining at a lavish Tokyo restaurant. After he had sampled numerous delicacies, the pièce de résistance was served: a live fish still flopping on the platter was brought to the table; the maitre d' then delicately sliced the live fish and served it to the guests (Axtell, 1993).

MEXICO

Shaking hands is the usual greeting in Mexico, and people also shake hands when saying goodbye. When introduced to a woman, a man will bow slightly and will shake hands if the woman initiates it. Address the person by his or her last name as first names are not used during initial encounters. Business cards are exchanged at a first meeting but remember to include the Spanish translation on your cards. Be sure to indicate your position with your company and your university degrees. Deference is shown to someone whose age, social status, or position warrants it. The altitude of Mexico City may affect your digestion so eat lightly and carefully. Always order bottled water since tap water is not considered safe. Although Mexicans will expect you to sample the fare, they will understand if you decline dishes such as *tripe* (stomach of sheep). Unlike many European cultures, they do not expect you to eat everything on your plate. You may wish to sample such national dishes as *mole poblano de guajolote* (turkey in a sauce of spices, herbs, and chocolate), *quesadillas* (folded tortillas filled with cheese), and *frijoles refritos* (mashed and fried cooked beans). If invited to a Mexican home, send flowers ahead of time; avoid marigolds (used to decorate cemeteries) and red flowers (used for casting spells). Appropriate gifts include gadgets such as an electric can opener, U.S. cigarettes, a gold cigarette lighter, gold pen, art books, or a bottle of Scotch. (Devine & Braganti, 1988).

A helpful rule to remember in most cultures is to follow the lead of the people in the other culture. If they shake hands, so do you. Eat what they eat and when they eat. If the other person gives you a gift, be prepared to reciprocate. Researching the country before you travel is always good advice.

Terms

- Caste system
- Continental eating style
- Dissing
- Etiquette
- Flaming
- Netiquette
- Protocol
- Shouting
- Spamming
- U.S. eating style

EXERCISE 8.1

Instructions: Circle T for true or F for false.

1. T F   In Japan, a business card should be presented with both hands.
2. T F   Throughout Latin America, the main meal of the day is in the evening.
3. T F   Flaming and dissing are terms associated with "netiquette."
4. T F   Introductions are more formal in Germany than in the United States.
5. T F   Bolivians expect visitors to eat everything on their plate.
6. T F   Tipping is more common in the United States than in China and Japan.
7. T F   The practice of serving a glass of water with meals is universal.
8. T F   In China, the gift of a clock is considered a symbol of good luck.
9. T F   In Germany, business gifts are usually exchanged at the beginning of formal negotiations.
10. T F   When selecting travel attire, the main consideration is comfort.

Questions and Cases for Discussion

1. How do introductions vary between the United States and other cultures?
2. Describe cultural variations in business card exchange.
3. Explain class distinctions in the United States and India.
4. How are gender and age related to position and status in the United States?
5. Identify some guidelines for proper telephone etiquette.
6. Explain the difference between the terms *flaming* and *shouting* in relation to network etiquette.
7. What are some advantages and disadvantages of using e-mail?
8. Identify some cultural differences in dining practices.
9. Explain the difference between the U.S. and Continental eating styles.
10. What are some guidelines for tipping appropriately? How do tipping customs vary with various cultures?
11. What are some guidelines for effective business gift giving in the United States?
12. What are some cultural differences in gift-giving practices? What gifts are considered appropriate for a person from the United States to give to someone in another culture?
13. Identify some cultural taboos concerning giving flowers as gifts.
14. What are some guidelines for airline travel attire?
15. List some suggestions for proper behavior during air travel.

CASE 1

Mark was in charge of a negotiating team sent to Japan. Upon learning the importance of gift giving to a successful business relationship in this culture, prior to departure he asked his secretary to wrap these gifts: a clock with the company logo, a leather briefcase, a country ham, and a pen and pencil set marked "Made in Japan." His secretary wrapped the gifts attractively in bright red paper and with matching bows and mailed them to his Japanese hosts. What rules for appropriate gift giving in this culture have been followed? Which have been violated?

CASE 2

A U.S. executive was invited to dine in the home of a Latin American businessman. The dinner invitation was for 9 p.m. The U.S. executive arrived promptly at 9 bearing a gift of an unwrapped bottle of Scotch for his host and a dozen yellow and white chrysanthemums for the businessman's wife. Discuss the appropriateness of the U.S. executive's behavior.

CASE 3

Joe Anthony, a U.S. graduate student, was beginning a semester-long internship in Mexico City with an international healthcare products firm. After he had been there about a week, some male employees invited him out to a bar to sample the local specialty, bull's testicles. Joe had heard about this practice considered a sign of young Mexican *machismo* (male power). The idea did not appeal to him since something he had eaten recently had made him queasy. What are Joe's options? What are the possible implications or consequences of each option? What would you do?

CASE 4

When Sara Canton boarded her flight to Barcelona in New York City, she was seated in the middle with an unkempt person who apparently had not bathed recently on one side and a crying baby on the other. The person in front of her immediately reclined his seat. Sara knew she would not be pleased making a seven-hour trip under these circumstances. What can Sara do to make the trip more bearable?

Activities

1. Practice introducing your U.S. manager to each of the following:
   a. An Italian manager, John Giovanni, with a college degree.
   b. Chung Lo Wang, a manager from China.
   c. Marco Comerlato Velasquez, a business associate from Brazil.
   d. Thomas Edward Peacock, a British associate who has been knighted.
2. Role play to show how a business card is presented to someone from Japan.
3. Review back issues of the *Wall Street Journal* or a news magazine such as *Time* and make a copy of an article related to a cultural faux pas committed by either a person from the United States when traveling abroad or by someone from another culture when visiting the United States. Share your information with the class.
4. Research the dining practices of such countries as Zimbabwe, Samoa, and Tanzania; write a one-page summary identifying major differences between dining practices in the United States and these countries.
5. Research the tipping practices of a European and an Asian country of your choice and make a comparison with tipping practices in the United States. Report your findings to the class.
6. Research the gift-giving practices of one of the following countries and make a brief report to the class: Japan, Taiwan, Egypt, Argentina, Germany. Include appropriate and inappropriate gifts and other related information such as gift presentation and reciprocation.

References

Axtell, R. E. (1993). *Do's and taboos around the world.* New York: John Wiley & Sons, Inc.

Axtell, R. E. (1990). *Do's and taboos of hosting international visitors.* New York: John Wiley & Sons, Inc.

Axtell, R. E. (1998). *Gestures: The do's and taboos of body language around the world.* New York: John Wiley & Sons, Inc.

Baldrige, L. (1993). *Letitia Baldrige's new complete guide to executive manners.* New York: Rawson Associates.

Barnum, C., & Wolniansky, N. (1989, April). Glitches in global gift giving. *Management Review,* 61–63.

Bosrock, M. M. (1997). *Put your best foot forward: South America.* St. Paul, MN: International Education Systems.

Bosrock, M. M. (1994). *Put your best foot forward: Asia.* St. Paul, MN: International Education Systems.

Braganti, N. L., & Devine, E. (1992). *European customs and manners.* New York: Meadowbrook Press.

Copeland, L., & Griggs, L. (1985). *Going international.* New York: Random House.

Devine, E., & Braganti, N. L. (1988). *The travelers' guide to Latin American customs and manners.* New York: St. Martin's Press.

Dosick, W. (1993). *The business bible.* New York: HarperCollins Publishers.

Dresser, N. (1996). *Multicultural manners.* New York: John Wiley & Sons, Inc.

Engholm, C. (1991). *When business East meets business West: The guide to practice and protocol in the Pacific Rim.* New York: John Wiley & Sons, Inc.

Fussell, P. (1983). *Class.* New York: Ballantine Books.

Glassman, A. (1998). *Can I FAX a thank-you note?* New York: Berkeley Books.

Kenton, S. B., & Valentine, D. (1997). *Crosstalk: Communicating in a multicultural workplace.* Upper Saddle River, NJ: Prentice Hall.

Kim, J. Y. (1993, July 11). Clinton couldn't get protocol right to save his Seoul. *The Commercial Appeal,* p. A5.

Mitchell, M. (1996). *The complete idiot's guide to etiquette.* New York: Alpha Books.

Mole, J. (1990). *When in Rome . . . .* New York: AMACOM.

Ricks, D. A. (1993). *Blunders in international business.* Cambridge, MA: Blackwell Publishers.

Rossman, M. L. (1990). *The international businesswoman of the 1990s.* New York: Praeger.

Sabath, A. M. (1998). *Business etiquette: 101 ways to conduct business with charm and savvy.* Franklin Lakes, NJ: Career Press.

Samovar, L. A., & Porter, R. E. (1988). *Intercultural communication: A reader.* Belmont, CA: Wadsworth Publishing Company.

Segaloff, N. (1998). *The everything etiquette book.* Holbrook, MA: Adams Media Corporation.

Stewart, M. Y. (1997). *The new etiquette.* New York: St. Martin's Press, Inc.

Yager, J. (1991). *Business protocol: How to survive & succeed in business.* New York: John Wiley & Sons, Inc.

CHAPTER

9

Business and Social Customs

Objectives
Upon completion of this chapter, you will:

- learn greeting customs as well as customary verbal expressions of persons of various countries.

- understand the importance of a knowledge of male and female relationships to successful intercultural communication.

- learn the role that humor, superstition, and taboos play in understanding people of other cultures.

- understand the role that dress and appearance play in interacting with persons from other countries.

- learn the importance of knowing about the customs associated with holidays and holy days of the country in which you are traveling or conducting business.

- understand that office customs vary from culture to culture.

- understand the importance of appropriate demeanor/behavior in intercultural encounters.

- recognize that bribery is culturally relative and plays an unofficial role in doing business in many cultures.

- recognize special food and meal customs considered typical of various cultures and how to show respect for consumption taboos of other countries.

Customs are behaviors generally expected in specific situations and are established, socially acceptable ways of behaving in given circumstances. Customs vary not only by country but by regions or locations within a country. For example in the United States, customs differ along north-south lines and urban-rural lines (Althen, 1988). In addition, religious backgrounds and ethnic identities account for differences in customs.

169

People of the United States have customary behaviors associated with certain holidays such as eating turkey on Thanksgiving, giving gifts at Christmas, and staying up until midnight on New Year's Eve. Other customary behaviors are associated with greetings and verbal expressions, male/female relationships, dress and appearance, use of humor, belief in superstitions, and special foods and consumption taboos. While it is impossible to identify all customs of a particular culture, certain customs are important to conducting business interculturally.

Greeting and Handshaking Customs

Customary greetings vary from culture to culture. Persons from other cultures are struck by the informality of U.S. Americans who often say "Hi!" to complete strangers. In most countries of the world, this practice is uncommon. People of the United States are often perceived as insincere when they use the standard greeting "Hi, how are you?" which does not mean that they are actually inquiring on the state of one's health. This outward show of friendliness is often misleading since people from the United States are in reality private and slow to form friendships. The use of "Hello, I'm pleased to meet you" is preferable as it conveys a more sincere message.

> British-born journalist Henry Fairlie, in writing "Why I Love America," recalled this encounter with a four-year-old boy riding his tricycle in the suburbs shortly after his arrival in the United States:
> "As I passed him, he said Hi!—just like that. No four-year-old boy had ever addressed me without an introduction before. Recovering from the culture shock, I found myself saying in return: Well—hi! He pedaled off, apparently satisfied."
> Fairlie, who comes from a country where one can tell another person's class from their greeting, observed that the greeting "Hi!" is a democracy. In America, anyone can say "Hi!" to anyone else (Fairlie, 1983).

In addition to the informal "Hi!" when meeting someone, persons of the United States engage in other ritualistic greeting behavior. When greeting an office colleague, one person will say, "Good morning, how are you?" The appropriate response is, "Fine, thank you. And how are you?" Some people make the mistake of forgetting that this is only a ritual and will proceed to tell you in great detail the state of their health. Remember, the appropriate response is, "Fine, thanks."

> Guenther Lengues, an exchange student from Germany, recalled his experience with ritualistic greetings when he returned to the campus apartment he shared with three U.S. students following his first day of classes.
> When one of his roommates said, "Hey, man, what's going on?," he was impressed that they seemed interested in how his day had gone and proceeded to recount his experiences in his classes. Noticing the strange expressions on his roommates' faces, he asked, "Did I say something wrong?" They then explained to him, "When we say, 'hey, man, what's going on?,' we don't really want to know. You're supposed to say, 'Not much, man, and what's going on with you?'; then we'll say, 'Not much.'"

When greeting people, the handshake is customary in many countries. While a firm handshake is considered the norm in the United States, it may be considered impolite in some cultures. Handshakes in other cultures vary from the soft grasp of the British to the brusk grasp of Germans. Thiederman (1991) presented the following summary of how various cultures differ in their ideas of a proper handshake:

Culture	*Type of Handshake*
U.S. American	Firm
Asian	Gentle (shaking hands is unfamiliar and uncomfortable for some; the exception is a Korean who usually has a firm handshake)
British	Soft
French	Light and quick (not offered to superiors); repeated upon arrival and departure
German	Brusk and firm; repeated upon arrival and departure
Latin American	Moderate grasp; repeated frequently
Middle Eastern	Gentle; repeated frequently

Source: Adapted from Lexington Books, an imprint of Macmillan, Inc., from *Bridging Cultural Barriers for Corporate Success* by Sondra Thiederman. Copyright 1991 by Sondra Thiederman.

Whereas embracing is considered inappropriate as a form of greeting in the United States, in other countries it is customary. For example in Saudi Arabia, the handshake is accompanied with a light kiss; even males in Saudi Arabia kiss both cheeks after a handshake. In the Russian states, the "bear hug" may follow a strong, firm handshake between good male friends; neighboring Finns, on the other hand, do not hug, kiss, or have body contact with strangers. People in Latin American countries also embrace, often accompanied by a couple of slaps on the back (Figure 9.1).

Asians, northern Europeans, and most North Americans are uncomfortable with touching and hugging. People of Greece have no firm customs for greeting others; they may shake hands, embrace, and/or kiss a person at the first meeting or at every meeting. Bowing is the customary form of greeting in Japan. In China, bowing is customary, but a handshake is also acceptable. When conducting business with people of Japan or

FIGURE 9.1

Greetings in Latin American countries are accompanied by an embrace.

FIGURE 9.2

Greetings in Japan involve bowing at the waist.

China, the handshake is often combined with a bow so that each culture shows the other proper respect (Baldrige, 1993) (See Figure 9.2).

Verbal Expressions

Although you are not expected to learn the language of every country where you conduct business, if you plan an extended relationship with a particular culture, learning to speak the language, especially commonly used expressions, is important since you may have to communicate with persons who do not speak your language.

Make an effort to learn to say such basic expressions as *please* and *thank you*, greetings, and other terms commonly used by people in the culture. Examples of such terms in French, German, and Spanish follow.

English	*French*	*German*	*Spanish*
Good day	Bonjour (bawn-JHOOR)	Guten Tag (GOO-tun TAHK)	Buenos días (BWAY-nos DEE-ahs)
Goodbye	Au revoir (o reh-VWAHR)	Auf Wiedersehen (owf VEE-der-zeyn)	Adiós (ah-DYOS)
Please	S'il vous plait (seel-voo-PLEH)	Bitte (BIT-teh)	Por favor (POR fah-vor)
Thank you	Merci (mehr-SEE)	Danke (DUNK-uh)	Gracias (GRAH-see-ahs)
Good evening	Bonsoir (bawn-SWAHR)	Guten Abend (GOO-tun AH-bent)	Buenas noches (BWAY-nahs NO-chase)
Excuse me	Excusez-moi (ex-kyou-zay MWAH)	Verzeihung (fare-TSY-oong)	Perdóneme (per-DOH-nay-may)

In addition to these expressions, a knowledge of other verbal expressions customarily used in a culture is useful. In the United States, people often respond to someone with a one word reply: "sure," "okay," and "nope." While such brevity seems blunt and abrupt by foreign standards, it is simply an indication of the informality typical of U.S. persons. Some expressions are used only in certain regions of the United States. For example, people in the southern United States will often say "Y'all come to see us" when bidding someone good-bye. The expected reply is "Thanks! Y'all come to see us, too."

This verbal exchange should not be taken as an invitation to visit but is rather only a friendly ritual. In many other cultures and certain regions in the United States, however, such an expression is meant to be an actual invitation to visit.

Other expressions such as "Don't mention it" and "Think nothing of it" in response to a courtesy or favor are considered rude by persons of other cultures. These expressions, however, are consistent with the U.S. custom that people should be modest and should not brag on themselves. Some persons feel awkward when people compliment or thank them and simply do not know how to respond (Lanier, 1996). When being thanked for a courtesy, a response of "You are welcome" is preferable. Other confusing verbal expressions used in the United States include "What's up?" and "How's it going?" Persons for whom English is a second language have no idea what the phrases mean. Using idioms and slang when conversing with new speakers of English should be avoided because they rely on the literal translation of words. For example, a newcomer to the United States did not accept a job on the "graveyard shift" since he thought he would be working in a cemetery (Dresser, 1996).

Upon meeting someone for the first time, U.S. persons engage in **chitchat** (small talk or light conversation). Small talk is important in getting to know another person before concentrating on business. In most cultures, starting business without light conversation is rude and insensitive. Chitchat often includes comments about the weather, the physical surroundings, the day's news or almost anything of a nonsubstantive nature (Althen, 1988; Baldrige, 1993). People of the United States excel at small talk as do Canadians and Australians. The British and the French are likewise masters of small talk. In the United States, small talk would not include topics related to politics, religion, personal income, or discussions of one's personal life. Likewise in Saudi Arabia, conversations about family members are usually inappropriate. In Latin America and Mexico, on the other hand, it is not only appropriate to inquire about the health of family members but to have lengthy discussions about their well-being. Any inquiries about one's family in the United States would be brief: "How is your wife?" would be answered with "Fine, thanks" (Althen, 1988). Small talk seems to pose problems for people of some cultures. Germans, for example, simply do not believe in it. Swedes, usually fluent in English, have little to say in addition to talking about their jobs which lasts 10 to 15 minutes. The Japanese are frightened by the idea of small talk as are people of Finland who actually buy books on the art of small talk (Lewis, 1996).

South Americans can talk incessantly for hours despite their relatively deficient foreign language skills. Author Richard Lewis reported attending an all-Latin American cocktail party in Caracas that lasted from 7 p.m. to 1 a.m. He said: "There were 300 people present, very little to eat, nobody stopped talking, except to draw breath, for six hours flat; I do not remember a single word that was said" (Lewis, 1996, p. 152).

When engaging in chitchat with someone of another culture, the best advice is probably to follow the other person's lead. If they talk about their family, you would talk about yours. If they initiate discussions of a political nature, you would continue the discourse with your own perceptions.

Male and Female Relationships

In high-context societies such as the Arabic culture, people have definite ideas on what constitutes proper behavior between males and females. In low-context cultures such as the United States, little agreement exists. Thus, both people of the United States and visitors from other cultures have difficulty knowing how to proceed in male/female relationships in the United States since a wide range of behaviors may be observed.

A problem with understanding acceptable male/female relationships in any culture is the stereotypes that exist. For example, a stereotype of U.S. women is that they are domineering and "loose" (have no inhibitions regarding having sexual relationships with a variety of men). Correspondingly, U.S. American men are viewed as weak who permit women to dominate them. Stereotypes of women in other cultures include that Asian women are nonassertive and submissive; a stereotype of Latin American males is that they are predatory and constantly pursue women for sexual relationships (Althen, 1988).

One tall and handsome Middle Eastern graduate student said he had come to the States with the notion that women were readily available for sexual activities with people such as himself. Everything that happened to him during his first two years in the States confirmed his opinion. After about two years, though, he began to realize that the women who were so readily available were not representative of the whole society. They were a certain type of person—insecure, socially marginal, apparently unable to find satisfactory relationships with American men so they turned to foreign students (Althen, 1988, p. 89).

The equality of men and women in the workplace has been a sensitive issue in the United States. Although 60 percent of U.S. women of employment age work, they still do not receive equal pay and responsibility. Some U.S. men feel threatened by the more assertive roles many women are assuming. However, most people accept that men and women can work side by side in the workplace (Lanier, 1996) and that they can have a friendship which does not have a sexual component. U.S. men and women often have business colleagues of the opposite gender. These work relationships may involve business travel, and no assumption is made about any sexual involvement.

In other countries, however, treatment of men and women in the workplace differs substantially from that of the United States. In Mexico, for example, male supervisors customarily kiss their female secretaries on the cheek each morning or embrace them. Despite this custom (seen as undue familiarity by U.S. managers), problems with sexual harassment and gender discrimination are uncommon according to Mexican managers. U.S. managers interviewed, however, reported the opposite (Stephens & Greer, 1995).

Humor in Business

As more and more companies conduct business internationally, frequent opportunities exist for businesspersons to interact in an attempt to develop a good relationship. Using humorous anecdotes is a way of breaking the ice and establishing a relaxed atmosphere prior to the start of business in international meetings.

While humor is a universal human characteristic, what is perceived as humorous varies from culture to culture. In the United States, presentations are often started with a joke or cartoon related to the topic to be covered. In addition to the United States, most European countries use humor during business meetings. The British, especially, intertwine humor in business discussions. When this same technique is used with Asian audiences (except for Koreans who seem to appreciate everybody's jokes), few are amused. Asian humor finds little merit in jokes about sex, religion, or minorities; however, they will laugh out of politeness when a joke is told. They take what is said quite literally and do not understand U.S. American humor. Germans, too, find humor out of place during business meetings. They take business seriously and do not appreciate joking remarks during negotiations. When a presentation in Germany was begun with a cartoon deriding European cultural differences, no one laughed. As the week progressed, people started laughing, both in and out of the sessions. Later the presenters learned that cartoons were not appropriate in a professional setting of strangers (Trompenaars & Hampden-Turner, 1998). At the conclusion of negotiations, though, Germans enjoy relaxing and telling jokes in local bars or restaurants.

Is there such a thing as international humor? Yes—some humor is acceptable internationally, e.g., slapstick, restaurant jokes, and humorous stories about golfers. Even in international jokes, however, people have their own nuances to make the jokes/anecdotes amusing to members of their own culture. In the United States, for example, sarcasm and kidding accompany humor; in Australia, humor is barbed and provocative (Lewis, 1996).

Some businesspersons with global experience recommend that jokes be avoided with people of diverse cultures; they maintain that American humor is hard to export and appreciate. Even though the intention of humor is to put your international colleagues at ease and create a more relaxed environment, the risk of offending someone of another culture or of telling a story that no one understands, is great (Thiederman, 1991). In short, we do not all laugh at the same things.

A New York businessman who frequently traveled to Japan on business, often used a translator for his speeches. After one such speech, he learned that the Japanese interpreter's version of his opening remarks went like this:

"American businessman is beginning speech with thing called joke. I am not sure why, but all American businessmen believe it necessary to start speech with joke. (Pause) He is telling joke now but frankly you would not understand joke so I won't translate it. He thinks I am telling you joke now. Polite thing to do when he finishes is to laugh. (Pause) He is getting close. (Pause) Now!"

The audience not only laughed appreciatively but stood and applauded as well. Later he commented to the translator: "I've been giving speeches in this country for several years, and you are the first translator who knows how to tell a good joke" (Axtell, 1990).

Superstitions and Taboos

Superstitions are beliefs that are inconsistent with the known laws of science or what a society considers to be true and rational. Examples of superstitions include a belief that special charms, omens, or rituals have supernatural powers. Superstitions which are treated rather casually in Europe and North America are taken quite seriously in other cultures. While few U.S. persons consult astrologers or fortune tellers for advice on business matters, in other cultures spiritualists are highly regarded and may be consulted in making business decisions. When doing business with persons who take business advice from seers, it is best to respect these beliefs. In parts of Asia, for example, fortune telling and palmistry are considered influential in the lives and business dealings of the people. In fact, one can find a "supermarket for one-stop fortune-telling shopping" (Victor, 1992, p. 111) located in one of Tokyo's trendy sections.

In many cultures, bad luck and even death are associated with certain numbers. People of the United States, for example, think that 13 is an unlucky number. Most U.S. American hotels do not have a thirteenth floor, and even a hotel number ending in 13 may be refused. Friday the thirteenth is perceived as an unlucky day. Many U.S. persons will not schedule important events such as weddings or major surgery on this day. The Chinese, who also believe that good or bad luck is associated with certain numbers, feel that four is the most negative number because it sounds like their word for death. Hotels in China, Hong Kong, and Taiwan often have no fourth floor, and some Asian airports have no Gate 4. Conversely, some numbers have positive meanings in China. For example, the number six represents happiness and nine represents long life. The number of people in a photograph also has significance. Many Chinese believe that having an uneven number of people in a photograph will bring bad luck and that having three people in a photograph will result in dire consequences—the middle person will die (Dresser, 1996). Those who take pictures as mementos for their Chinese business friends should keep this in mind. Additional superstitions regarding numbers and gift giving (e.g. the number of flowers to give as a gift) were covered in the preceding chapter on gift-giving etiquette.

Other superstitions held by persons in some cultures include:

- Events on New Year's Day predict what will happen for the entire year.
- Sweeping the floor on New Year's Day may sweep away one's good luck for the coming year; likewise, bathing on this day will wash away one's good luck.
- Performing certain rituals will protect a newborn child from evil spirits.
- Attaching old shoes to the car of newlyweds assures fertility.
- Walking under a ladder or breaking a mirror will bring bad luck.
- Giving too much attention to a newborn child would place the child in jeopardy; the evil spirits will harm the baby if it receives a lot of attention (Dresser, 1996).

Many South Americans respect these superstitions:

- Bringing coral or shells into your home will bring bad luck.
- Putting your purse on the floor will result in your money running away.
- Passing salt hand-to-hand will bring bad luck.
- Avoiding the scheduling of important events on Tuesday the thirteenth as this is an unlucky day (Bosrock, 1997).

Taboos are practices or verbal expressions considered by a society or culture as improper or unacceptable. Taboos often are rooted in the beliefs of the people of a specific region or culture and are passed down from generation to generation. In Arabic countries, for example, it is considered taboo to ask about the health of a man's wife. In Taiwan, messages should not be written in red ink as this has death connotations. Writing a person's name in red also has negative associations in Korea, parts of Mexico, and among some Chinese (Lewis, 1996).

> An American English teacher made comments and constructive criticisms in red ink on her students' papers. Although U.S. students were accustomed to this practice, her Korean students were not. These red-inked notes sent shock waves through the families of Korean students who associated red ink with death. When the families told the principal of this taboo, he asked all teachers to refrain from using red ink on any student's paper (Dresser, 1996).

In Malaysia, pointing with one's index finger is taboo, but one may point with the thumb. Indonesia has certain taboos related to the head. Since the head is considered a sacred part of the body, it should not be touched by someone else. The practice in the United States of patting young children on the head would be cause for great concern in Indonesia. Another taboo concerns making sure one's head is not in a higher position than the head of a senior person. People of the Russian states have numerous taboos: no whistling in the street, no coats worn indoors, and no lunches on park lawns. Taboos of the people of Madagascar are perhaps the most unusual: pregnant women are forbidden from eating brains or sitting in doorways; women may not wash their brothers' clothes; and children are not permitted to say their father's name or make reference to any part of his body (Lewis, 1996).

Dress and Appearance

What you wear sends a nonverbal message about you and your company. Since clothes can enhance or destroy your credibility, it is advisable to determine what attire is customary in the countries you visit. According to Axtell (1993) in his book, *Do's and Taboos Around the World,* the general rule for business everywhere is be "buttoned up": conservative suit and tie for men and dress or skirted suit for women.

> An American television program investigated the impact of an attractive, well-groomed appearance in both social and business situations. "Well-groomed men and women were placed in identical situations with less polished participants who had neglected their appearance. Every single time, the more highly groomed individual got not only the date or the help with a flat tire but also the job offer and the higher salary" (Bixler, 1997, p. 16).

According to U.S. researchers and image consultants, people who wear suits, whether male or female, are perceived as more professional than those who wear any other type of attire. Wearing professional attire is recommended when one wishes to be taken seriously: for men, this is very dark suits in charcoal gray or navy blue pinstripe with a white, pastel, or pinstripe long-sleeved cotton shirt; for women, a medium-range or navy blue suit with a white blouse. A second choice for women is a beige suit with a light blue blouse (Baldrige, 1993; Molloy, 1996). Fabric is also important in projecting credibility, status, and power. Fabrics of pure fibers (silk, wool, and cotton) convey higher credibility and status than synthetic fibers such as polyester. The recommended suit for both men and women is 100 percent wool (Molloy, 1996).

Business dress in Canada, Great Britain, France, Germany, Japan, and Mexico is similar to that worn in the United States with slight variances. In Canada, people dress more conservatively and formally than people in the United States. The French are very fashion-conscious since France is considered a leader in fashion. When conducting business in Europe, remember that dress is very formal; coats and ties are required for business. Jackets stay on in the office and restaurants even when the weather is hot. Dress in Japan is also formal. Japanese women dress very conservatively and wear muted colors to the office. Care should be exercised in wearing very casual attire in public in these countries as this practice is considered inappropriate (Devine & Braganti, 1986).

Dress standards in the U.S. workplace have become increasingly casual in the 1990s. A study conducted by Levi Strauss in 1997 of 900 white collar workers determined that 53 percent now wear casual dress to work every day and 90 percent are permitted to wear casual attire at least occasionally (McShulskis, 1998). However, this trend toward casual office attire is not just a U.S. phenomenon. Over half of the companies in Europe now have a casual dress policy. Of the European countries, Sweden has the greatest percentage (81 percent) of companies with casual dress policies while traditionally conservative England is on the other end of the spectrum with only 23 percent of companies permitting casual business attire (Elsberry, 1997). Despite this trend toward casual dress, a number of companies are concerned with their corporate image as many employees seem to be unable to distinguish between casual and slovenly. As a result, some companies are revoking casual dress policies because casual attire is wreaking havoc on the workplace (Jarman, 1998). Since people, particularly those from other cultures, tend to make assumptions about another person's educational level, status, and income based on dress alone (Gray, 1993), those interested in career advancement and in careers in international business should probably follow Molloy's (1996) rule for business casual: clothing should be conservative, upperclass, and traditional.

> At a Washington firm, a group of Japanese businessmen who came for a meeting on a Friday found a room full of casually dressed people. They made a hasty retreat, believing they had the wrong office (Alvarez-Correa, 1996, p. 134).

Casual attire that is even more informal than the norm in the United States is appropriate in certain cultures. In the Philippines, men wear the barong—a loose, white or cream-colored shirt with tails out and no jacket or tie. In Indonesia, batiks (brightly patterned shirts worn without tie or jacket) are worn (Axtell, 1993).

Although Western business dress has been widely adopted among other cultures, you may wish to learn cultural distinctions in appropriate business attire. When visiting Saudi Arabia, for example, the Saudi might wear the traditional Arabic white flowing robe and headcloth. You would not, however, attempt to dress in a similar manner. You would dress in the same manner as you would for an important meeting in your U.S. office.

Color of clothing is also a consideration because in some cultures, color has strong associations. Do not wear black or solid white in Thailand because these colors have funeral connotations. Avoid wearing all white in the People's Republic of China as white is the symbol of mourning. In the United States, black is typically worn at funerals but has no special significance in business situations.

Shoes are considered inappropriate in certain situations in various cultures. They should not be worn in Muslim mosques and Buddhist temples. Shoes should also be removed when entering most Asian homes or restaurants. Place them neatly together facing the door you entered. Following the host's lead is good advice; if the host goes without shoes, so do you. Remember that in the Arabic culture, the soles of the feet should not be shown, so keep both feet on the floor or the bottoms of your feet covered.

Women who conduct business abroad should be very careful to conform to local customs concerning appropriate attire. Women conducting business in the Arabian countries, for example, should avoid wearing slacks and should wear clothes that give good coverage such as long-sleeved dresses and dress/skirt lengths below the knees. In Europe, women do not wear slacks to the office or to nice restaurants. Ask before you go; consult a colleague who is familiar with the culture (Axtell, 1993; Devine & Braganti, 1986, 1988).

Dress is an important factor in most women's careers. Research shows that when a woman dresses for success, it does not guarantee success, but if she dresses poorly or inappropriately, it almost always ensures failure (Molloy, 1996, p. xi).

Customs Associated with Holidays and Holy Days

An awareness of the holidays and holy days of other cultures is important in scheduling telephone calls and business trips.

Holidays may celebrate a prominent person's birthday (Washington's Birthday), a historic event (Independence Day), or pay homage to a group (Veterans' Day and Memorial Day). Holy days are associated with religious observances (Ramadan, Christmas, Easter, and Yom Kippur). Since business may not be conducted on some of these special days, you will want to consider this information when planning a trip abroad.

People who travel to the United States, for example, should understand that it is not customary to conduct business on Christmas Day or Thanksgiving. Business is rarely conducted on the Fourth of July when Independence Day is celebrated with fireworks, picnics, parades, and parties. Many businesses, with the exception of retail establishments, are closed on Sunday which is the Sabbath for many religions. The Sabbath in Israel, on the other hand, is observed on Saturday while the Arabs observe the Sabbath on Friday.

In some countries, holidays are similar to those celebrated in the United States. Some Catholic countries such as Germany, have a carnival season (similar to New Orleans' Mardi Gras) which is not a good time for conducting business. Many countries celebrate the New Year; the nature, duration, and time of the year of the celebration may vary. In Mexico, for example, the two-week period including Christmas and New Year's Day is not a good time to conduct business nor is the two-week period prior to Easter. Businesspeople are usually traveling with their families during this time.

The holidays observed in the United States and those observed by the six countries with which the United States conducts most of its international business are listed below (Beach, Hinojosa, & Tedford, 1991; Casady, 1993; Kenton & Valentine, 1997).

United States	New Year's Day (January 1)
	Birthday of Martin Luther King, Jr. (third Monday in January)
	President's Day (third Monday in February)
	Memorial Day (last Monday in May)
	Independence Day (July 4)
	Labor Day (first Monday in September)
	Columbus Day (second Monday in October)
	Veteran's Day (November 11)
	Thanksgiving (fourth Thursday in November)
	Christmas (December 25)
Canada	New Year's Day (January 1)
	Easter Sunday and Monday*
	Labor Day (May 1)
	Victoria Day (third Monday in May)
	Canada Day (July 1)
	Thanksgiving Day (second Monday in October)
	All Saints' Day (November 1)
	Remembrance Day (November 11)
	Christmas (December 25)
	Boxing Day (December 26)
	Québec has two additional holidays: The Carnival de Québec (February) and St. Jean Baptiste Day (June 24)
Great Britain	New Year's Day (January 1)
	Good Friday*
	May Day*
	Easter Sunday and Monday*
	Spring Bank Holiday*
	Late Summer Holiday*
	Christmas (December 25)
	Boxing Day (December 26)
France	New Year's Day (January 1)
	Mardi Gras (Shrove Tuesday)*
	Easter Sunday and Monday*
	Labor Day (May 1)

	Liberation Day (May 8)
	Ascension Day*
	Whit Monday*
	Bastille Day (July 14)
	Pentecost*
	Assumption of the Virgin Mary (August 15)
	All Saints' Day (November 1)
	World War I Armistice Day*
	Christmas (December 25)
Germany	New Year's Day (January 1)
	Good Friday*
	Easter Sunday and Monday*
	Labor Day (May 1)
	Ascension Day*
	Whit Monday*
	Day of German Unity (October 3)
	All Saints' Day (November 1)
	Day of Prayer and Repentance*
	Christmas (December 25)
Japan	New Year's Day (January 1)
	Coming of Age Day (January 15)
	National Foundation Day (February 11)
	Vernal Equinox (March 21)
	Greenery Day (April 29)
	Constitution Day (May 3)
	Children's Day (May 5)
	Bon Festival (August 15)
	Respect for the Aged Day (September 15)
	Autumnal Equinox (September 23)
	Sports Day (October 10)
	Culture Day (November 3)
	Labor Thanksgiving Day (November 23)
	Emperor Akihito's Birthday (December 23)
Mexico	New Year's Day (January 1)
	St. Anthony's Day (January 17)
	Constitution Day (February 5)
	Carnival Week*
	Birthday of Benito Juarez (March 21)
	Easter*
	Labor Day (May 1)
	Cinco de Mayo (May 5)
	Corpus Christi*
	Assumption of the Virgin Mary (August 15)
	President's Annual Message (September 1)
	Independence Day (September 16)

Columbus Day (October 12)
All Saints' Day (November 1)
All Souls' Day (November 2)
Revolution Day (November 20)
Day of the Virgin Guadalupe (December 12)
Christmas (December 25)

*Dates vary

In addition to their holidays, some countries have other times when business is curtailed. Do not expect to conduct business in Europe during August as this is considered the vacation month, and many people close their businesses during this time. In addition to the Sabbath, little business is conducted with the Arabs during Ramadan, the month-long Islamic fast. In Japan, many companies close from April 29 to May 5 to celebrate various holidays and birthdays.

Office Customs and Practices

Office customs and practices include typical hours of work, lunch, and breaktimes, degree of formality, and hiring/firing.

Customarily hours of work in United States offices are 9 a.m. to 5 p.m. Employees are expected to start work promptly and to stay busy even during slow periods. In other words, employees are expected to find work to do and never be idle. In many countries, on the other hand, employees feel free to read the newspaper or visit with colleagues when there is nothing pressing, especially when the supervisor is out of the office (Lanier, 1996).

Office hours in other countries vary. In Iran, for example, business hours are from 9:30 a.m. to 1 p.m. and 2 to 5 p.m., Monday through Friday. In some South American countries such as Brazil and Colombia, the workweek is 8 a.m. to 6 p.m., Monday through Friday. Some offices and stores close from noon to 2 p.m. for lunch. Peru has one of the longest workweeks in the world: 48 hours with businesses open at least six days a week (Bosrock, 1997).

The lunch period in United States firms may vary from 30 minutes to an hour, and breaktimes are usually one 15-minute period in the morning with a second 15-minute period in the afternoon. These should be kept to the time specified because extended periods would result in a reprimand because in the United States "time is money." U.S. persons, who are time- and productivity-conscious, seriously question the workday customs commonplace throughout Europe. For example, Europeans have a 1- to 1½-hour lunch break, 20 minute morning and afternoon breaks (often including beer or wine), and 15 minutes at the end of the workday for cleanup time. Thus, their nine-hour workday is, in reality, a seven-hour workday (Utroska, 1992).

Hiring and firing practices vary according to the culture. In the United States, people are hired with the understanding that retention and promotions depend upon performing the job satisfactorily and getting along with their colleagues. In other words, hiring and retention are based on job effectiveness and job performance. While workers cannot legally be fired without cause, it is understood that no job is permanent. In Europe, on the other hand, everyone in the firm has a contract that virtually guarantees permanent employment regardless of the financial condition of the company (Utroska, 1992). Likewise, in such countries as Japan, employers consider an employee's job to be permanent unless the person breaks the law or is guilty of a moral turpitude. In such socialist countries as France and England, the only grounds for job termination are criminal behavior. Employees who are dismissed receive generous severance pay by U.S. standards. Employees receive a three-months' notice at full salary and benefits while they look for a new job. Executives would receive an even more generous severance package: a full year's salary plus one month's pay for each year of company service plus accumulated vacation pay (Utroska, 1992). In many Asian cultures, the company is considered an extension of the family. In the United States, workers are simply employees, and the company does not serve as an extended family (Lanier, 1996). Problems sometimes arise when Japanese companies take over U.S. firms. Since Japanese managers assume their employees will be with them their entire careers, they think they are entitled to ask personal questions related to the prospective employee's home life and can even make recommendations regarding the improvement of their personal appearance. They then discover that such questions and comments are illegal in the United States (Dresser, 1996).

The degree of formality found in U.S. offices varies; in major corporations, especially financial institutions and those in large cities, more formality often exists than in smaller companies in rural areas. Characteristics of an informal atmosphere include the use of first names at all levels, frequent small talk and joking, and, in recent years, more casual attire. This informal atmosphere does not indicate a lack of respect as would be the case in many European countries.

Another important aspect of office relationships is the appropriateness of showing emotions at work. Cultures that are primarily affective feel it acceptable to show emotions; those who are emotionally neutral would control or mask their feelings. In an exercise reported by Trompenaars and Hampden-Turner (1998), participants from various cultures were asked whether they would express their feelings openly if they became upset about something at work. The highest percentage of persons who would not show their emotions openly were from Ethiopia, Japan, and Poland while the lowest percentage of persons who would not express emotions were from Kuwait, Egypt, Spain, and Cuba. No pattern was apparent by continent; the United States was in the middle range with 43 percent of persons indicating they would not show emotions at work.

Customary Demeanor/Behavior

What is considered customary behavior in one culture may be unacceptable in another. **Demeanor** involves one's conduct or deportment and is influenced by culture. Behavior in public places is culture specific. U.S. Americans speak louder in public than people of Germany, and people from Brazil or Nigeria speak louder than people of the United States. The type of public place also affects the voice volume that is considered acceptable. At sporting events, it is acceptable to make more noise than inside a shopping mall or health club. Good advice to follow in a foreign country is to observe the behavior of the nationals and avoid calling attention to yourself by speaking louder than those around you.

The following rules apply to appropriate behavior in public places in the United States:

- Keep to the right when walking in malls or on the street;
- Wait your turn when standing in line at the post office, bank, or theater;
- Give priority to the first person who arrives (rather than to people who are older or wealthier as is done in Asian cultures);
- Do not block traffic;
- Do not block someone's view at a ballgame or other public event;
- Be considerate of nonsmokers;
- Treat clerks, taxi drivers, and other service personnel with courtesy and respect since in the United States the principle of equality prevails.

Courtesy is, in fact, important in most areas of the United States. The use of "please" when you are making a request is expected; "thank you" is considered appropriate when someone has granted a request or performed a service. People of all social and educational levels are accorded equal courtesy.

Another behavior that varies with the culture is the degree of touching in public places. People in the United States usually avoid situations in which they would be touching strangers in public. They avoid getting on a crowded elevator because they are quite uncomfortable with physical contact. If they must get on a crowded elevator, they observe "elevator etiquette," refraining from speaking, facing the front, and watching the floor indicator. One exception seems to be subway trains where people are often too crowded to move. People in South America, on the other hand, think nothing of squeezing onto a crowded bus or elevator and pushing through a crowd.

A behavior of U.S. Americans that seems unusual to those of many other countries is doing "menial" jobs. In fact, the United States is often referred to as a "do-it-yourself" society. Regardless of wealth, position, or social standing, people of the United States are often found mowing their lawn, washing their car, or building a patio. Reasons for this custom vary; some U.S. persons point out that hiring household help or a gardener represents a loss of privacy. Others reason that they prefer to do the work themselves and use the money they would spend on service personnel for vacations, sports, and labor-saving appliances. When both adults work, home cleaning services or domestic help may be used for a limited number of hours each week (Lanier, 1996). In many European and South American countries, on the other hand, numerous service people are often employed by businesspersons, government officials, and professionals. Households commonly have a cook, maid, and gardener.

Bribery

A custom that has undergone close scrutiny in the past few years is bribery. **Bribery** is the giving or promising of something, often money, to influence another person's actions. In Mexico, bribes are known as *mordida;* in southeast Asia, *kumshaw;* and in the Middle East, *baksheesh.* While bribery is not officially sanctioned or condoned in any country, it is unofficially a part of business in many cultures. The practice is often referred to as "greasing the palm" and is considered neither unethical nor immoral in a number of countries. In Nigeria, for example, one must pay the customs agent in order to leave the airport while in Thailand and Indonesia getting a driver's license involves giving a tip to an agent (Engholm & Rowland, 1996).

The United States has the most restrictive laws against bribery in the world. Companies found guilty of paying bribes to foreign officials can be fined up to $1 million, and guilty employees may be fined up to $10,000 (Engholm, 1991). Many U.S. competitors including Italian, German, and Japanese firms not only use bribery in international transactions but may deduct the amount of the bribe on their taxes as a necessary business expense.

> Mike Lorelli of Pizza Hut shared this experience related to bribery in other cultures:
>
> In the Middle East or Brazil, they would think you are crazy for not offering a bribe because to them there is absolutely nothing wrong with bribery. You're an oddball, but there is not a thing you can do about it (Engholm & Rowland, 1996, p. 133).

Managers in the United States are faced with situations that are considered illegal in their country that are not only lawful but are an accepted part of doing business in other countries. They must, therefore, be aware that as business becomes globalized, different perceptions exist regarding the appropriateness of certain incentives. What is perceived as bribery is culturally relative just as a person's conscience can become "culturally conditioned." What is considered a tip (to ensure promptness) in one culture is considered illegal in another (Harris & Moran, 1996). Although people of the United States are not legally permitted to accept bribes, many U.S. businesspersons provide favorite clients with box seats at sporting events or entertain them lavishly (Dresser, 1996). Some would consider this practice a form of bribery. Additional information on bribery is presented in chapter 12.

Special Foods and Consumption Taboos

Most cultures have unusual foods that are viewed with surprise or even disdain by persons in other cultures. Foods that are common in the United States that people in other cultures find unusual include corn on the cob (in some countries considered a food for animals), grits, popcorn, marshmallows, and crawfish (Althen, 1988; Axtell, 1993). (See Figure 9.3.)

FIGURE 9.3

Popcorn (a), crawfish (b), and corn on the cob (c) are considered unusual U.S. foods.

Foods in other cultures that concern some U.S. Americans include Japanese sushi (raw fish), dog meat in South Korea, and sheep's eyeballs in Saudi Arabia. In parts of Mexico, chicken soup may contain the chicken's feet; in China, you may be served duck's feet. (See Figure 9.4.)

> A college professor from the United States who had just arrived in La Paz, Bolivia, for a two-year teaching assignment at the local university, was invited to dine with U.S. colleagues at a well-known local restaurant. She was assured that the eatery's specialty was mixed grill—a variety of meats grilled at the table. After consuming one chewy morsel, she made the mistake of asking what it was. The reply: stuffed cow's teats!

Since you are expected to eat what you are served in other countries, you may find it advisable to swallow quickly, avoid asking what it is, or pretend to eat by moving the food around so that it changes form. People who are experienced travelers also advise cutting the food into very thin slices and imagining that the unusual food, such as snake or dog meat, looks or tastes like something palatable (for example, chicken).

> Master of five languages, Patrick Larbuisson eats sheep intestines to help grease business deals in Saudi Arabia. He swallows with a smile but is "sick like hell the next day" (Jones, 1993).

Knowing consumption taboos of the host culture is important. People in the United States, for example, do not knowingly eat horse meat although there is no religious taboo associated with this practice. South Koreans, on the other hand, consider dog meat a delicacy. Strict Muslims do not consume pork (or any animal that is a scavenger) or al-

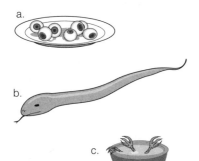

FIGURE 9.4

Sheep's eyeballs (a), snake (b), and chicken soup containing the feet (c) are foods in other countries considered unusual by U.S. standards.

cohol. Orthodox Jews eat neither pork nor shellfish. They also observe such rules as not serving meat and dairy products together and requiring that cattle or fowl must be ritually slaughtered, i.e., kosher. Strict Muslims also observe ritual slaughtering. Hindus do not eat any beef because the cow is considered sacred. People from countries such as India are often vegetarians because of personal or religious beliefs (Axtell, 1993).

Since business encounters are often conducted in social settings, you will want to become familiar with special foods associated with the host culture as well as consumption taboos so that your lack of knowledge of cultural eating habits will not negatively affect the communication process. The following section identifies special foods and consumption practices/taboos associated with the United States and with the six countries with which the United States conducts the majority of its international business. To secure information about countries not specifically identified, consult such sources as Brigham Young University's *Culturgrams* (David M. Kennedy Center for International Studies, Brigham Young University, Provo, UT 84602). The 1998 edition contains briefings on over 100 countries.

UNITED STATES

The majority of U.S. people eat the meat of animals except for certain parts of the animal such as the feet and eyes. Most U.S. people do not feel uncomfortable eating something they cannot easily identify. Meats that are consumed are beef, pork, and poultry as well as fish and shellfish. Fresh vegetables and fruits are enjoyed and easily obtained year round. (*Culturgram '98, U.S.A.,* 1997).

U.S. Americans are great supporters of the fast-food industry, frequenting such restaurants as McDonald's, Wendy's, Kentucky Fried Chicken, and Taco Bell. In metropolitan areas, ethnic and international cuisine is readily available.

CANADA

Although the majority of Canadians eat many of the same foods as people in the United States, the French influence is apparent in restaurants in many parts of Canada. Canadians along the Atlantic seaboard maintain a diet of seafood including lobster and seaweed. Canadians along the Pacific Ocean are partial to smoked salmon. Canadians living in the interior eat more grain products and red meats. As in the United States, ethnic and international cuisine is readily available in the metropolitan areas (*Culturgram '98, Canada,* 1997).

GREAT BRITAIN

Although similarities exist between consumption practices of the United States and Great Britain, differences are numerous. Kippers (smoked herring) and kidneys are often served at breakfast. Another difference is the serving of tea every afternoon from 3:30 to 4:30, a tradition that might include serving small sandwiches of cucumber, watercress, and egg as well as cookies and cakes. British food tends to include a lot of meat and potatoes. Popular meats include beef, mutton, and fish. Sauces and fancy preparations are not considered necessary. Cooked vegetables are also an important part of the meal. Tea and beer are popular drinks and mixed drinks, as in much of Europe, are served with no ice or with one ice cube (Braganti & Devine, 1992).

FRANCE

Foods typical of certain regions of France considered somewhat unusual by U.S. standards include *tripes à la mode de Caen* (a stew of tripe, cider, and vegetables), *escargots à la bourguignonne* (snails served in garlic butter), and *lamproie à la bordelaise* (eels cooked in red wine). The French are renowned for their fine wines and cuisine. Eating is an art in France, and the presentation of the meal is as important as the food. French sauces, soups, breads, and pastries have been the measure of fine cooking in the Western world since the Middle Ages (Braganti & Devine, 1992).

GERMANY

Germany, like Great Britain, tends to have a cuisine that is meat-and-potatoes oriented. Since many cuts of meat tend to be tough in texture, most foods are cooked for a lengthy time or cut up and served with sauces. Foods considered unusual by U.S. standards include *eisbein* (pig's knuckle), *schavelfleish* (raw hamburger), and *hasenpfeffer* (rabbit stew). The serving of warm beer, wine, and soft drinks is common in Germany (Braganti & Devine, 1992).

JAPAN

An example of a food a U.S. person would consider unusual is dried squid, a food that is symbolic of happiness and served at New Year's in Japan. Another unusual food is *fugu*, blowfish or glowfish which requires special preparation as the liver and ovaries contain a dangerous poison. The Japanese diet consists of very little meat and large quantities of rice and vegetables. Coffee has surpassed tea as the preferred drink. Food presentation is a very important part of the meal (Devine & Braganti, 1986).

MEXICO

Typical Mexican cuisine includes tortillas, beans, and various soups such as *sopa de lima* (chicken and lime soup). An hors d'oeuvres people of the United States find unusual is *chicharrón* (pork crackling served with a piquant sauce). In some parts of Mexico, a favorite dish is *pollo borracho* (chicken flavored with a tequila sauce). Other foods include *ceviche* (raw fish with onions, tomatoes, lime juice, and chiles) and *huevos motuleños* (corn tortillas with black beans, ham, fried eggs, and tomato sauce). Many foods are highly spiced; bland foods such as breads and rice are used to temper the hot seasonings (Devine & Braganti, 1988).

Terms

- Bribery
- Chitchat
- Customs
- Demeanor
- Superstitions
- Taboos

EXERCISE 9.1

Instructions: Circle T for true and F for false.

1. T F U.S. greetings are considered informal by persons of other cultures.
2. T F The handshakes of U.S. persons and the British are quite similar.
3. T F The cost of items is an appropriate topic for small talk in most cultures.
4. T F People in Mexico do not waste time with "small talk" but get right down to business.
5. T F A stereotype of U.S. women is they are domineering.
6. T F What is perceived as humorous in the United States may not be humorous in Japan.
7. T F When conducting business in another country, wear what the people in that country typically wear.
8. T F In some cultures, bad luck is associated with certain numbers.
9. T F In the United States, employees consider their jobs to be permanent.
10. T F What is perceived as bribery is culturally relative.

Questions and Cases for Discussion

1. Explain the difference in handshaking customs of U.S. Americans and French citizens.
2. Identify some verbal expressions used in the United States which, when translated literally, have little meaning and are confusing to persons for whom English is a second language.
3. Give examples of how variations in the English language exist within regions of the United States.
4. How do you say "Good day" in French, German, and Spanish?
5. Explain differences in the use of humor in business in the United States and Germany.
6. Explain how women in business are treated differently in the United States and Mexico.
7. What superstitions relating to numbers are held by people of the United States and China?
8. In what countries is business dress similar to that worn in the United States?
9. Identify cultures in which business dress may be different from that worn in the United States.
10. What guidelines for business dress should women observe in cultures other than their own?
11. Describe how hiring/firing practices of the United States and Japan differ.
12. Identify some rules for appropriate behavior in public places in the United States.
13. How is a knowledge of holidays and holy days helpful when conducting business with another culture?
14. What U.S. foods do people of other cultures find unusual? What foods of other cultures do people of the United States consider unusual?
15. List some consumption taboos of people in various cultures.

CASE 1

Your organization is having a large party for its worldwide distributors in the United States. Since there will be people from all over the world, what would you serve for meals to avoid offending anyone?

CASE 2

You have unknowingly arrived in Mexico during Carnival Week. Because people are busy partying and celebrating, they are not interested in meeting with you to discuss business. However, since you are here, they have invited you to join in their activities. Should you accept or reject their invitation?

CASE 3

A Japanese businessman on his first visit to the United States was pleased to be invited to a U.S. executive's home for cocktails. He arrived promptly at 7 p.m. The host introduced him to a small group of people, then returned to the front door to greet others who were arriving. The Japanese businessman apparently had nothing to contribute on the seemingly mindless topics that were discussed. After a few minutes, the others in the group wandered off to join other groups, and he was left alone. Since the host did not return to introduce him to others at the party, he left and returned to his hotel. What, if any, rules of proper etiquette were breached?

CASE 4

At his first meeting with Mina Van Buren, a U.S. manager, Juan Velasquez, an Argentine businessman, complimented her on her appearance and invited her out for drinks and dinner that evening. Ms. Van Buren refused, saying that she preferred to keep their relationship on a professional level. Discuss the appropriateness of Mr. Velasquez' invitation and Ms. Van Buren's response and the implications for building a solid business relationship.

Activities

1. Research appropriate business and social dress in one of the following countries: India, Israel, Thailand, or Saudi Arabia.
2. List some religious taboos associated with food consumption in a subculture of the United States or a culture of your choice.
3. Write a paragraph summarizing your experience in trying a U.S. American dish for the first time and a food in another culture.
4. Practice saying the following in French, German, and Spanish: please, thank you, good-bye, and excuse me.
5. Research superstitions of a country of your choice and make an oral report to the class.

References

Althen, G. (1988). *American ways.* Yarmouth, ME: Intercultural Press, Inc.

Alvarez-Correa, W. (1996, October). Relax, it's Friday. *The Washingtonian,* 134–137.

Axtell, R. E. (1993). *Do's and taboos around the world.* New York: John Wiley & Sons, Inc.

Axtell, R. E. (1990). *Do's and taboos of hosting international visitors.* New York: John Wiley & Sons, Inc.

Baldrige, L. (1993). *Letitia Baldrige's new complete guide to executive manners.* New York: Rawson Associates.

Beach, L., Hinojosa, B. L., & Tedford, A. K. (1991, November/December). Holiday express. *Instructor, 25–34.*

Bixler, S. (1997). *The new professional image.* Holbrook, MA: Adams Media Corp.

Bosrock, M. M. (1997). *Put your best foot forward: South America.* St. Paul, MN: International Education Systems.

Braganti, N. L., & Devine, E. (1992). *European customs and manners.* New York: Meadowbrook Press.

Casady, M. J. (1993). Strategies for teaching international concepts in business courses. *Instructional strategies: An applied research series, 9* (2), 1–6.

Culturgram '98. (1997). Provo, UT: Brigham Young University's David M. Kennedy Center for International Studies.

Devine, E., & Braganti, N. L. (1986). *The travelers' guide to Asian customs and manners.* New York: St. Martin's Press.

Devine, E., & Braganti, N. L. (1988). *The travelers' guide to Latin American customs and manners.* New York: St. Martin's Press.

Dresser, N. (1996). *Multicultural manners.* New York: John Wiley & Sons, Inc.

Elsberry, R. B. (1997, September). Clothes call. *Office Systems, 14* (9), 25, 60.

Engholm, C. (1991). *When business East meets business West.* New York: John Wiley & Sons, Inc.

Engholm, C., & Rowland, D. (1996). *International excellence.* New York: Kodansha International.

Fairlie, H. (1983, July 4). Why I love America. *The New Republic,* p. 12.

Gray, J., Jr. (1993). *The winning image.* New York: AMACOM.

Harris, R. R., & Moran, R. T. (1996). *Managing cultural differences* (4th ed.). Houston: Gulf Publishing Company.

Jarman, M. (1998, June 28). Casual dress in the workplace. *The Arizona Republic,* D1.

Jones, D. (1993, September 14). More business travelers going global. *USA Today,* 1e.

Kenton, S. B., & Valentine, D. (1997). *Crosstalk: Communicating in a multicultural workplace.* Upper Saddle River, NJ: Prentice Hall.

Lanier, A. R. (1996). *Living in the U.S.A.* (5th ed.). Yarmouth, ME: Intercultural Press, Inc.

Lewis, R. D. (1996). *When cultures collide: Managing successfully across cultures:* London: Nicholas Brealey Publishing.

McShulskis, E. (1998, February). Rising numbers of workers are dressing down. *HR Magazine, 43* (2), 28.

Molloy, J. T. (1996). *New women's dress for success.* New York: Warner.

Stephens, G. K., & Greer, C. R. (1995, Summer). Doing business in Mexico: Understanding cultural differences. *Organizational Dynamics, 24* (1), 39–56.

Thiederman, S. (1991). *Bridging cultural barriers for corporate success.* New York: Lexington Books.

Trompenaars, F., & Hampden-Turner, C. (1998). *Riding the waves of culture* (2nd ed.). New ed.). New York: McGraw-Hill.

Utroska, D. R. (1992, November). Management in Europe: More than just etiquette. *Management Review,* 21–24.

Victor, D. A. (1992). *International business communication.* New York: HarperCollins Publishers.

Intercultural Negotiation Process

Objectives
Upon completion of this chapter, you will:

■ be able to define the intercultural negotiation process.

■ be able to distinguish between negotiation models.

■ understand different cultural conflict perspectives.

■ understand conflict resolution in intercultural negotiations.

■ be able to decide if alternatives to negotiation are justified.

The increasing globalization of industries will necessitate an increase in strategic alliances and hence intercultural negotiations. **Intercultural negotiation** involves discussions of common and conflicting interests between persons of different cultural backgrounds who work to reach an agreement of mutual benefit (Moran & Stripp, 1991). Some of the reasons global joint ventures and strategic alliances are on the increase include economic deregulation, rapid technological changes, large capital requirements, government-supported industries, economic maturation, and improved communications.

Characteristics of Effective Negotiators

Effective negotiators are observant, patient, adaptable, and good listeners. They appreciate the humor in a situation but are careful to use humor only when appropriate. Good negotiators are mentally sharp. They think before they speak, and they are careful to speak in an agreeable, civil manner. They do their homework on the countries with whom they are negotiating and become knowledgeable about their history, customs, values, and beliefs. Effective negotiators know that in many cultures history is revered, and displaying a knowledge of the country's past can do much to pave the way to smooth negotiations. Good negotiators praise what is praiseworthy and refrain from criticizing anything about the negotiators or their country. They keep their promises and always negotiate in good faith (Moran & Stripp, 1991).

Negotiators, however, cannot escape their own cultural mindset. Even professional training cannot erase the deep-seated perceptions from childhood (Cohen, 1998). These perceptions must not be vocalized, though, because nothing is to be gained by denouncing the behavior or customs of others simply because they do not fit your cultural mindset. Since such factors as social skills, gender, age, experience in intercultural relations, and background may be important in a specific culture, considering these factors when selecting negotiators is recommended.

Noted negotiator Dr. Chester L. Karrass says, "In business, you don't get what you deserve; you get what you negotiate. Why take 'no' for an answer? Successful people don't. They get what they want by negotiating better deals for both parties" (Karrass, 1996).

Cross-cultural Negotiation Considerations

Fisher (1980) identifies five considerations that should be addressed before negotiating with persons from another culture: the players and the situation, decision-making styles, national character, cultural noise, and use of interpreters and translators.

THE PLAYERS AND THE SITUATION

According to Fisher (1980), you should learn how the negotiators and negotiating teams were selected. Try to determine the background of the players to anticipate the opponent's behavior. Determine the expectations of the other negotiators, their negotiating style, and the role they have played in past negotiations. Attempt to provide an environment that is free of tension and conducive to an exchange of ideas and problem resolution.

DECISION-MAKING STYLES

The way members of the negotiating team reach a decision as well as individual negotiating styles must be taken into consideration. Although negotiators usually reflect the mindset of their particular culture, this may not always be the case. For example, negotiators from the United States are by nature very individualistic; their attitude on making a decision on exports would be "anything is permitted unless it is restricted by the state." In another culture the attitude might be "nothing is permitted unless it is initiated by the state" (Vernon, 1974).

> Stereotyping can be dangerous! A U.S. businessman was going to be negotiating with a Japanese group. He asked a U.S. professor who was knowledgeable about intercultural negotiations to recommend some references. After carefully reading them, he went to the meeting understanding some of the differences he might encounter. The main Japanese negotiator had negotiated many contracts in the United States and had adapted to the U.S. way of negotiating. The U.S. businessman said it was just like negotiating any other U.S. contract.

Items that affect decision-making styles include cultural mindset differences such as views of contracts, interests, and the inclusion of lawyers. Therefore, the way business matters are presented and discussed will tend to vary across cultures. In an intercultural business situation, you need to add information that generally is not necessary when negotiating in the United States.

NATIONAL CHARACTER

According to Fisher (1980, p. 37), "patterns of personality do exist for groups that share a common culture." The question then becomes: How much does this idea of national character affect the negotiation process? The answer is: a great deal. As has been mentioned in earlier chapters, people of the United States value time; punctuality is very important. To a large degree, they also believe they determine their own fate. The people of Latin American countries, on the other hand, are less concerned with time and stoically accept their fate. While numerous other differences exist between the values of the two cultures, these two attitudes could hamper negotiations considerably, regardless of the attractiveness of the terms offered.

CULTURAL NOISE

Cultural noise includes anything that would distract or interfere with the message being communicated. Nonverbal messages such as body language, space, and gift giving can impede or expedite negotiations. For example, giving an inappropriate gift or one wrapped improperly is a form of cultural noise. In addition, what a person says can result in cultural noise; e.g., negotiators who criticize their competitor or make disparaging comments about their competitors' products.

USE OF INTERPRETERS AND TRANSLATORS

Using interpreters and translators can affect the negotiation process both positively and negatively. On the positive side, you have more time to think about your next statement while your previous statement is being translated. Because of the time it takes to translate, you are also more careful to state the message succinctly. On the negative side, since language and culture are intertwined, translators may not convey the intended message because of nuances of the languages involved. Additional suggestions for using interpreters and translators were given in chapter 5.

Variables Affecting Intercultural Negotiations

According to Moran and Stripp (1991, p. 92), four components which are divided into 12 variables, affect the outcome of intercultural negotiations:*

1. Policy	–Basic concept of negotiation
	–Selection of negotiators
	–Role of individual aspirations
	–Concern with protocol
	–Significance of type of issue
2. Interaction	–Complexity of language
	–Nature of persuasive argument
	–Value of time
3. Deliberation	–Bases of trust
	–Risk-taking propensity
	–Internal decision-making systems
4. Outcome	–Form of satisfactory agreement

Utilizing these 12 variables can help negotiators develop a profile of their counterpart's philosophy that will be useful in the negotiation process.

Protocol is important in understanding which negotiation strategy you should follow. Basically there are three fundamental classifications: tribal, collective, and pluralist. Tribal involves the family unit, close relationships, and a connection to the past. Collectivism is an extension of tribal and includes larger groups such as a town, nation, or race. The pluralist society has many different groups and combinations of groups, and individuals are free to join those they wish. Most countries fit one of these three protocol classifications (Leaptrott, 1996).

The chart on page 196 compares the three protocol types (Leaptrott, 1996, pp. 4–7).

The three styles of strategies are very different in some areas and similar in others. This makes the way variables of policy, interaction, deliberation, and outcome are used vary depending upon the two cultures involved in the negotiation. In addition, remembering to consider the situation from the other culture's viewpoint yet maintaining one's own cultural viewpoint will avoid problems in many instances.

Although all cultures share the need for honesty, courage, respect for human dignity, fairness, and love, these values can have very different meanings in different cultures (Burke & Stewart, 1992). Reality is difficult to assess when two cultures do not share the same definition of needs. If the expectations are not met and the perceptions are wrong, disastrous business consequences are usually the result (Mu, 1998).

---

*From *Dynamics of Successful International Business Negotiations* by Robert T. Moran and William G. Stripp. Copyright © 1991 by Gulf Publishing Company, Houston, TX. Used with permission. All rights reserved.

TABLE 10-1 Protocol Characteristics			
Area	*Tribal*	*Collective*	*Pluralist*
Person's responsibility	Support family and follow rules of society	Group contribution, honor, conformity	Personal growth, achievement, independence
Expectations of others	Mutual support and absolute loyalty	Humility, respect, support	Integrity, performance, competence
Interaction with others	With stranger aloof and formal; friends warm, welcoming, trusting	Does not stand out, friendly yet noncommittal to strangers; loyal, firm relationship with friends	Informal, direct communication
Traits respected	Status, strength, cunning	Strength with humility, cleverness, knowledge	Creativity, personal achievement, status
Attitude toward foreigners	Cautious, defensive, formal, distrustful	Cautious, aggressive, defensive	Open, curious, nonhostile
Reason to work	Works to live	Works to live	Lives to work
Life objective	Respect of group, contribute to family	Succeed at work, to get opponent to concede something	Success beyond goals
Definition of winning	Receiving what is asked for	Zero-sum, win-lose	Zero-sum or win-win
Business environment	Strong vertical hierarchy, leaders inaccessible, open offices for lower levels, offices for managers	Shared power, no one stands out, open offices, location important	Layered hierarchy, private spaces, best spaces for top management
Conducts business	Must control, manipulative, correspondence limited	Divided responsibilities; strategy and ritual important; correspondence open, shared	Direct, formality with strangers, correspondence to many
Learning style	Visual, data, coaching generalized; repetition helpful	Shown, learns with others best	Detailed information, verbal text, verification
Feedback	Avoids details, not accountable, subjective feedback	Within the group, consensus a must, nothing negative	Direct, specific, objective, impersonal

TABLE 10-1 Protocol Characteristics (*Continued*)

Area	*Tribal*	*Collective*	*Pluralist*
Decision making	Decisions at the top; pride, emotion before objectivism	Consensus, final decisions from the top	Independent, rational process, mid-management approval
Attitude toward time, schedules, plans, and change	Linear time, process oriented, changes are okay, no detailed plans	Process oriented, no definition of length of time necessary, need for changes seen as errors	Linear time, punctual, detailed plans, change expected
Approach to problem solving	Blame assessment more important than solving problems and consequences for those who are to blame	Problems are evaded; someone loses face; conflict; no problem admitted	Addressed quickly, rationally; analyze after the fact

An example of differences in perception: A group of U.S. businessmen are visiting China and are exploring the possibility of building a factory in China. While the Chinese are showing them sites, the U.S. people ask the level of the available water pressure. The Chinese are perplexed and ask why. The U.S. people say because they need to be sure the water pressure is sufficient to fight fires for insurance purposes. The Chinese answer that they have sufficient water pressure but want to know why the U.S. people are speaking of bad luck before they begin the project because that will assure bad luck. What one culture sees as planning and necessary, another culture may perceive differently (Mu, 1998).

For negotiations to proceed expeditiously, examining the negotiation process which involves defining, observing, analyzing, and evaluating what happens between negotiators, is important.

Defining the Process

In defining the negotiation process, you will choose where the meeting will be held. If a meeting is held on your turf, you, of course, have more power but you also have more responsibility for seeing to your opponent's comforts. If the meeting is held on your opponent's turf, he or she has the power and responsibilities. If it is held at a neutral location, you are each responsible for your own comforts. In intercultural negotiations, you also need to consider the differences in tactics, strategies, power, social expectations, conflict perspectives, and conflict resolution that may be used during the negotiation by your opponents.

Distinguishing the opponents' interests in the negotiation from the issues on which positions are taken is important. Issues are points of conflict (Sebenius, 1992).

A negotiator's checklist of items to be completed prior to negotiating include: selecting the location, determining the cultural protocol of the location, gathering information about the members of the other negotiation team, defining objectives, preparing a strategic plan, gathering ideas on applying your strategies within the protocol, researching the etiquette rules of the other culture, and viewing negotiations as an obstacle course to complete in order to achieve your goal (Leaptrott, 1996).

Observing, Analyzing, and Evaluating

As negotiations proceed, you will have to be very observant of changes from your initial expectations, carefully analyze the differences, and adapt your negotiation strategy accordingly. Constant evaluation of verbal, nonverbal, and group interaction will be necessary if you are to negotiate from the best position possible.

In order for negotiations to be successful, the negotiations must allow for both parties to gain something—a win-win situation—though the parties probably will not gain equally.

Analysis involves defining the problem by separating and subjectively assessing probabilities, values, risk attitudes, time preferences, structuring and sequencing of the opponents' choices, and the unknown (Sebenius, 1992). In addition, the people who are involved in the negotiation, their style of negotiating, the national culture, the differences in the two cultures, and the interpreters and translators, need to be analyzed and evaluated. The developmental process of observing, analyzing, and evaluating is completed for each of the following eight steps in negotiation (Moran & Stripp, 1991):

1. Physical location of the negotiations
2. Agenda or issues in the negotiation
3. Preliminary statements and limitations
4. Solution of some issues and identification of the issues of no agreement
5. Preliminaries to final negotiations
6. Final negotiations
7. Contract or confirmation of agreement
8. Implementation of the agreement

Intercultural negotiation assumes the parties are from different cultures and may not share the same values, beliefs, needs, and thought patterns. During the interaction periods of the negotiation, the values, beliefs, needs, and thought patterns that are not shared by both groups can cause many unanticipated problems. As a negotiator, one must become adept through continual observation, analysis, and evaluation at catching the problems and adapting the negotiation strategy accordingly. The following list shows factors that must be considered when negotiating interculturally (Casse & Deol, 1985, pp. 3–4).

NEGOTIATION IS . . .	**INTERCULTURAL IMPLICATIONS**
• A situation	• Appreciation of cultural differences is essential in cross-cultural situations

- Mutual understanding

- Communication

- Need satisfaction

- Compromise or settlement

- A deal

- A bargaining process
- Anticipation

- Persuasion

- Achieving consensus

- Practicing empathy

- Searching for alternatives

- Conflict management

- Winning

- A means of getting what you want from others
- Gaining the favor of people from whom you want things
- Managing power and information

- Time and opportunity management

- More of an art than a science

- Selling
- Least troublesome method of settling disputes

- A conscious endeavor to manage cultural differences is required
- Both parties must be in a position to communicate clearly and overcome cultural barriers to effective communication
- Ascertain expectations and then work for their achievement
- Narrow down differences and emphasize commonalties of interest
- Both written and unwritten aspects of negotiation are important
- Prepare to give and take
- Familiarize yourself with management styles and assumptions of others to anticipate their moves
- Establish your credibility, be soft while not losing your grip on the problem
- Reduce differences to reach an agreement
- Appreciate problems and limitations of your "opponents"
- Be systematic and simple (don't try to impress with complex models)
- It is possible to manage conflicting interests
- It can create problems and generate bad feelings
- It also means giving what others expect of you
- It is easier gaining favors when acting in a genuine and rational manner
- Know in advance the limitations of your power; gain information while managing the process of negotiation
- Timely actions based on opportunity analysis provide the needed edge in highly competitive situations
- Be natural; don't play on others' sensibilities
- Create the need first
- Use of intercultural negotiating styles, modes, and skills is important

Intercultural Negotiation Models

The model you choose to use when negotiating interculturally will depend on the people with whom you are negotiating as well as your own personal biases. Since research has shown that social, cultural, political, and legal issues, timing of delivery, payment, terms of payment, role of consultants, and authority to make binding decisions take up most of the negotiation time, researching a particular company and culture could greatly reduce the time spent in negotiation (Ghauri, 1983).

People tend to negotiate interculturally as they do intraculturally unless they realize they need to adapt to another culture. The effect of culture in intercultural negotiation is one of relative, not absolute, values. The negotiations will proceed as smoothly as the abilities of all participants to be empathetic and to adapt to each other's cultural constraints. For example, the Russian negotiating tactics include a need for authority, a need to avoid risk, and a need to control. Negotiating style is not neutral; it is culturally based and somewhat subconscious. A clash of negotiating styles can lead to a breakdown in the negotiation (Cohen, 1998).

Protocol helps to maintain the cultural values of a country. Therefore, business people who are going to negotiate outside their own culture need to learn as much about the other culture as possible. When you understand the opposition, you will be able to formulate a course of action more accurately and obtain your goals (Leaptrott, 1996).

> Game theory holds that protocol ensures that the rules of behavior are the same for both parties; however, if one party does not understand the rules, that party will not win in the negotiations.
>
> For example, the Japanese protocol is to never say "no." A negotiator must know and understand the many variations of "yes" to know whether a contract is forthcoming or not (Leaptrott, 1996).

SOCIO-PSYCHOLOGICAL MODEL

The **socio-psychological model** has five parts: the goals the parties want to reach, the communication and actions leading to the negotiations, the expected outcomes for each, the pre-existing relationship and cultural factors of both parties, and the conditions under which the negotiations are conducted. The model assumes a certain amount of ethnocentrism because the national character of the negotiators cannot be overcome and may lead to certain negative interpretations being made incorrectly by each side (Ghauri, 1983).

PRINCIPLES MODEL

The **principles model,** also known as the *comparative model,* has two assumptions with four parts. It is assumed that the negotiators are problem solvers and that the negotiators share a goal that they wish to reach efficiently and amicably. The four parts are the people are separate from the problem, the focus is on interests, the options have mutual gains, and the criteria used to judge the gains are objective. The model assumes both parties would prefer to negotiate in this manner and there would be no use of power or

other negative tactics; the long-term relationship would be stressed because this negotiation model does not give enough attention to the power/dependence characteristic
in negotiations. The model assumes the negotiators have knowledge of each other's behaviors (Ghauri, 1983).

DIRECTIONAL MODEL

The **directional model** is based on the prediction that tough or soft moves will be followed by similar moves by the other negotiating party. The parties using this model have
fallen into a pattern of reciprocal moves from which they do not seem to be able to escape. The directional model has been used extensively in the past in intercultural negotiations when foreign buyers had few alternatives and products made in the United
States sold themselves even though they may not have entirely met the needs of the
users (Ghauri, 1983).

INTERACTION MODEL

The **interaction model** includes four aspects: environment, atmosphere, parties, and
process. The environment includes political, social, and cultural variables that regulate
the negotiation process. Atmosphere includes distance (the space between their positions that will need to be bridged), conflict, cooperation, power, dependence, and expectations. The corporate and national cultures of the parties affect the negotiations. The
process includes the history and preconceived ideas of the negotiators (Ghauri, 1983).

PACKAGE DEAL MODEL

The **package deal model** has four parts: background factors, process, atmosphere, and outcome. Background factors include the objectives, environment, market position, third
parties, culture, and negotiators. The process includes time, issues, and contacts. Atmosphere includes cooperation/conflict, distance, power/dependence, and expectations.

Outcome allows for win-win, lose-lose, or continued negotiations. The model includes cultural factors and background research before beginning the negotiation
process (Ghauri, 1983).

Perspective Conflicts

Being able to identify the conflict in which you are involved is important. Issues form
out of substantive and relationship-based differences. The substantive issues include the
use and control of resources. The relationship-based issues center on the long-term
friendship or partnership. Negotiations should be conducted in such a way as to protect
future relations.

The conflict may be seen from the point of view of both negotiators or may be seen
from the point of view of only one negotiator. The conflict may involve a deadlock, behavior difference, lack of a common goal, communication problems, poor translators,
misunderstandings, secrets, lack of feedback, or unfamiliar tactics. Some of these factors may be due to the negotiators' perceptions of reality and their unconscious ability
to block out information that is inconsistent with their cultural beliefs. Negotiation

breakdown or deadlock may be identified by the negotiators' repeating themselves by using the same arguments. The negotiators may not be saying anything constructive but merely allowing the passage of time, or non-negotiation tactics may be used to try to change the attitudes of the other side (Fells, 1989).

Cognitive dissonance, as defined by Jervis (1998, p. 452), is: "two elements are in a dissonant relation if, considering these two alone, the obverse of one element would follow from the other." Cognitive dissonance, logic and reasoning differences normally due to cultural differences, is often the focus of such conflicts because your perspectives are based upon your cultural training, and your oppositions' perspectives are based on their cultural training. Cognitive dissonance may generate the following emotions and actions: frustration, regression, fixation, resignation, repression, projection, and aggression (Cohen, 1998). If you are aware of the possible cultural shocks before entering negotiations, it will be easier to adapt your negotiation style to accommodate both your own and others' ethnocentrism and maintain your patience while dealing with the differences. Part of negotiation is being able to discern what is going on mentally with the negotiators on the other side of the table. By studying the psychological predisposition of the other culture, you will be familiar with at least some of the variations between the two cultures. Communicating adequately is difficult when the cultural programming of the negotiators differs. Within a culture, there is normally an internal consistency to the beliefs and values of that culture. In intercultural negotiation, people need to be cognizant of not projecting their cultural thinking onto the other side. Be sure to discuss every point and not attribute motives to the other side that may, in fact, be nonexistent. The conceptualization of information, how the information is used, and how causes and effects are associated change from culture to culture.

In order to prepare for behavioral differences, you must train yourself to perceive the differences and adjust your reasoning accordingly. Developing "an efficient and coherent mental cross-referencing system" (Fisher, 1997, p. 22) that automatically adjusts your reactions saves time, money, and problems. While it is not possible in the international setting, much less in our day-to-day activities, to have a built-in response to all situations, if you build a mechanism to screen, sort, code, and store differences, you are able to respond more quickly. In other words, you develop a new mindset. This new cognitive structure allows us to share a defined culture and way of acting and thinking. Because our cognitive structures are programmed to our own cultures, reprogramming is disturbing to the existing system. Our mind inherently tries to make cognitive dissonance fit our current cognitive system rather than expanding the system by recognizing the difference and developing more storage cognitively (Fisher, 1997).

Interpreters and translators, if not well versed in both cultures, may unintentionally (though well intended) translate your communications inaccurately. Care should be exercised in selecting interpreters and translators to be certain they enhance rather than impede the negotiation process (Cohen, 1998).

Because lifestyles within cultures vary, so does the vocabulary that develops to explain the culture. When cultures are different, the words that develop will also be different. The subjective meaning of the translation can be very important. The United States is a very individual-oriented society. The Japanese equivalent of the word for individual has a negative connotation because the Japanese are a group-oriented culture. Education in the United States means academic achievement and is associated with school attendance. In the Spanish language cultures, however, education includes being polite, well-bred, and sensitive as well as covering school attendance and academic achievement. The idea of "fair play" is an example of a concept that does not exist in any other language yet is used frequently in U.S. business, sports, and other aspects of life. Since fair play is a culturally bound phrase, other cultures cannot be expected to understand its meaning. Gestures, tone of voice, and cadence further complicate the translation situation (Cohen, 1998).

Conflict Resolution

Conflict resolution involves a series of questions: How do we know if there is conflict? Is the conflict increasing or decreasing? Is the time to resolve the conflict now? What are the tactics to resolve the conflict? Is the conflict unresolvable? How do you tell if there is conflict or simply a lively debate? What is often an emotional, verbal disagreement for one culture may be a display of sincerity for another. In many countries and cultures, courts are third-party intermediaries (Weaver, 1998).

Negotiator selection is an important aspect of conflict resolution. Negotiators should be selected for their background (technical or social), emotional makeup, values, and viewpoints. It is important to find a negotiator whose qualifications most closely fit the requirements for the negotiations that are going to take place. Some important areas to be considered are gender, age, political affiliation, social class, cooperativeness, authoritarianism, and risk-taking propensity. Evaluating the negotiators from the other perspective will be helpful in selecting or adapting your strategy (Cohen, 1998).

Evaluating yourself as an intercultural negotiator within the constraints of the situation is important. Be sure you clearly perceive your objectives, know the facts, and have chosen your strategies and tactics carefully. Negotiation is essentially communication with an encoder and a decoder. To the extent that the encoder and decoder share the same perceptions is the degree to which their communications will be sent and received as intended. Communicating successfully with someone in your own society is often difficult; when you add different cultural concepts, different experiences, and different languages and word meanings, the possibility for miscommunication increases (Cohen, 1998).

> Even in the United States, mainstream whites present arguments for conflicts differently. White Americans use a factual-inductive approach, stating facts first then ending with an unemotional conclusion. African Americans use an affective-intuitive approach that starts with an emotional conclusion, followed by the facts (Weaver, 1998).

In decoding and encoding messages, the careful choice of ideas, words, or descriptions is crucial to all parties drawing matching semantic assumptions. Negotiators from different cultural backgrounds cannot rely on shared experiences or word meanings. For example, the Korean and United States meanings for the word "corruption" are negative for both cultures. However in the United States, corruption carries a connotation of being morally wrong while for the Koreans it implies being socially unfortunate.

If you consider these factors consciously as you are negotiating, then you will be better prepared to resolve the conflicts that arise (Cohen, 1998).

Learning the social system and cultural values of the other negotiators will help you identify the signs of conflict or prevent the conflict from developing. Knowing whether to cultivate a personal relationship, being conscious of rank and position, having an understanding of the thought patterns of other negotiators, and knowing how to establish trust are essential to successful conflict resolution. Because of culture differences, negotiators may focus on different aspects of the negotiations as being more important. A U.S. negotiator, for example, may focus on legal and financial agreements while the Mexican or Japanese negotiator may emphasize the personal relationship (Herbig & Kramer, 1991). Communicating respect, being nonjudgmental, realizing that perceptions are personal, showing empathy, and tolerating ambiguity can help you negotiate successfully (Mu, 1998).

If you have done your homework and are still having conflicts that defy resolution, you may wish to turn to a third party, a consultant, or apologize to the other negotiators and ask them to explain the problem. When you are in another culture, it is very important to live as its members live. Practicing cultural relativism is part of the empathy that needs to be utilized in intercultural negotiations. Judge people in a culture by their own standards and realize that for their geographical, historical, and social context, their cultural views are valid (Moran & Stripp, 1991).

The best way to avoid conflict is to prepare, plan, and respect the culture with whom you are negotiating before the negotiations commence. Be sure you know and respect the customs of the other negotiator's culture and be careful of gestures, nuances in meanings, and taboos of the other culture. Avoid using jargon, idioms, or slang. Realize that even if you are using a bicultural interpreter, quite often equivalent concepts do not exist between different languages. Many times a picture will help with explanations; therefore, you may wish to bring photographs, drawings, overhead transparencies, samples, or anything that can assist in the other side's understanding your presentation.

According to Lewicki, Litterer, Saunders, and Minton (1993), a mediator can sometimes productively solve disputes. A mediator would first stabilize the setting including greeting the participants, designating seating, identifying each person, stating the purpose of the mediation, and confirming his or her own neutrality. After setting this stage, the mediator would get a commitment from the participants to proceed in a businesslike manner.

The second step is helping the parties to communicate in an orderly fashion. The mediator would decide who is to speak first and would provide a rationale to the group. As each participant speaks, the mediator would take notes, actively restate the points being made, be a calming influence, and focus on the issues. Then the mediator would summarize, asking the speakers for their agreement. Next, the mediator would help the participants set priorities.

Step three would be to assist the parties in solving their disagreements. The negotiator would ask everyone to list alternative possibilities for settlement and a workable alternative, increase understanding of the alternatives, and rephrase them if necessary.

Finally, step four involves clarifying the agreement, checking to be sure both sides are in agreement and understand the terms, establishing a timetable for follow-up, emphasizing that the agreement belongs to the parties not the mediator, and congratulating the negotiators on their resolution.

Additional training and education in the art of intercultural negotiation will be needed for many managers and their management teams. Learning techniques including language classes, cultural assimilator sessions, and other cultural training, are part of becoming an effective intercultural negotiator able to deal with shared decision making, outsiders' ideas, and building long-term relationships.

Stereotypes that Affect Intercultural Negotiations

The way people of a culture view themselves and the way they are actually viewed by persons of other cultures often have an impact on intercultural negotiations. (A discussion of stereotypes of persons of selected cultures was included in chapter 1.)

According to Ruch (1989, p. 37), a disparity exists between the way U.S. people think of themselves and the way they are viewed by foreigners:

U.S. PERSONS' VIEWS	FOREIGNERS' VIEWS OF U.S. PERSONS
• Informal, friendly, casual	• Undisciplined, too personal, familiar
• Egalitarian	• Insensitive to status
• Direct, aggressive	• Blunt, rude, oppressive
• Efficient	• Obsessed with time, opportunistic
• Goal/achievement oriented	• Promise more than they deliver
• Profit oriented	• Materialistic
• Resourceful, ingenious	• Work oriented, deals more important than people
• Individualistic, progressive	• Self-absorbed, equating "new" with "best"
• Dynamic, find identity in work	• Driven
• Enthusiastic, prefer hard-sell	• Deceptive, fearsome
• Open	• Weak, untrustworthy

Negotiators from the United States should, therefore, take into consideration this disparity in viewpoints and should make a concerted effort to change some of the negative stereotypes such as being rude and obsessed with time when interacting during negotiations.

Intercultural negotiators need to be selected very carefully. People who can negotiate well in their own culture may not be successful at negotiating interculturally. Intercultural negotiators need to be able to ascertain where their opposition "is coming from." The negotiator must be able to grasp the situation and be able to answer such questions as: Are the opposition's negotiators bound by their culture or do they take on some of your own cultural characteristics? Being able to discern role behavior and knowing the proper deference is important in intercultural negotiations (Moran & Stripp, 1991).

A brief comparison of the negotiation styles of different cultures follows (Elashmawi & Harris, 1993; Ruch, 1989);

ELEMENT	U.S. AMERICANS	JAPANESE	ARABIANS	MEXICANS
Group composition	Marketing oriented	Function oriented	Committee of specialists	Friendship oriented
Number involved	2–3	4–7	4–6	2–3
Space orientation	Confrontational; competitive	Display harmonious relationship	Status	Close, friendly
Establishing rapport	Short period; direct to task	Longer period; until harmony	Long period; until trusted	Longer period; discuss family
Exchange of information	Documented; step-by-step; multimedia	Extensive; concentrate on receiving side	Less emphasis on technology, more on relationship	Less emphasis on technology, more on relationship
Persuasion tools	Time pressure; loss of saving/making money	Maintain relationship references; intergroup connections	Go-between; hospitality	Emphasis on family and on social concern; goodwill measured in generations
Use of language	Open/direct; sense of urgency	Indirect; appreciative; cooperative	Flattery; emotional; religious	Respectful; graciousness
First offer	Fair +/−5 to 10%	+/− 10 to 20%	+/− 20 to 50%	Fair
Second offer	Add to package; sweeten the deal	−5%	−10%	Add incentive
Final offer package	Total package	Makes no further concessions	−25%	Total
Decision-making process	Top management team	Collective	Team makes recommendation	Senior manager and secretary
Decision maker	Top management team	Middle line with team consensus	Senior manager	Senior manager
Risk taking	Calculated; personal responsibility	Low group responsibility	Religion-based	Personally responsible

The following summary of the negotiating styles of the United States and other se-lected countries is not intended to be all inclusive. Individual differences exist in other cultures just as they do in the U.S. culture.

UNITED STATES

According to Graham and Herberger (1983), the following statements are characteris-tic of the U.S. style of negotiating:

- "I can handle this by myself" (to express individualism).
- "Please call me Steve" (to make people feel relaxed by being informal).
- "Pardon my French" (to excuse profanity).
- "Let's get to the point" (to speed up decisions).
- "Speak up; what do you think?" (to avoid silence).
- "Let's put our cards on the table" (to convey the expectation of honesty).
- "A deal is a deal" (to indicate an expectation that the agreement will be honored).

In addition, Ruch (1989) emphasized that the space requirements in the United States have a direct bearing on negotiations. Entering the intimate space (up to 18 inches) of a person from the United States causes great discomfort. Another consideration when negotiating with people of the United States is related to their attitude toward saving face. Since people of the United States are not as concerned with saving face as people of other cultures, they may be quick with "constructive criticism" that may be a source of humiliation or discomfort for persons in other cultures.

CANADA

Recently, a large group of Hong Kong businesspeople immigrated to Canada in fear of the takeover of Hong Kong by the Peoples Republic of China; this move has introduced another culture into the country (Harris & Moran, 1996). Canada is a bilingual country with French as the primary language in the province of Québec and English in the other provinces. The English spoken is closer to British English than U.S. English. Canadians appear to be open and friendly, yet they are reserved, conservative, and very formal. They are also patriotic, lawful, and observe strict rules of etiquette. Canadians are not and do not like being considered to be the same as U.S. people or that their country is part of the United States. Canadians tend to be individualistic and speak a variation of British English. Respect the fact that the Canadians are very proud of their heritage and that they did not fight for independence from England. Otherwise, negotiation practices are similar to those in the United States.

CHINA

The Chinese have the largest population in the world. The Chinese are reserved and known for their hospitality and good manners. China has been very ethnocentric due to its chosen isolation behind the Great Wall for some 2,300 years. Westerners have had difficulty doing business with the Chinese because of a lack of understanding of the Chinese culture. The Chinese believe they are the center of human civilization and as such should be revered. Protocol to follow during the negotiation process would include giving small, inexpensive presents. The Chinese do not like to be touched, so a short bow and brief handshake will be used during introductions. Last names are used in conversation and printed first when written. Business cards may or may not be used by the Chinese. Alcoholic beverages are not consumed during meals until the host proposes a toast; the guest should toast the other people at the table throughout the meal. In China it is proper for the guest of honor to leave first; this should be shortly after the meal is finished. The Chinese consider mutual relationships and trust very important. Therefore, time will be spent in the beginning enjoying tea and social talk. However, they are some of the toughest negotiators in the world. Technical competence of the negotiators is necessary, and a noncondescending attitude is important because the Chinese research their opponents thoroughly to gain competitive advantage during negotiation. Nothing is final until it is signed; they prefer to use an intermediary. The Chinese delegation will be large. They rarely use lawyers, and interpreters may have inadequate language skills and experience. Although Chinese negotiators imply that there is no compromise or third choice, in reality there is ample room for compromise (Axtell, 1993; Cohen, 1998; Moran & Stripp, 1991).

GREAT BRITAIN

The British consider their English superior to U.S. English. British negotiators reflect their cultural characteristics; they are very formal and polite and place great importance on proper protocol. They are also concerned with proper etiquette. The British are not as casual or quick to make friends as U.S. persons nor is this considered necessary to conducting any business in Great Britain. The British can be tough and ruthless; they excel at intelligence gathering and political blackmail. Because they sometimes appear quaint and eccentric, negotiators from other cultures may underestimate their skill. As U.S. law is based on English law, understanding the meaning of a British contract is relatively easy (Harris & Moran, 1996).

FRANCE

France was the largest country in western Europe before the reunification of Germany. Needless to say, this change has not added to French self-esteem. The French expect everyone to behave as they do when conducting business including speaking their language. They are very individualistic and have a sense of pride that is sometimes interpreted as supremacy. The French enjoy conversation for the sake of conversation, but they are also very pragmatic about details of the proposed agreement during negotiations. During conversations, keep in mind that the French are world leaders in fashion, art, literature, cuisine, and diplomacy. The French follow their own logic referred to as "Cartesian" logic when negotiating. Their logic is based on principles previously established; it proceeds from what is known, in point-by-point fashion, until agreement is reached.

Protocol, manners, status, education, family, and individual accomplishments are keys to success when dealing with the French (Moran & Stripp, 1991). Trust has to be earned; they are impressed by results. The French prefer detailed, firm contracts.

The difference in the United States–French cognitive patterns and styles can be seen in their reaction to the Richard Nixon and Bill Clinton presidential scandals. The French have a very difficult time understanding the U.S. people and why they would want to drive a President from office over a moral or ethical issue. The French view the U.S. need to be morally correct in international situations to be unnecessary.

GERMANY

With the dismantling of the Berlin Wall in late 1989, there is now one unified Germany. In business, Germans are typically group oriented; however, as a people they are rather individualistic. Protocol is very important and formal. Dress is conservative, and correct posture and manners are required. Germans tend to use a handshake at the beginning and end of meetings. Remember to use titles when addressing members of the negotiating team and to use *please* and *thank you* freely. Since the Germans believe friendships and personal relationships can complicate negotiations, they prefer to keep a distance between themselves and the other team of negotiators. German is the official language of Germany; however, most Germans speak several languages.

Since Germans tend to be detail oriented, having technical people as part of the negotiation team is important. Being punctual is expected. Contracts are firm guidelines to be followed exactly. Corporate decisions are made at the top but with a great deal of input from workers. Quality is important, and decisions are pondered and carefully scrutinized to be sure such quality exists in any projects they undertake. To a U.S. person, Germans may seem pessimistic because of their ability to entertain every conceivable negative point possible. Once they accept a project, however, they give 100 percent to its successful implementation (Moran & Stripp, 1991).

INDIA

India is the second most populous country and tenth most industrialized country in the world. India has been influenced by Britain which ruled that country until 1947. Although the educated people speak English, Hindi is spoken by 30 percent of the population. Besides English and Hindi, there are 14 other Indian languages. Indians are family oriented and religious.

Business is conducted in a formal yet relaxed manner. Bribery is common, and having connections is important. Remember to avoid using the left hand in greetings and eating; request permission before smoking, entering the room, or sitting (Moran & Stripp, 1991). Building relationships is important, and an introduction is necessary. Use titles to convey respect. A knowledge of local affairs is important to people of India.

Intermediaries are commonly used. Since people of India place importance on building relationships, the negotiation process can be rather long by U.S. standards. Indian management is paternalistic toward subordinates. Due to status differences, group orientations are generally not used by the Indians. Indians, in an effort to maintain harmony, may tell the other party what it would like to hear. People of India do not approve of displays of emotion, and negotiators must use patience and allow the Indians to take the lead in the negotiations (Moran & Stripp, 1991).

JAPAN

The Japanese people are the most homogeneous culture on the globe and consider themselves to be very ethnocentric. The Japanese business culture is very different from that in the United States. The Japanese wish to maintain harmony and group consensus in all aspects of business. The importance of the individual has been suppressed. Signs that this may be changing in Japan, however, include the position women are taking in business and the trend toward changing jobs rather than staying with one company for a lifetime.

Business etiquette is extremely important in Japan. A business meeting should be arranged by an intermediary who has a relationship with both parties. Negotiating parties normally consist of five people. Business cards are exchanged ritualistically at the first formal meeting. The business cards should be printed in Japanese on one side and English on the reverse side. The Japanese are addressed by their titles or last names. Last names are printed in front of first names unless they have westernized their business cards. The senior negotiator sits in the middle of the team on one side of the table, and the other negotiating team sits on the opposite side of the table.

Social meetings are very important in building a relationship of trust and friendship. Eventually the real negotiations will go on behind the scenes at social meetings, allowing everyone to maintain face in the formal negotiation meetings. The development of a relationship based on trust is very important to good business negotiations. Completing a deal quickly is not important to the Japanese. Unless the U.S. negotiators view the negotiations as part of a long-term commitment, the Japanese are not interested in negotiating or becoming involved with the U.S. company. The Japanese are interested in fairness and will offer a proposal that they feel is correct and reasonable.

The negotiating practices of the Japanese companies are based on the keiretsu systems. A **keiretsu system** is a company group formed by the principal company and the partner companies that supply parts, equipment, financial support, or distribution of the final products. In Japan, every company in the keiretsu works to provide the customer the best product for the lowest price while maintaining an acceptable return on investment. A keiretsu group is viewed as a long-term commitment (Yonekura, 1991).

Communication is very complex with the Japanese. In order to avoid having someone lose face, lose the group harmony, or disappoint another person, the Japanese use very subtle and complex verbal and nonverbal cues. You need to read between the lines in order to interpret what has been said, and you will need to use more silence and less eye contact than is considered normal for U.S. Americans. Because the Japanese do not use *no* and have such subtle cues, ask a number of questions to be certain you understand the intent of what is being communicated (March, 1989).

Silence is an important Japanese nonverbal communication and should not be interrupted. Standing at the table, slouching, doodling, crossing the legs, or other informal behavior by sellers is considered disrespectful (Engholm, 1991).

If a problem is found even after a written agreement is signed, the Japanese will resolve the difference through mutual agreement with the other party as they always consider contracts flexible instruments. Since Japan has very few business lawyers by U.S. standards, the Japanese will be very suspicious of a negotiating team that includes lawyers (March, 1989).

LATIN AMERICA

Latin America includes Mexico and Central and South America. The people are from Spanish, Aztec, and Mayan descent with German, Italian, Portuguese, English, African, ancient Polynesian, and Japanese influences in given geographical areas. The people are significantly different from the United States in how they conduct business. Developing a warm relationship or friendship is necessary to a successful negotiation process (which can be lengthy).

Since Latin Americans may believe that U.S. Americans have taken advantage of them, a negotiator must be careful to maintain the self-esteem of the Latins. If your trust is questionable or lost, the opportunity to negotiate will probably be lost. Relationships are important because of the need to have contacts. Since bribery is common, the local contacts can help you determine who should be approached to get the business moving. The government is very involved in business.

Latins emphasize general principles more than problem solving. A story told by a U.S. businessman illustrates the difference in approaches. The U.S. businessman was invited by a Guatemalan to supply equipment for a cereal factory the Guatemalan was planning to open in his country. The U.S. supplier focused on the financing of the purchases, the Guatemalan's credit rating, and how the Guatemalan was going to pay the supplying company. A German contractor, who eventually received the production line order, concentrated on how the production line was going to operate and how to meet the Guatemalan's needs. The German even sent a representative of the company to live on-site for the first three months of production. The U.S. interest in the financial aspects of the contract was a turnoff to the Guatemalan (Axtell, 1991).

Negotiators will be chosen based on their family connections, political influence, education, and gender. Female negotiators should be in the background rather than the foreground of the negotiation. Latins are very individualistic in business; however, they are very group oriented concerning family and friends.

Social competence is paramount in Latin business. Handshaking and asking about the health and well-being of business contacts and their families are expected. In business, people are addressed by their titles and maternal and paternal surnames. Business cards are exchanged and should include the negotiator's academic degrees.

Since most agreements are consummated over lunch, suitable, informal luncheon accommodations are important. Many meetings will be held to allow a personal relationship to develop. The negotiations will begin with social and personal conversations that are sensitive but formal. Numerous meetings will be the norm, and time is not seen as important. Latins are people oriented rather than task oriented. Since body language is important and different from that in the United States, research nonverbal messages of the people; such behavior as putting your hands in your pockets should be avoided. Another gesture that should be avoided is placing the hands on the hips which is a sign of a challenge. Hands should be on the top of the table. As you become more friendly with Latins, you may be treated as a member of the cultural family. Latins tend to stand and sit close together when talking; they touch one another and often place a hand on another's shoulder.

Mexico and Central and South America cover a large geographical area, so important negotiating differences exist between countries within the area. Negotiators need to learn as much specific information as possible about the particular country, company, and people with whom they will be negotiating (Harris & Moran, 1996).

NIGERIA

The Nigerian people have been strongly influenced as a tribal society by the British and by the Islamic and Christian religions. Although more than 250 different languages and their dialects are spoken, many Nigerians are educated in English. The official language of the country is English.

Negotiation in the form of bargaining in the marketplace is practiced by all Nigerians from childhood. Because of this, they are very skillful negotiators. Since they are an individualistic society, negotiations are viewed as a competitive process. Age is equated with wisdom and is an important criterion when selecting negotiators. Gender, cultural background, and educational credentials are also important considerations.

Tribal loyalties are very strong, and it is best not to mix tribes. Nepotism is practiced because of the responsibility to support family and tribe members. Developing a personal relationship is important to the success of the negotiators. Time is not particularly important; therefore, negotiations will take a while to complete. Titles and last names are used in business, and an intermediary should make the initial introductions. Being well dressed is important, and a conscious demonstration of courtesy and consideration is expected. A successful negotiation is completed when the parties reach a verbal understanding. Contracts are considered flexible and may be oral or written. A bribe in the form of a mobilization fee may be required to expedite business (Stripp & Moran, 1991).

RUSSIAN STATES

The Russian states are now divided into 15 republics with 130 languages although Russian is the official language. Ethnic groups include eastern Slavic, Turkish, Baltic, Mongolian, and Inuits. In 1991, the government and production facilities were decentralized.

Political and economic changes have occurred rapidly. The Russians want to learn and take part in western management practices. Currently there is a lot of opportunity for joint ventures that include industrial modernization. Russia has had no business schools. People were formally trained as specialists (in engineering or the sciences) rather than as generalists.

Some negotiation tactics may remain the same, but many tactics will probably change as other management practices are initiated. In the past, negotiation sessions with the Russians have been long with the Russians controlling the agenda. Russians seem to be concerned with age, rank, and protocol. They are addressed by their full name and tend to be somewhat formal. Like U.S. people, Russians see time as money, and friendships are not crucial to business. Russians are not concerned with equality between business partners but are concerned with maximizing their own profits. Contracts are interpreted rigidly (Moran & Stripp, 1991; Elashmawi & Harris, 1993).

As Moran and Stripp (1991, p. 1) emphasize: "Negotiating on a global scale can present tremendous opportunities." Corporations can expand their markets, increase their profits and productivity, and lower their costs by negotiating globally.

Terms

- Cultural noise
- Directional model
- Interaction model
- Intercultural negotiation
- Keiretsu system
- Package deal model
- Principles model
- Socio-psychological model

EXERCISE 10.1

Instructions: Circle T for true and F for false.

1. T F   In intercultural negotiation, the meeting location is associated with power and responsibilities.
2. T F   Russian negotiating strategies include a need to control.
3. T F   The socio-psychological negotiation model assumes no use of power or negative tactics.
4. T F   The principles negotiation model assumes a certain amount of ethnocentrism.
5. T F   The interaction negotiation model involves environment, atmosphere, parties, and process.
6. T F   Social class is unimportant in negotiator selection.
7. T F   Gender is important when negotiating in Latin American countries.
8. T F   The Japanese prefer negotiating teams rather than a single negotiator.
9. T F   Bribery is a common part of conducting business in India.
10. T F   Protocol is very important when dealing with the French.

Questions and Cases for Discussion

1. Intercultural negotiations have many implications. Discuss how two of these implications would affect negotiations between a U.S. negotiation team and a Japanese negotiation team. Discuss how two of these implications would affect negotiations between a Japanese negotiation team and a Mexican negotiation team.
2. Explain why following the saying, "When in Rome, do as the Romans do," is appropriate to the negotiation process.
3. Are most negotiation conflicts culturally based?
4. How can you prepare for cultural shock in negotiations?
5. What are the issues you need to consider when choosing a negotiation process model?
6. List the three ways you may recognize a negotiation deadlock.
7. What does the intercultural negotiation process involve?
8. Give three reasons why global joint ventures and strategic alliances are increasing.
9. When analyzing a negotiation problem, what are the factors to consider?
10. Which negotiation model would you choose when negotiating with Canadians?

CASE 1

A U.S. corporation has sent four people to meet with a group from a Russian organization. As the groups have had previous negotiations and contact, the U.S. group is hoping to go home with an agreement. The first meeting lasts 12 hours and ends in a deadlock. After agreeing to meet the next day, one of the U.S. negotiators notices the Russians leaving for an evening on the town. The next morning the meeting is a repeat of the first except that it is cut short so the Russian negotiators can play golf. All agree to meet the next morning. The U.S. lead negotiator asks his company for time to wait out the Russians. Three weeks later (after many repeat meetings with no concessions), the Russians begin to make concessions. What do you know of the Russian culture that could explain what happened? Did the U.S. negotiator make the right move or would pressure have made the Russians move faster?

CASE 2

A U.S. salesman is in Spain negotiating a contract with a Spanish company. He has expressed to his Spanish colleagues an interest in attending a bullfight, so they invite him to one. As the first bull is released, the salesman jokingly says, "So who's going to win? I'll put my money on the bull." The Spaniards remained silent. The salesman felt very uncomfortable during the rest of the bullfight. Explain the salesman's faux pas and the negative effects it may have on his progress. If the salesman had taken time to research bullfighting, how might he have better handled the situation?

CASE 3

International negotiators must diagnose meaning, motive, and intention on the spot if they are to get the contract or the sale. How does one become nonethnocentric and "do as the Romans do" in order to get the order? How much will previous experience help or hinder the progress of the sale? Why does the visible part of the iceberg overshadow the hidden parts of the iceberg?

CASE 4

The following is a comparison chart for a U.S. person wishing to sell a Chinese person a piece of expensive equipment. As you can see, the two gentlemen are not interpreting, perceiving, or expecting the same thing. Using this list, discuss what will probably happen to these negotiations and why.

Expectations and Behaviors of U.S. American and Chinese

	EXPECTATIONS	EXPECTED CONVERSATIONS	BEHAVIORS	UNFULLFILLED EXPECTATIONS
U.S. American	Complete job; obtain contract; close deal	Equipment; specification; price; contract terms	Professional; technically-oriented	Disappointed and confused
Chinese	Establish long-term relationship; obtain contract; confirm relationship built; begin working on future	Background; introduction to company; training and services	Hospitable; less technically-oriented	Hurt and not respected

(Mu, 1998, pp. 553.)

Activities

1. Invite three or four businesspersons who have had experience in international negotiation to serve as a panel to discuss "Negotiating with the Japanese" (or another culture of your choice).
2. Prepare a negotiation profile for a person who will be negotiating with representatives of a manufacturing firm in Mexico. Include verbal and nonverbal do's and don'ts.
3. Select a recent book containing information on international negotiation such as Dean Allen Foster's *Bargaining Across Borders* or Roger E. Axtell's *The Do's and Taboos of International Trade* and prepare a one-page summary of nonverbal aspects of negotiating with persons of a culture of your choice.
4. Review recent issues of a business journal or news magazine for an article related to international negotiation to be used as a basis for class discussion.
5. Prepare a list of possible problems U.S. businesswomen might encounter when negotiating with Asians.

References

Axtell, R. E. (1991). *The do's and taboos of international trade.* New York: John Wiley & Sons, Inc.

Axtell, R. E. (1993). *Do's and taboos around the world.* New York: John Wiley & Sons, Inc.

Burke, C. G., & Stewart, K. (1992). *The drivers of organizational behavior and culture.* Working paper of University of Southern California.

Casse, P., & Deol, S. (1985). *Managing intercultural negotiations.* Washington, DC: Sietar.

Cohen, R. (1998). *Negotiating across cultures.* Washington, DC: United States Institute of Peace Press.

Elashmawi, F., & Harris, P. (1993). *Multicultural management; New skills for global success.* Houston, TX: Gulf Publishing Company.

Engholm, C. (1991). *When business East meets business West.* New York: John Wiley & Sons, Inc.

Fells, R. (1989). Managing deadlocks in negotiation. *Management Decision, 27*(4), 32–38.

Fisher, G. (1980). *International negotiation.* Yarmouth, ME: Intercultural Press.

Fisher, G. (1997). *Mindsets: The role of culture and preparation in international relations.* Yarmouth, ME: Intercultural Press.

Ghauri, P. N. (1983). *Negotiating international package deals.* Doctoral dissertation, Acta Universitatis Upsaliensis Studia Oeconomiae Negotiorum.

Graham, J., & Herberger, R. (1983). Negotiators abroad—Don't shoot from the hip. *Harvard Business Review, 61,* 160–169.

Harris, P. R., & Moran, R. T. (1996). *Managing cultural differences.* Houston: Gulf Publishing Company.

Herbig, P. A., & Kramer, H. E. (1991). Cross-cultural negotiations: Success through understanding. *Management Decision, 29*(8), 19–31.

Jervis, R. (1998). Cognitive dissonance and international relations. In Weaver, G. R. (Ed.). *Culture, communication, and conflict.* New York: Simon & Schuster.

Karrass, C. L. (1996). *In business, you don't get what you deserve; you get what you negotiate.* Los Angeles, CA: Stanford Street Press.

Leaptrott, N. (1996). *Rules of the game: Global business protocol.* Cincinnati: Thomson Executive Press.

Lewicki, R. J., Litterer, J. A., Saunders, D. M., & Minton, J. W. (1993). *Negotiation.* Homewood, IL: Irwin.

March, R. M. (1989). No-nos in negotiating with the Japanese. *Across the Board, 26*(4), 44–51.

Moran, R. T., & Stripp, W. G. (1991). *Dynamics of successful international business negotiations.* Houston: Gulf Publishing.

Mu, D. P. (1998). Culture and business: Interacting effectively to achieve mutual goals. In

Weaver, G. R. (Ed.) *Culture, communication and conflict.* New York: Simon & Schuster.

Ruch, W. V. (1989). *International handbook of corporate communication.* Jefferson, NC: McFarland & Company, Inc., Publishers.

Sebenius, J. K. (1992). Negotiation analysis: A characterization and review. *Management Science, 38*(1), 18–38.

Vernon, R. (1974). Apparatchiks and entrepreneurs: U.S.–Soviet economic relations. *Foreign Affairs, 52*(2), 249–262.

Weaver, G. R. (Ed.). (1998). *Culture, communication and conflict.* New York: Simon & Schuster.

Yonekura, S. (1991). *What's the "keiretsu?"* Paper written at Hitotubashi University, Japan.

CHAPTER

Intercultural Negotiation Strategies

Objectives
Upon completion of this chapter, you will:

■ be able to differentiate between negotiation strategies.

■ understand the effects of different personal constructs.

■ recognize and use successful intercultural negotiation guidelines.

■ understand various trade agreements that affect intercultural negotiation.

Intercultural negotiation requires choosing the appropriate communication channels. As you learned earlier in this text, a knowledge of protocol for communicating effectively in your culture is important. When you negotiate in another culture, the protocol will probably change. Differences to consider include the chain of command, organizational decision making, nonverbal communication, the proper environment of negotiations, the gender of negotiators, and the consequences of different strategies on different cultures. The greater the difference between cultures, the greater the likelihood that miscommunication could result in negative outcomes.

Strategies

Negotiation strategies are plans organized to achieve a desired objective. Because strategies are used to elicit desired responses, negotiations can take many forms. Predicting the opponent's response is essential to strategic planning. Intercultural negotiation strategies differ from intracultural styles for most cultures.

> Mark McCormack explained in his book *What They Don't Teach You at Harvard Business School* how negotiations can be win-win:
> I find it helpful to try to figure out in advance where the other person would like to end up—at what point he will do the deal and still feel like he's coming away with something. This is different from 'how far will he go?' A lot of times you can push someone to the wall, and you still reach an agreement, but his resentment will come back to haunt you in a million ways (1984, p. 149).

On what are negotiation strategies based? Assuming that people act on the basis of their own best interests, the question then becomes: How do I determine whether this is the deal I should accept, or more broadly, what is the truth? Different cultures arrive at truth in negotiations in one of three ways: faith, fact, and feeling. Persons operating on faith care that your religious or political ideology matches theirs. For example, small nations who believe in self-sufficiency may reject a good deal simply because they want their own people to do the work, even though your product is clearly superior and lower priced. Thus, presenting facts to these persons is futile. Persons who believe in facts are often quite predictable; they give the contract to the lowest bidder. Most of the people in the world are more concerned with feelings and relationships; they believe in building a relationship over time and will not buy from someone else just because they can get a lower price (Morrison, Conaway, & Borden, 1994).

U.S. Americans tend to make fewer adjustments to their opponent's behavior, and they change their negotiation strategy less than other cultures when dealing interculturally. U.S. persons lack sufficient motivation to change their behavior in negotiation encounters because, in the past, the world wanted what the United States produced.

One's negotiating strategy may achieve a compromise agreement or an integrative agreement. The **compromise agreement** is reached when two parties find a common ground between their individual wishes that results in lower joint benefit. For example, if one side offers to sell a product for $35 per unit and the other side offers to buy it for $25, a compromise of $30 can be reached that yields a lower joint benefit. With an **integrative agreement,** the two parties reconcile their interests to yield a high joint benefit. Negotiators should seek integrative agreements rather than compromise agreements because integrative agreements tend to be more stable, more mutually rewarding, and usually benefit the broader community represented by the two parties. The five methods of reaching integrative agreements described by Pruitt (1998) are expanding the pie, nonspecific compensation, logrolling, cost cutting, and bridging. Expanding the pie involves receiving additional resources. Nonspecific compensation involves repaying the party who does not receive what he or she requests in some unrelated way. Logrolling, which may be viewed as a variant of nonspecific compensation, involves both parties, rather than only one, being compensated for making concessions requested by the other party. Each party makes concessions on low-priority issues in exchange for concessions on high-priority issues. The cost cutting solution involves the reduction of one person's costs while the other person gets what he or she wants. Bridging involves devising a new option for situations in which neither person gets his or her initial demands (Pruitt, 1998).

A cease-fire in the Yom Kippur War found the Egyptian Third Army surrounded by Israeli forces. A dispute arose about the control of the only road available for bringing food and medicine to this army, and the two parties appeared to be at loggerheads. After a careful analysis, the mediator, Henry Kissinger, concluded that Israel wanted actual control of the road while Egypt wanted only the appearance that Israel did not control it for the sake of public relations. A bridging solution was found that involved continued Israeli control but the stationing of United Nations soldiers at checkpoints on the road so that they seemed to control it (Pruitt, 1998, p. 513).

Negotiation strategies include group oriented, individual oriented, media, and face-to-face (Copeland & Griggs, 1985).

GROUP ORIENTED

Group orientation ideally results in a solution that is good for everyone since all points of view are supposedly considered. Negotiations with group-oriented negotiators would be detail oriented in order to determine the proper solution. Your identity belongs to the group of which you are a member. The group would have to reach a consensus on any and all decisions, and this probably would not be done during the negotiation sessions. The individuals in the group would avoid making an individual decision. Individuals who are not group oriented may feel that group-oriented negotiators appear to stall, are not interested in the negotiations, and give ambiguous statements. Group-oriented cultures tend to view contracts as flexible (Hofstede, 1991).

The Japanese are the most group-oriented culture in our world due to the number of years they were physically segregated from other cultures. Although the Japanese culture is particularly different from that of the United States, Japan and the United States do have a common work ethic—hard work is applauded by both. Even though the original management styles were very different, as joint ventures and subsidiaries of Japanese companies become part of the U.S. economy, U.S. corporations are beginning to utilize some of the Japanese management concepts. Both cultures are gaining an understanding of their differences and are learning to cope. Other cultures that are also very group oriented are the Chinese, Polynesians, Native Americans, and Africans (Hofstede, 1991). This group approach assumes that the action taken is conservative and well thought out and that all options were considered in the decision (Foster, 1992).

Armaco was losing money on one of its trucking operations in Saudi Arabia. Finally, an Arab was able to buy the franchise and set up his own system. Knowing his own people, he worked out a series of complex reinforcement schedules for each truck and driver. He even penalized them for every valve cap that was missing and rewarded drivers when nothing that was supposed to be there was missing. Oil levels in the crankcase, maintenance schedules, time schedules, everything was examined and recorded. The cost per ton-mile dropped to a third of what it had been under American management (Weaver, 1998, p. 14).

INDIVIDUAL ORIENTED

If you are individually oriented, you will be concerned with the best contract for your company and may not be concerned about whether the agreement is good for the other company. If there is more than one negotiator on your team, one person will probably control the negotiations and make the final decision concerning the various issues being discussed. Usually much individual sparring has taken place with members of the other team before the negotiation meeting. The individually-oriented person would tend to interpret the contract very rigidly.

The U.S. American culture is probably the most individualistic culture in the world. Another individualistic culture is Latin America. According to Foster (1992), a Latin negotiation is frequently an internal contest of individual will battling for position and power. Other cultures that are very individualistic include British, French, Australian, and Canadian (Hofstede, 1991).

FACE-TO-FACE

Face-to-face strategies are concerned with negotiating in person rather than through the mail, fax, telephone, telegraph, lawyers, or other intermediaries. People in many cultures will only negotiate on a face-to-face basis. The Japanese, in particular, do not like to make commitments over the telephone or in writing until numerous face-to-face meetings have taken place. In many European countries as well as India and Japan, contracts are considered an insult to the trust of the partners. They place great importance on face-to-face encounters and oral agreements (Prosser, 1985).

Role of the Media

Representatives of the media—TV, radio, and newspapers—have a unique position in creating multicultural understanding and misunderstanding. Most of the views you have of other cultures have been gained through the media window. The media has been used in various ways including supporting and tearing down political candidates and office-holders and defining and distorting numerous messages. Media people also represent a culture and have cultural biases. The media tends to have a stereotypical view of business. Media members have generally presented other cultures through the bias of the U.S. perceptual grid.

Advertisers make up the largest group of negotiators in the world—they all compete for consumers' dollars. Advertisers use media extensively and have learned that differences in culture necessitate different delivery and content if an ad is to successfully promote a product (Prosser, 1985).

An example of media influence in the world today was the CNN (Cable News Network) broadcasts during Desert Storm. CNN coverage was watched by the antagonists and protagonists in the battle and everyone else in the world who had access to satellite television broadcasts. Another example of media influence is the number of teenagers worldwide who wear jeans and listen to the same music and watch the same movies.

Movies are big promoters of stereotypes. Many times the wrong perception of a culture is gained from the subject matter presented in movies or a television series that is broadcasted in foreign countries. Many of the stereotypes foreigners have of U.S. Americans (such as all carry guns) are due to movies and television series. Likewise, U.S. Americans hold views of other cultures (such as the belief that all followers of Islam do not drink alcoholic beverages) based on movie and television messages. Since perceptions of other cultures are often acquired through the media and may be brought to the negotiation table, an awareness of the role of the media is important.

Personal Constructs

Personal constructs refer to individual belief systems and attitudes. The individual belief system, attitudes, or personal constructs differ from culture to culture and often from person to person within a given culture. What you expect to happen cognitively is based on your life experiences. No two people in the world have the same set of life experiences. Cultural stereotypes are dangerous even though they provide clues to the behavior of the "average" person in the culture.

The reason "birds of a feather flock together" is such a powerful adage is because we like to spend time with those who are like us. This is one of the reasons people say "They're in America; they should act like Americans." The Americans who make these statements, however, do not understand they need to reciprocate and adopt certain foreign behaviors when they visit another country. Of course, without a lot of time and willingness, it would be very difficult "to do as the Romans do."

The question has been raised as to whether it is possible for a person to become a "native" of another country (Francis, 1991). Perhaps not, but it is possible to learn about the culture, customs, and traditions and to be sensitive to them. People react more positively to people who shift their communication style toward the new culture; however, the other culture may become threatened if the group distinctiveness is threatened. Moderate levels of adaptation seem to improve relations, but large levels of adaptation may have negative effects. Moderate adaptation reflects respect and sensitivity toward another culture. Those who choose strong adaptation may unintentionally be perceived as having an uncomplimentary view of the new culture, a similar view held of individuals who choose not to adapt at all (Francis, 1991).

During the Gulf War, the soldiers from various countries were restricted to the military compounds because the Saudi Arabians were afraid that if they had contact with the Saudi civilians, it would threaten the Saudi way of life.

Everyone is ethnocentric to a great degree. Because losing ethnocentrism means changing, it is a very powerful construct. Resistance to change is a universal construct (Copeland & Griggs, 1985; Herbig & Kramer, 1991). Negotiations take place within the political, economic, social, and cultural systems of the countries involved; these are the environmental issues of negotiation.

The cultural systems involved in the negotiation may be similar or divergent. Negotiations take place within the context of the four Cs: common interest, conflicting interests, compromise, and criteria (Moran & Stripp, 1991).

Alfonso Lopez-Vasquez has researched Hispanic work styles brought into the Anglo workplaces. One of his main findings has been that both sides, the U.S. Americans and the Hispanics, have misconceptions and apprehensions about each other. One of the mistakes U.S. Americans have made is to treat the Hispanic workers as if there are no differences in the two cultures. In order to get the kind of work they want, U.S. Americans have to understand the cultural differences (Staa, 1998).

Common interest considers that both parties in the negotiation share, have, or want something that the other party has or does. Without a common goal, there would be no need for negotiation. Areas of conflicting interests include payment, distribution, profits, contractual responsibilities, and quality. Compromise includes areas of disagreement. Although a win-win negotiated settlement would be best for both parties, the compromises that are negotiated may not produce that result. The criteria include the conditions under which the negotiations take place.

Communication is plagued with misinterpretations. When perspectives, environment, the four Cs, and the negotiation situation are all considered together, the possibility of misinterpretations is magnified. When the negotiators are from different cultures, they have different mindsets or differing cognitive systems for reacting to situations. For example, ethics and ethical behavior which are always near the surface can confound negotiations if the two cultures have very different views on proper business ethics. For example, the Japanese consider a contract to be an adaptive tool rather than a rigid legal document as most U.S. Americans would interpret it. Nigerians, Mexicans, and the Chinese find bribes placed in the proper places help business run smoothly, but such behavior is considered unethical in the United States.

Businesspeople's mindsets have developed to give stability and are mutually compatible with other businesspeople in their field in their culture. When cognitive dissonance is acknowledged due to a different culture, our peace of mind is lost and we strive to reestablish a new peace of mind. Realizing we are locked into our own mindset is important. Acknowledging that the other culture's representatives are having the same mindset difficulties we are is crucial. When negotiating with another culture, we will find beliefs we do not share and will have cognitive dissonance. The more abstract a subject is, the more difficult it will be to view it from your counterpart's mindset (Fisher, 1997).

An example of how cognitive dissonance works and how we try to make something fit into our current mindset can be seen by the following visual perception example.

In the West, we are surrounded by right angles—rooms, windows, doors, furniture, buildings. If someone asks you what the shape of the filing cabinet across the room is, you would say rectangular. However, unless you are looking at the object directly from above or in front, you would be seeing the object from an angle, and it would not appear to have 90-degree angles. Because from experience we know these things have 90-degree angles, we know we have a rectangular object. These are preconceived cognitives that we have learned to trust. If we are placed in a room that has been devised to elude our senses because it is not built proportionally, we will try to make objects in the room fit our cognitive model. It is almost impossible for persons to visualize reality as it is rather than how it is in their mind (Fisher, 1997).

If friendship and trust are important, it may be necessary to plan a number of social activities. These activities are essential in building personal relationships before negotiations begin or before a solution can be reached in the negotiations. In many cultures, business is conducted with family and friends, and personal relationships are considered important for the long run. In other cultures, friendships are not important to business relationships.

ENVIRONMENT

The environment in which the negotiations take place is particularly important for intercultural negotiations. If meetings are held at the office of one of the parties, then that party has control and responsibility as host to the other party. When one of the parties is at home, they have "home court" advantage—the advantage of access to information and human resources. When negotiators are on their home territory, they are likely to be more assertive than when in the host's territory. Reasons for this include conditioning. We are taught it is rude to be impolite to someone in his or her home or office. The host negotiators may also have a feeling of superiority since the other team is coming to them. (Lewicki & Litterer, 1985). One way to avoid this competitiveness is to choose a neutral site. The neutrality of the site eliminates the psychological advantage of the home ground.

The actual room where the negotiations will take place could play an important role if the room makes one of the negotiating teams feel comfortable and the other team uncomfortable. Cultural differences need to be considered when choosing the site. Details to consider include the physical arrangement of the room, the distance between people and teams, and the formal or informal atmosphere of the room.

The arrangement of the table and chairs can also make a difference. Some cultures ascribe a title to people according to the seating arrangement. Those same cultures also would expect the other team to have the same number of negotiators and negotiators of rank equal to theirs. The Japanese particularly have been surprised when the United States sends a younger person of a lower rank to meet with a top official of their company. Because the Japanese conduct side negotiations with their counterpart in the opposing company, it is necessary for everyone to know his or her counterparts. Two ways of arranging seating in a meeting to accomplish this purpose are shown in Figures 11.1 and 11.2 (Funakawa, 1997).

POWER AND AUTHORITY

Power is the ability to influence others; **authority** is the power to give commands and make final decisions. With the ability to influence comes the responsibility of the action taken. Power has the ability to make people and companies dependent or independent. Power can be an advantage or a disadvantage depending on how it is used, but it must be used within the bounds of moral and ethical behavior (Lewicki & Litterer, 1985).

In order for power to be meaningful, it has to be accepted. When you accept power, you are giving it the authority to exist to the extent it is acceptable to you. The personal constructs of the receiver of the power determine the strength of the power exerted.

An example of the use of power and authority would occur in a meeting between the Chinese, who do not believe in a time schedule for negotiations, and time-conscious U.S. Americans. The Chinese would have the power of time on their side and possibly could make the U.S. Americans feel pressured to make compromises. Japanese negotiators have observed that they can make U.S. negotiators agree to concessions because they can "outwait" the impatient Americans (Engholm, 1991) (See Figure 11.3).

PERCEPTION

The process by which individuals ascribe meaning to their environment is strongly affected by their culture. The stress of negotiation can cause misperception but more often

FIGURE 11.1 Seating Arrangement A

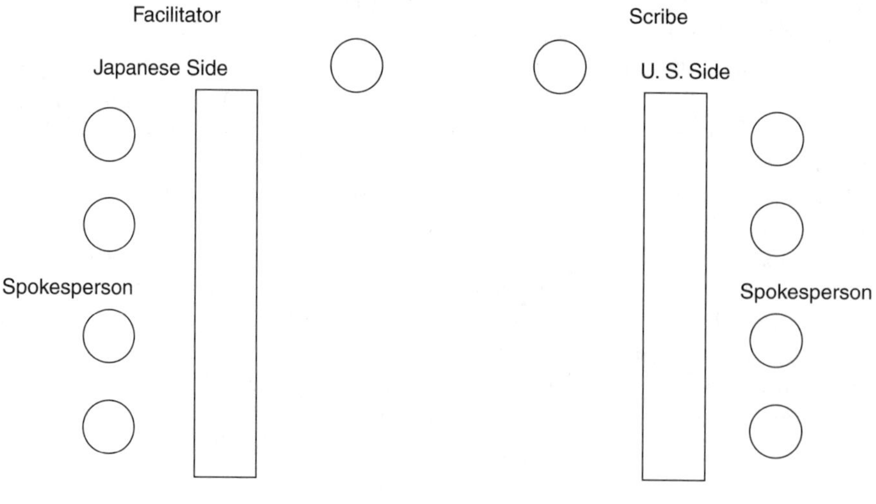

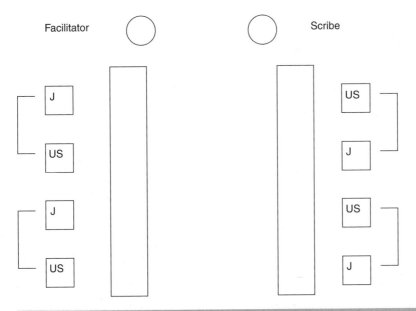

FIGURE 11.2 Seating Arrangement B

it will be due to the different meanings of verbal and nonverbal cues in the cultures involved. An example of misinterpreted nonverbal messages would be U.S. Americans "talking" with their hands to clarify or exaggerate a particular point during negotiations with a German negotiating team. The Germans could incorrectly interpret the motions as spontaneous emotional displays that they consider impolite. In an additional example, if a company were to send only one person to negotiate with the Japanese, the Japanese would assume the company was not serious about negotiating an agreement (Lewicki & Litterer, 1985).

Stimuli have both a physical size and socioenvironmental meaning that can be different for each individual within and across cultures. Our experiences determine to what stimuli we are sensitive or insensitive. While it is obvious to the Japanese and U.S. Americans that the two cultures are very different, it may not be so obvious that U.S.

FIGURE 11.3 The Negotiation Waiting Game

citizens and Canadians also have many cultural differences. Sometimes thinking we are alike can be more dangerous than knowing we are different and being careful of our verbal and nonverbal behaviors.

TACTICS

Tactics are maneuvers used for gaining advantage or success. The attributes the receiver attaches to the tactic used can be so distracting that the receiver has a distorted perception of the point communicated. Jokes often used by people of the United States to "break the ice" are examples of such tactics. Although these work well when the negotiations are between U.S. companies, jokes generally do not translate well to other cultures. Jokes are often derogatory toward a particular person and in group-oriented cultures these may be considered offensive (Moran & Stripp, 1991).

Distracting tactics can be detrimental to the negotiation process. Allowing insufficient time for the negotiations is typical of cultures that want to get "right to business." By doing so, the other negotiating team may feel you are uninterested in a long-term relationship and, consequently, are not interested in what your team may have to say.

Whether the climate during negotiations is supportive or defensive depends on how the cultures negotiating view each other. What one culture considers defensive, dominating, retaliatory, and threatening may be considered normal by the other culture. However, if a negotiator is perceived, rightly or wrongly, as defensive or supportive, the other team will respond according to its perceptions and not according to what was intended. Climate is a very important area to research to read your opponents correctly. One way to avoid being defensive is to ask questions and learn what your opponent is thinking. Clarify or restate what you understand to have been said and ask if that is correct. Try to follow the other side as it explores the issues rather than always taking the leadership role. Use role reversal to understand and appreciate the other side's position.

MEDIATION

Mediation is the use of a third party to settle differences between negotiating teams to bring them to common agreement. Mediation may be the fastest road to discovering the negotiation barriers. If you are dealing with members of a culture who do not like confrontation, who are afraid of losing face, or causing you to lose face, using a mediator may be the best path to follow (Moran & Stripp, 1991).

Many times it will be necessary to have a common friendship, business relationship, or other contact to obtain an appointment for business. Even if the other negotiating team speaks your language, it is a good idea to bring your own interpreter and translator. Because languages do not translate word for word, you need to have someone you can depend on for translation quality (see chapter 7). Remember that in many countries lawyers are not involved in the negotiation sessions, and your foreign hosts may feel intimidated or distrustful if you bring a lawyer with you (Casse and Deol, 1991).

GENDER

Although women have made significant strides in the U.S. business world, there are still many parts of the world where women are not welcome in business. In some countries, women are in support functions or simply "window dressing" for the firm. Women are considered as equals at the negotiation table in the United States, Israel, Great Britain, France, Switzerland, and India but are beginning to gain equality in other parts of the world.

A key challenge for Anglo businesswomen can be Latin America's very patriarchal society. Yet, in a survey conducted by Wederspahn's firm, "We found that U.S. American women in management and executive roles in foreign countries can do just as well as U.S. American men. Their biggest problem was convincing their companies to give them the assignments." (Staa, 1988, p. 8).

Intercultural Negotiation Guidelines

Effective negotiators will generally be successful in their negotiation attempts, and their ideas will be feasible to implement. Skilled negotiators consider a number of alternatives, are not as concerned about the sequence of the items to be negotiated, emphasize areas of agreement, and consider the long-term consequences of their agreements.

Kozicki (1998) presents a four-stage negotiation model—investigative, presentation, bargaining, and agreement. The investigative stage includes preparation or knowledge gathering about the other side and their goals. The presentation stage is a challenge because of cultural, perceptual, environmental, and power differences. The bargaining stage style depends on cultural differences and the ability to stay disciplined and controlled. The agreement stage is the point at which the negotiators finalize the deal and set the stage for a continued relationship. Often people think of negotiations only at the bargaining stage, but negotiations are much more than bargaining.

Copeland and Griggs (1985) have developed 20 rules for intercultural negotiation.* The rules are a starting point for negotiators. Other points will probably be added with experience.

BEFORE THE NEGOTIATION

Rule 1: Determine that the negotiation is feasible.
Rule 2: Define the objectives to be gained from the negotiation.
Rule 3: Research your facts such as culture-specific information and business style.
Rule 4: Decide on your strategy.

---

*From *Going International* by Lennie Copeland and Lewis Griggs. Copyright © 1985 by Lennie Copeland and Lewis Griggs. Reprinted by permission of Random House, Inc.

Rule 5: Send the proper team including your own interpreter; if consultants are proper, include them. Do not change negotiators.

Rule 6: Allow plenty of time. Do not, however, tell the other side your timetable.

BEGINNING THE NEGOTIATION

Rule 7: Make sure the environment is correct; be familiar with the agenda, physical arrangements, and the area where the negotiations will take place.

HARD BARGAINING

Rule 8: Control the information you give your opponents.

Rule 9: Watch your use of idioms, slang, and other verbal and nonverbal communication.

Rule 10: Put your thought processes on the same mindset as your opponents. Remember that they are not U.S. Americans and that your persuasion techniques need to be flexible.

Rule 11: Adjust to the way of life in the host culture. Remember the well-known adage, "While in Rome, do as the Romans do."

Rule 12. Talk informally away from the pressure.

Rule 13: Remember to save face for everyone.

Rule 14: Avoid a deadlock; neither side wins and both sides lose.

Rule 15: Do not agree to a bad deal; be prepared to walk away.

Rule 16: Make sure the agreement is signed before you leave.

Rule 17: Be sure both parties understand the meaning of what they signed.

Rule 18: Be flexible in your view of the definition of a contract.

BEYOND THE CONTRACT

Rule 19: Discuss differences and come to agreements rather than legal settlements.

Rule 20: Maintain a good relationship with the other side.

By using these guidelines, planning properly, treating people individually rather than stereotyping them, and learning from your mistakes, you will have made a good start to becoming a successful intercultural negotiator.

U.S. Americans, in particular, need to be aware of their shortcomings which are well known to many of their opponents. To people of many cultures, people in the United States always seem to be in a hurry. It is generally known that U.S. negotiators are often in a rush and may not be as completely prepared as the other side.

A young U.S. businessman related a story about negotiating a joint-venture with a Japanese company. As they negotiated, it was very apparent the Japanese company knew everything about the U.S. company—who its customers were, production capacity, sales history, financial status—and the U.S. firm only had a little data on the Japanese firm. The Japanese had expected the U.S. firm to be better prepared for their visit and took their business elsewhere.

During negotiation orientations, U.S. Americans need to learn to take advantage of the opportunity to learn more about the personalities of their opponents. U.S. Americans tend to rush through this stage or fail to note its importance. The orientation allows each side to gain valuable information about the opponents.

Due to the self-imposed time constraints of U.S. Americans, concessions are often made prematurely. Many times the size of the concession is larger than would have been necessary had more time been taken. If a concession is made too soon or if a large concession is made, the opponent is not as likely to see the concession as much of a gain. The Russians and the Chinese are very good at making such concessions work for them.

People of the United States also look at negotiations from a legal point of view. Most cultures are not as concerned with the legal view but are concerned with having a good agreement, a shared perception, and a trust of the other side (Moran & Stripp, 1991).

Mistakes made most often in intercultural negotiations include the following (Cellich, 1997):

1. Making a negative initial impression.
2. Failing to listen and talking too much.
3. Assuming understanding by the other culture.
4. Failing to ask important questions.
5. Showing discomfort with silence.
6. Using unfamiliar and slang words.
7. Interrupting the speaker.
8. Failing to read the nonverbal cues.
9. Failing to note key points.
10. Making statements that are irritating or contradictory.
11. Failing to prepare a list of questions for discussion.
12. Being easily distracted.
13. Failing to start with conditional offers.
14. Failing to summarize and restate to ensure understanding.
15. Hearing only what you want to hear.
16. Failing to use first-class supporting materials.

Points as identified by Axtell (1991) that need to be considered in distributor agreements include the following:

1. Effective dates of the agreement
2. Options at the end of the agreement
3. Place of jurisdiction
4. Terms of termination before agreement ends
5. Arbitration
6. Geographical boundaries of agreement
7. Degree of exclusivity
8. Description of products being distributed
9. Agreed upon sales quotas
10. Responsibility for import duty, freight, and insurance
11. Responsibility for warehousing, inventory control, and accounting

12. Information that must be reported to the sourcing company
13. Currency to be used for payment
14. Terms of payment
15. Provisions for secrecy
16. Competitive products that can or cannot be carried
17. Responsibility for warranty and repairs
18: Responsibility for advertising, merchandising, and public relations
19. Protection of patents and trademarks
20. Responsibility for drop-shipping
21. Provisions for payment of commissions and bonuses
22. Responsibility for taxes
23. Responsibility for indemnification
24. Responsibility for translation
25. Consideration of legal assignment, waivers, force majeure, notices, severability, Foreign Corrupt Practices Act
26. Responsibility for setting prices
27. Responsibility for payment of drop-shipments

Many of these points can be handled ahead of negotiations and would be controlled by lawyers during the negotiations between U.S. firms. However, when you are dealing interculturally and multinationally, these points need to be addressed so that everyone understands both the letter and intent of the contract.

When there are barriers that develop during the negotiations, the negotiators will need to be creative if the negotiations are important to their company. The negotiators will have to sift through the information to look for the conflict, look at the goals that underlie the demands, seek ways to reconcile the two sides, and if agreement is not reached, decide whether to pursue by changing the goals (Pruitt, 1998).

Trade Agreements

Trade agreements are the laws under which U.S. business must function when exporting. All exports are controlled by the U.S. government. General and validated are the two types of trade agreement licenses. Because the general license is never actually issued, many firms do not realize they are operating under such a license. The validated license is very specific, and the Department of Commerce will assist you with the regulations that apply. The validated license allows a specific exporter to export specific products to specific places. To learn more about validated licenses, obtain a copy of *Export Administration Regulations* from the Department of Commerce.

Other books from the Department of Commerce that will prove useful to the overseas negotiator include: *Basic Guide to Exporting, Exporters' Guide to Federal Resources for Small Business, Government Periodicals and Subscription Services,* and a nongovernment magazine titled *Export Today* (Write to: P.O. Box 28189, Washington, DC 20038).

Free trade zones, (FTZ) are zones of international commerce where foreign or domestic merchandise may enter without formal customs entry or custom duties. The

North American Free Trade Agreement (NAFTA) is an expansion of the FTZ concept as is the European Economic Community (EEC).

The NAFTA agreement between the United States, Canada, and Mexico, was ratified in 1993 (See Figure 11.4) and took effect January 1, 1994. In 2008, all import and export taxes on qualified goods between the three countries will be revoked and all qualified materials and service will flow freely among the three countries. NAFTA deals with trade in goods, technical barriers to trade, government procurement, investment, services and related matters, intellectual property, and administrative and institutional provisions. The objectives of the NAFTA are to:

1. eliminate barriers to trade and facilitate cross-border movement of goods and services.
2. promote fair competition.
3. increase investment opportunities.
4. provide adequate and effective protection for intellectual property.
5. develop effective procedures to handle disputes.
6. expand cooperation and increase benefits to the three countries (NAFTA, 1992).

Many different products are covered by NAFTA, and tariff implementation varies from 1993 to 2006. Other regional trade associations include one in each of the following regions: Central America, southeast Asia, and Latin America.

The **General Agreement of Tariffs and Trade** (GATT) is a multinational trade agreement of which the United States is a member. The problem with this agreement is that all nations currently doing business with the United States are not members. For example, China and Taiwan account for 24.3 percent of the clothing and textiles imported into the United States, yet they are not members of GATT. GATT provisions are continually being negotiated or renegotiated. Many stalemates have occurred as countries vie to protect specific industries or commodities. GATT deals with intellectual

FIGURE 11.4 Before and After NAFTA

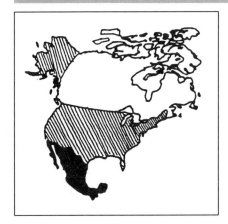

property, services, national treatment for services (members must treat other nations' members equal to or better than service suppliers in their own nation), market access for services, foreign investment, antidumping, subsidies, textiles, agriculture, market access, dispute settlement, and telecommunications. Small modifications to a product can change tariff classification.

The **European Economic Community** is a FTZ currently involving 15 countries: Austria, Belgium, Denmark, Finland, France, Germany, Greece, Ireland, Italy, Luxembourg, The Netherlands, Portugal, Spain, Sweden, and the United Kingdom. The EEC is still working out problems due, in part, to the breakdown of the communist block countries, but the popularity of the EEC is expected to grow in the future. Agenda 2000 of the EEC is programmed to strengthen growth, competitiveness and employment extending beyond the community itself to the Ukraine, Belarus, Moldova, Hungary, Poland, Estonia, the Czech Republic, and Slovenia. The EEC is expecting the first accessions as early as 2001 but definitely by 2003. Their overall plan is to include as many countries as possible.

As of 1987, the number of active trade agreements between the United States and other countries for specific products was 512. The trade agreements are indexed in the *UST Cumulative Index* which is a cumulative index to the U.S. slip treaties (loose paper treaties before binding) and agreements.

The U.S. **antiboycott regulation** prohibits U.S. firms or their employees from refusing to do business with friendly nations or in any way responding to a boycott. If a company is approached to boycott a country, the company is required by law to notify the Department of Commerce or be subject to large fines.

Terms

- Antiboycott regulation
- Authority
- Compromise agreement
- European Economic Community (EEC)
- Free trade zones (FTZ)
- General Agreement of Tariffs and Trade (GATT)
- Integrative agreement
- Mediation
- Negotiation strategies
- North America Free Trade Agreement (NAFTA)
- Personal constructs
- Power
- Tactics
- Trade agreements

EXERCISE 11.1

Your negotiating team has just finished telling the Japanese negotiating team about the technological lead your company has on the competition and what the new technology will cost the Japanese. In response to the proposal, the Japanese say "yes" and become silent. You should:

a. Take this to mean agreement and acceptance of these additional costs by the Japanese.

b. Take this as a negative response to your proposal.

c. Interpret this as neither positive nor negative.

```
                        EXERCISE 11.2
```

Instructions: Circle T for true and F for false.
1. T F Protocol changes when negotiating with another culture.
2. T F U.S. Americans tend to make more adjustments in their negotiation strategies than their opponents.
3. T F Group-oriented negotiations are generally positive for both sides.
4. T F Some cultures adjust more easily to negotiation differences.
5. T F The room environment including the physical arrangement, distance between people and teams, and the formality of the room is important to negotiations.
6. T F If the United States were to send only one person to negotiate with the Japanese, they would assume the U.S. company was serious.
7. T F Mediation may be the best way to find out what the negotiation barriers may be.
8. T F A woman can negotiate as well in Japan, Saudi Arabia, and France as she can in the United States.
9. T F During negotiations, it is a good idea to have informal talks away from the negotiation site.
10. T F Trade agreements are laws that affect business functioning within the United States.

Questions and Cases for Discussion

1. Describe your strategy for negotiating with people whose culture believes that to win is everything. How would your strategy change if you believe that if you trust people they will take advantage of you?
2. Discuss differences in negotiating with people who are group oriented versus those who are individual oriented. Give examples of cultures that are group oriented and those that are individual oriented.
3. Explain how media affect intercultural communication. Give examples of media-induced stereotypes.
4. Explain what is meant by personal constructs and how they affect the negotiation process.
5. How can misperceptions and cultural tactics negatively affect the negotiation process?
6. Discuss how courtesy is an important element in negotiation. How do perceptions of courtesy differ in various cultures?
7. What role does mediation play in the negotiation process?
8. Explain how gender can have an impact on successful negotiation. Identify cultures in which women are treated as equals at the negotiation table and cultures in which they are not.
9. Identify guidelines to effective negotiation.
10. Describe your strategy for negotiating with people whose culture believes no one should lose face, negotiation is an ongoing process, and consensus is the only way to reach an agreement.

11. Describe your strategy for negotiating with people whose culture believes that being very emotional in a negotiating setting is good, that it is not important to know facts or details, and that status is important.
12. How can the negotiation situation and environment affect the participants in the negotiation if it is held in the home country, the opponent's country, or a neutral country?
13. Identify three personal constructs you hold that would differentiate you from most of your country's people, and explain how these may confuse a negotiator who has a stereotype in his or her mind about your country's culture.
14. Would it be easier for a U.S. American to negotiate with a Canadian, a Mexican, or a Japanese? What support can you give for your answer?
15. Regional FTZs are becoming popular. What are the negative and positive points of such trade zones? How will they help or hinder global organizations?
16. What is NAFTA? What is GATT? Explain their relationship to intercultural negotiation.

CASE 1

Your instructor will separate the class into two negotiation teams. One team is from the United States; the other team is from Mexico. You are to respond from the cultural perspective of your country (either the United States or Mexico). The U.S. corporation desires to lower its cost of production and believes it can do so by manufacturing in Mexico. However, since the U.S. firm does not have experience manufacturing in Mexico, it wishes to negotiate with Agua Manufacturing in Mexico. The management of Agua Manufacturing is anxious to do the production for the U.S. corporation because it has excess capacity. The negotiations will take place in Mexico so that the U.S. representatives will be able to see and evaluate the facilities. Answer the following questions from the point of view of the Mexican negotiation team and the U.S. negotiation team. You will probably need to research the cultural background of Mexico and the United States. Remember that even if you were born and raised in the United States, it is sometimes difficult to see yourself as others see you.

a. Explain what the negotiation perspective, environment, and negotiation situation would be.
b. Where would you expect there to be common interests, conflicting interests, and compromises? What would be the criteria for achievement?
c. What would your negotiation strategy be? Your tactics?
d. How important is culture in this situation?

CASE 2

A U.S. American woman executive is sent to negotiate a contract with a corporation in Saudi Arabia. She dresses conservatively in a dark business suit and completes her makeup and hair as she would in the United States. She find the Arabs to be very aloof. She is asked when her boss will be arriving and is basically feeling ignored. What mistakes have been made? What can be done to correct such a situation?

CASE 3

Your company has chosen to use an export management company that will handle all the sales and financial transactions for your products overseas. In what way could this be an advantage, and how could it be a disadvantage? Does the size of the firm matter?

CASE 4

A group of high-powered businessmen from New York arrives in Mexico City to give a presentation. They have timed, detailed agendas; a long contract; and specific plans for a joint venture. They distribute the materials, say they are pressed for time, and need to complete the meeting so they can catch their plane. The Mexicans sat very quietly during the presentation. After the presentation, the New Yorkers on their way home congratulated themselves on their success. The Mexicans, however, felt they would not be able to work with these New Yorkers. Why do the two sides view the meeting differently?

Activities

1. Write a paragraph on the role that holidays and religion might play when negotiating in Saudi Arabia.
2. Consult a book on etiquette such as Letitia Baldrige's *New Complete Guide to Executive Manners* that contains a chapter on International Business Manners, and write a one-page summary on the role that gift giving plays when negotiating with the Japanese.
3. Consult a book on nonverbal communication such as Roger E. Axtell's *Gestures: The Do's and Taboos of Body Language Around the World* and prepare a one-page summary of the role that nonverbal communication plays when negotiating with persons in a South American country of your choice.
4. From recent issues of the *Wall Street Journal* or your local newspaper, find an article related to trade agreements between the United States and another country. Make a short oral report summarizing the article.
5. Be prepared to discuss the role that bargaining plays when negotiating with persons in different cultures.
6. Underline unacceptable behavior in the following scenario: The ABC Corporation's negotiating team has been invited to dine with the Mexican team at a Mexican restaurant. Some of the team members do not care for Mexican food. At the restaurant, Tom is uncomfortable and very hot and before sitting down takes his jacket off and loosens his tie. He now feels comfortable and starts talking with two of the Mexican team members. As Juan refers to him as Dr. Ross, Tom stops him and tells him to please call him Tom. Tom asks the Mexican team leader if there is some way in which they can compromise over an issue discussed during the day. The first course is served which is chicken soup with the chicken's feet in the dish. Tom winces as he sees the chicken's feet and pushes the bowl to the side.
7. The following is a self-assessment exercise you may take; the interpretation of the results follows.

Negotiation Skills Self-Assessment Exercise*

Please respond to this list of questions in terms of what you believe you do when interacting with others. Base your answers on your typical day-to-day activities. Be as frank as you can. For each statement, please enter on the score sheet the number corresponding to your choice of the five possible responses given below:

1. If you have never (or very rarely) observed yourself doing what is described in the statement.
2. If you have observed yourself doing what is described in the statement occasionally, but infrequently: that is, less often than most other people who are involved in similar situations.

3. If you have observed yourself doing what is described in the statement about an average amount: that is, about as often as most other people who are involved in similar situations.
4. If you have observed yourself doing what is described in the statement fairly frequently: that is, somewhat more often than most other people who are involved in similar situations.
5. If you have observed yourself doing what is described in the statement very frequently: that is, considerably more than most other people who are involved in similar situations.

Please answer each question.

1. I focus on the entire situation or problem.
2. I evaluate the facts according to a set of personal values.
3. I am relatively unemotional.
4. I think that the facts speak for themselves in most situations.
5. I enjoy working on new problems.
6. I focus on what is going on between people when interacting.
7. I tend to analyze things very carefully.
8. I am neutral when arguing.
9. I work in bursts of energy with slack periods in between.
10. I am sensitive to other people's needs and feelings.
11. I hurt people's feelings without knowing it.
12. I am good at keeping track of what has been said in a discussion.
13. I put two and two together quickly.
14. I look for common ground and compromise.
15. I use logic to solve problems.
16. I know most of the details when discussing an issue.
17. I follow my inspirations of the moment.
18. I take strong stands on matters of principle.
19. I am good at using a step-by-step approach.
20. I clarify information for others.
21. I get my facts a bit wrong.
22. I try to please people.
23. I am very systematic when making a point.
24. I relate facts to experience.
25. I am good at pinpointing essentials.
26. I enjoy harmony.
27. I weigh the pros and cons.
28. I am patient.
29. I project myself into the future.
30. I let my decisions be influenced by my personal likes and wishes.
31. I look for cause and effect.
32. I focus on what needs attention now.
33. When others become uncertain or discouraged, my enthusiasm carries them along.
34. I am sensitive to praise.
35. I make logical statements.

36. I rely on well-tested ways to solve problems.
37. I keep switching from one idea to another.
38. I offer bargains.
39. I have my ideas very well thought out.
40. I am precise in my arguments.
41. I bring others to see the exciting possibilities in a situation.
42. I appeal to emotions and feelings to reach a "fair" deal.
43. I present well-articulated arguments for the proposals I favor.
44. I do not trust inspiration.
45. I speak in a way which conveys a sense of excitement to others.
46. I communicate what I am willing to give in return for what I get.
47. I put forward proposals or suggestions which make sense even if they are unpopular.
48. I am pragmatic.
49. I am imaginative and creative in analyzing a situation.
50. I put together very well-reasoned arguments.
51. I actively solicit others' opinions and suggestions.
52. I document my statements.
53. My enthusiasm is contagious.
54. I build upon others' ideas.
55. My proposals command the attention of others.
56. I like to use the inductive method (from facts to theories).
57. I can be emotional at times.
58. I use veiled or open threats to get others to comply.
59. When I disagree with someone, I skillfully point out the flaws in the other's arguments.
60. I am low-key in my reactions.
61. In trying to persuade others, I appeal to their need for sensation and novelty.
62. I make other people feel that they have something of value to contribute.
63. I put forth ideas which are incisive.
64. I face difficulties with realism.
65. I point out the positive potential in discouraging or difficult situations.
66. I show tolerance and understanding of others' feelings.
67. I use arguments relevant to the problem at hand.
68. I am perceived as a down-to-earth person.
69. I go beyond the facts.
70. I give people credit for their ideas and contributions.
71. I like to organize and plan.
72. I am skillful at bringing up pertinent facts.
73. I have a charismatic tone.
74. When disputes arise, I search for the areas of agreement.
75. I am consistent in my reactions.
76. I quickly notice what needs attention.
77. I withdraw when the excitement is over.
78. I appeal for harmony and cooperation.
79. I am cool when negotiating.
80. I work all the way through to reach a conclusion.

Score Sheet

Enter the score you assigned each question (1, 2, 3, 4, or 5) in the space provided. (Note: The item numbers progress across the page from left to right.) When you have recorded all your scores, add them up vertically to attain four totals. Insert a "3" in any numbered space left blank

1. _____	2. _____	3. _____	4. _____
5. _____	6. _____	7. _____	8. _____
9. _____	10. _____	11. _____	12. _____
13. _____	14. _____	15. _____	16. _____
17. _____	18. _____	19. _____	20. _____
21 _____	22. _____	23. _____	24. _____
25. _____	26. _____	27. _____	28. _____
29. _____	30. _____	31. _____	32. _____
33. _____	34. _____	35. _____	36. _____
37. _____	38. _____	39. _____	40. _____
41. _____	42. _____	43. _____	44. _____
45. _____	46. _____	47. _____	48. _____
49. _____	50. _____	51. _____	52. _____
53. _____	54. _____	55. _____	56. _____
57. _____	58. _____	59. _____	60. _____
61. _____	62. _____	63. _____	64. _____
65. _____	66. _____	67. _____	68. _____
69. _____	70. _____	71. _____	72. _____
73. _____	74. _____	75. _____	76. _____
77. _____	78. _____	79. _____	80. _____
IN: _____	**NR:** _____	**AN:** _____	**FA:** _____

Negotiation Style Profile

Enter your four scores on the following bar chart. Construct your profile by connecting the four data points.

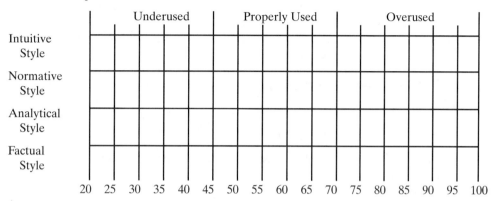

INTUITIVE

Basic Assumption: "Imagination can solve any problem."
Behavior: Making warm and enthusiastic statements, focusing on the entire situation or problem, pinpointing essentials, making projections, being imaginative and creative in analyzing the situation, switching from one subject to another, going beyond the facts, coming up with new ideas all the time, pushing and withdrawing from time to time, putting two and two together quickly, getting the facts a bit wrong sometimes, and being deductive.
Key Words: Principles, essential, tomorrow, creative, idea.

NORMATIVE

Basic Assumption: "Negotiating is bargaining."
Behavior: Judging, assessing, and evaluating the facts according to a set of personal values, approving and disapproving, agreeing and disagreeing, using loaded words, offering bargains, proposing rewards, incentives, appealing to feelings and emotions to reach a "fair" deal, demanding, requiring, threatening, involving power, using status, authority, correlating, looking for compromise, making effective statements, focusing on people and their reactions, judging, attention to communication, and group processes.
Key Words: Wrong, right, good, bad, like.

ANALYTICAL

Basic Assumption: "Logic leads to the right conclusions."
Behavior: Forming reasons, drawing conclusions, and applying them to the case in negotiation, arguing in favor or against one's own or others' position, directing, breaking down, dividing, analyzing each situation for cause and effect, identifying relationships of the parts, putting things into logical order, organizing, weighing the pros and cons thoroughly, making identical statements, and using linear reckoning.
Key Words: Because, then, consequently, therefore, in order to.

FACTUAL

Basic Assumption: "The facts speak for themselves."
Behavior: Pointing out facts in a neutral way, keeping track of what has been said, reminding people of their statements, knowing most of the details of the discussed issue and sharing them with others, clarifying, relating facts to experience, being low-key in their own reactions, looking for proof, and documenting their own statements.
Key Words: Meaning, define, explain, clarify, facts.

Guidelines for Negotiating with People Having Different Styles

1. Negotiating with someone with a factual style—
   Be precise in presenting your facts.
   Refer to the past (what has already been tried out, what has worked, what has been shown from past experiences).
   Be indicative (go from the facts to the principles).
   Know your dossier (including the details).
   Document what you say.
2. Negotiating with someone with an intuitive style—
   Focus on the situation as a whole.
   Project yourself into the future (look for opportunities).
   Tap the imagination and creativity of your partner.
   Be quick in reacting (jump from one idea to another).
   Build upon the reaction of the other person.
3. Negotiationg with someone with an analytical style—
   Use logic when arguing.
   Look for causes and effects.
   Analyze the relationships between the various elements of the situation or problem at stake.
   Be patient.
   Analyze various options with their respective pros and cons.
4. Negotiating with someone with a normative style—
   Establish a sound relationship right at the outset of the negotiation.
   Show your interest in what the other person is saying.
   Identify his or her values and adjust to them accordingly.
   Be ready to compromise.
   Appeal to your partner's feelings.

*Adapted by Pierre Casse from Interactive Style Questionnaire Situation Management Systems, Inc., in *Training for the Cross-Cultural Mind,* Sietar, Washington, DC, 1979.

References

Axtell, R. E. (1991). *The do's and taboos of international trade.* New York: John Wiley & Sons, Inc.

Casse, P., & Deol, S. (1991). *Managing intercultural negotiations.* Washington, DC: Sietar.

Cellich, C. (1997). Communication skills for negotiations. *International Trade Forum, 3,* 22–28.

Copeland, L., & Griggs, L. (1985). *Going international.* New York: Random House.

Engholm, C. (1991). When business East meets business West. New York: John Wiley & Sons, Inc.

Fisher, G. (1997). *Mindsets: The role of culture and perception in international relations.* Yarmouth, ME: Intercultural Press.

Foster, D. A. (1992). *Bargaining across borders.* New York: McGraw-Hill, Inc.

Francis, J. N. P. (1991). When in Rome? The effects of cultural adaptation on intercultural business negotiations. *Journal of International Business Studies, 22* (3), 403–429.

Funakawa, A. (1997). *Transcultural management.* San Francisco, CA: Jossey-Bass Publishers.

Herbig, P. A., & Kramer, H. E. (1991). Cross-cultural negotiations: Success through understanding. *Management Decision, 29* (8), 19–31.

Hofstede. G. (1991). *Cultures and organizations.* New York: McGraw-Hill.

Kozicki, S. (1998). *Creative negotiating.* Holbrook, MA: Adams Media Corporation.

Lewicki, R. J., & Litterer, J. A. (1985). *Negotiation.* Homewood, IL: Irwin.

McCormack, M. (1984). *What they don't teach you at Harvard Business School.* New York: Bantam Books.

Moran, R. T., & Stripp, W. G. (1991). *Dynamics of successful international business negotiations.* Houston: Gulf Publishing.

Morrison, T., Conaway, W. A., & Borden, G. A. (1994). *Kiss, bow, or shake hands.* Holbrook, MA: Adams Media Corporation.

North American Free Trade Agreement Between the Government of the United States of America, The Government of Canada and The Government of the United Mexican States. (1992). Washington, DC: U.S. Government Printing Office.

Prosser, M. H. (1985). *The cultural dialogue.* Washington, DC: Sietar.

Pruitt, D. G. (1998). Achieving integrative agreements in negotiation. In Weaver, G. R. *Culture, communication, and conflict.* Upper Saddle River, NJ: Simon & Schuster.

Staa, D. (1998). No need for inter-American culture clash. *Management Review, 87* (1), 8.

Weaver, G. R. (1998). *Culture, communication, and conflict.* Needham Heights, MA: Simon & Schuster.

 C H A P T E R

Laws Affecting International Business and Travel

Objectives
Upon completion of this chapter you will:

■ understand the difference between home country laws and host country laws.

■ understand why a contract has different meanings in different countries.

■ understand how ethics and laws relate.

■ know why international laws are being promulgated.

■ understand the importance of the nonwritten laws.

■ know how international travel is affected by the law.

Legal cultural research is the study of societies and how the societies develop their legal culture. The elements of legal culture include styles of legislation; court proceedings; adjudication (hearing and deciding a case); and the status, action, and acceptance by the members of the legal profession and of public officials (Blankenburg, 1988). Culture is relevant to the development of law. The current international trade agreements stress flexibility and a willingness to change, thereby showing an interest by participating countries in looking at the law from more than one country's point of view.

Understanding the law of a country allows insight into the moral and philosophical mindsets of the citizens. Laws are what a society already believes and values (Fisher, 1997). When laws or treaties are made or changed, those changes do not always represent all of the people and can take time to be accepted.

With over 170 nations, the world has numerous laws that affect international business. Laws are used to regulate the flow of products entering and leaving a country.

When a firm is engaged in international business, what the company representatives can legally do is controlled by both their nation and by the foreign nation with which they conduct business. Each nation can legally do as it wishes within its own boundaries without interference from other nations. This right is legally protected by the **Act of State Doctrine.**

"This market is exploding," said James Zimmerman of the San Diego law firm of Chapin, Fleming & Winet. "I spend most of my time putting together deals between U.S. firms and foreign firms. I think this is by far the fastest growing area of the law" (Bowler, 1997, p. 1A).

Home Country and Host Country Laws

Business communication between persons of different national origins is governed by the laws of both countries. Because of the large number of countries and laws, a knowledge of not only your home country's laws but the host country's laws is important. **Home country laws** are the laws, treaties, or acts that govern business within your country of citizenship and those governing your business with other countries. **Host country laws** are the laws, treaties, or acts that govern business within the foreign country in which you are conducting business.

Imports and exports are regulated in some manner by most countries. A lawyer who is knowledgeable of the laws of the foreign country with whom you are conducting business is as important as having a lawyer who is knowledgeable of your home country's laws and agreements with the foreign country.

There are three important legal requirements of U.S. citizens' actions during negotiations: antidiversion, antiboycott, and antitrust requirements (Axtell, 1991).

The **antidiversion requirement** states that the bill of lading and the invoice must clearly display that the carrier cannot divert the shipment to a country the U.S. government considers restricted.

Antitrust laws are primarily designed to ensure fair competition and low prices to U.S. consumers; they affect exporters in such areas as mergers or acquisitions of foreign firms, raw material procurement agreements and concessions, knowledge licenses (i.e., intellectual information), distribution channels, joint ventures for research, manufacturing, and construction (Murray & Evans, 1992).

WRITTEN INFORMATION LAWS

Written information is also controlled by most nations. The United States has several laws that govern the information that can be sent to specific countries.

The **Export Administration Act of 1985** requires federal licensing of technical information in business correspondence.

The **Arms Export Control Act of 1968** and the **Trading with the Enemy Act of 1917** prohibit the transfer of information on military material or defense-related materials.

The **International Emergency Economic Powers Act of 1977** governs information that is research oriented from being communicated to foreigners.

TECHNOLOGY LAWS

The area of technology law is currently being discussed in many countries. Mexico, Brazil, Venezuela, and the United States already have laws governing how technological knowledge may be transferred. The legal area of intellectual property licensing was helped considerably by the **Berne Convention Implementation Act of 1988** that recognizes the copyrights of all the signatory nations to the act. Trademarks are protected by the countries that are signatories of the **Madrid Convention;** however, the United States is not a signatory (Presner, 1991).

EMPLOYMENT LAWS

Employment regulations differ between nations. Most nations have legislation governing wages, hours, union-management relations, residence visas, and work permits. Restricting foreigners to the number and types of jobs they may hold is common; however, a great deal of variation exists between nations. Some nations require a certain ratio of nationals to foreigners; other nations require proof that no one in their nation can do the job; other nations allow foreigners to stay for a limited time period. Questions that can be legally asked of a potential employee also vary greatly by country. For example, in the United States, employers can ask if someone would be willing to work overtime; in other countries this is not the case.

MAQUILADORA LAW

Mexico has a maquiladora program which is governed by the **Presidential Decree for the Development and Operation of the Maquiladora Industry Program, 1983.** The program allows the duty-free import of equipment, machinery, and materials to assemble parts of products that are then returned to the home country. The U.S. Tariff Code allows the final product to be brought into the United States with only the final value added to the goods being taxed. Pacific Rim and European countries are also taking advantage of the maquiladora program. An important consideration in this program is the difference in form of law. The United States practices common law (except in Louisiana), but Mexico practices civil law. The difference is that the civil law rather than **precedent** (interpretations of the law in previous court decisions) is considered during litigation (Jarvis, 1990).

International Law

The **International Court of Justice,** also known as the **World Court,** is a specialized body of the United Nations that provides a means to settle international disagreements between countries rather than corporations. The **International Law Commission** is also a body of the United Nations; it produces laws on international commerce such as the Law of the Sea (rights of states or countries in rules of navigation).

The EEC, NAFTA, and GATT are three cross-national agreements that are trying to equalize the treatment of multinational organizations. A movement by institutions concerned with international business has encouraged the development of agreements and laws that are uniformly accepted in world trade. The institutions include: **International Chamber of Commerce, International Commercial Terms (Incoterms),** and the **Vienna Agreement** (Presner, 1991).

Unified laws have not produced unified judicial practices. Judges currently lack training or experience in international trade. Even in the signatory countries of an agreement, the judicial practices are not equal concerning the interpretation of the agreement. Currently multinational corporations must be flexible and willing to learn international contracts. Home country laws frequently have nothing in common with host country laws. Since different cultures may have divergent value conceptions, it is not surprising that they would also have divergent legal conceptions. Current changes facing corporate lawyers are central and eastern European nations, the Russian states, and EEC procedural changes as countries either embrace free market economics or join to form new economic units with new rules.

Quasi-international laws are rules for the relationship between legal entities and states that do not have national status such as private corporations (Presner, 1991). One such quasi-international law is **sanctions.** Sanctions prohibit U.S. companies from doing business in targeted countries. When the U.S. government does not approve of a country's politics, they attempt to reform the country by implementing sanctions. A problem that U.S. firms cannot foresee is which country the U.S. government will target next since any country that offends religious groups or environmentalists, violates human rights, or engages in political oppression may be subject to sanctions (Roberts, 1997).

Unocal, a U.S. oil company, was involved with the Burmese to develop the offshore natural gas that was to be sold to markets in Thailand. The U.S. government sanctioned Burma and Unocal could not expand its business. Texaco, who was also in the area, sold its interests to a British company. The sanctions hurt U.S. corporations and benefited other foreign competitors (Roberts, 1997).

Negotiations in international business situations play an important part in determining which laws will be followed. These negotiated contracts will eventually help to define an international body of law. **Macaulay's thesis,** in fact, states that intercultural business cultures are developing that consider the long-term, mutually beneficial relationship more important than the contract lawyers so laboriously draft. Macaulay explains that business' lack of consideration of the law is due to the long-term relationships and interdependencies that develop and their importance to the organizations involved. It is to the organizations' benefit to ignore, suppress, or compromise rather than litigate; few international contracts are litigated. Macaulay (1976) cites Luhmann's thematization process as applicable to his thesis. **Thematization** is the process by which a framework for mutual communication and satisfaction is reached; this process could be related to the law, economics, power, utilitarianism, or religion.

How the parties maintain their relationship over time is called the **governance structure** (Blegvad, 1990; Macaulay, 1976). There are four types of governance structures: (1) **market governance** which is contract based, (2) **trilateral governance** which adds an arbitrator, (3) **bilateral governance** which may not spell out details but has a strong recognition of a continuing economic relationship, and (4) **unified governance** in which no detail is negotiated in advance, maximum flexibility is provided, and only one party sets terms for both parties involved. Depending on the frequency of transactions, market replaceability, the firms' tolerances for uncertainty, and the relationship of the firms, one of these governance structures would cover their transactions. Consumer transactions fit the market governance structure. Trilateral governance fits transactions that involve idiosyncratic goods or services or a situation in which the establishment of the relationship is expensive. Bilateral governance is good for long-term relationships that involve uncertainty due to the mixture of goods or services that are to be included. Unified governance is appropriate for subsidiaries of a single organization (Blegvad, 1990).

The desire organizations have for long-term economic relationships that are privately governed are emerging as the preference over international laws and public governance. However, the time period that statistics have been kept is short, so this is an area that is still evolving. Modern business wants future-oriented solutions and cooperation rather than legal constraints. Time will tell if economic norms can acquire the status of laws or if laws will have to be written to guide private governance.

Contracts

In the United States, a **contract** is defined as an agreement between parties to do something that is oral, written, or implied through conduct. If a supplier ships goods to a customer that he or she believes the buyer needs and the buyer accepts the shipment, the buyer enters into a contract with the supplier. Purchase orders that are commonly used for the written form of a contract must contain a statement such as: Confirmation of contract entered into between the buyer and seller (and date of the oral contract). The word *contract* is important to the legal enforceability particularly in the United States (Murray, 1992).

In the United States, an oral contract is legally enforceable if the parties admit that the contract was made even if no written contract was made. Oral contracts are also enforceable if the contract is for custom-manufactured goods, and special materials have been purchased that are usable only for the custom order. An oral contract that has been partially fulfilled through shipment and goods have been accepted is also enforceable (Lewicki & Litterer, 1985).

In Japan, a contract can also be made verbally, in writing, or by conduct but is always considered open for renegotiation. Because Japanese corporate personnel are accustomed to working with a general trading company called a sogososha (which are very difficult to join and which look out for each other forever), when problems occur they are discussed and resolved without legal intervention.

Before the breakup of the Soviet Union, little need existed for contracts. Goods were allocated which meant the companies had to accept what was sent to them whether or not they needed the goods. With reforms, companies now have a right to refuse unneeded allocations and can modify or cancel contracts. When the Russian states moved to the theory of property rights, they recognized the eventual costs to the buyer and the consumer. By allowing the companies to plan and order what they needed, central planning and binding annual production plans were eliminated. The companies now operate very much as western companies do; they are responsible for their operational costs, income, expenses, and profit. Since the economic climate in the Russian states is still evolving, contract perception may change and should be taken into consideration when negotiating contracts in these states (Kroll, 1989).

Because of numerous differences that exist in various countries, having legal counsel to give advice on the proper way to negotiate contracts in individual countries is recommended. Reading a book on contract law for the particular country with which you will be conducting business would also suggest questions to ask your legal counsel. Unknown foreign laws and changes in foreign laws make international investing risky.

Panama Processes successfully negotiated a contract to protect its flow of dividends from a jointly owned Brazilian corporation in which Panama was the minority shareholder. After several years of compliance, Cities Service Co., the majority shareholder, decided to void the agreement and cause the jointly owned corporation to cease paying dividends. Panama filed a number of suits to protect its financial position only to discover that its contract could not be enforced due to the omission of a few normally insignificant points.

It is these few points, normally insignificant in a domestic situation but of pivotal importance in an international business arrangement. . . . Had Panama included even the least intrusive of these points in its original agreement, points to which Cities under the circumstances would have undoubtedly agreed, it could have enjoyed the fruits of its financial arrangements.

Basically the considerations that were omitted from the agreement between Panama and Cities were: (1) in the event that relations between the parties broke down, which court of law or other tribunal would referee their dispute, and (2) which set of rules or which country's laws would be used to determine the parties' respective rights and obligations? (McCubbins, 1994, p. 95)

Global Patents

Global patent concerns are important for companies involved in proprietary products or methods. Because it is impossible to file patents in all the nations in the world, companies tend to follow a strategy of filing for patents in key countries and regions of the world (Global, 1997). Currently, a corporation completes and files a patent application with the U.S. Patent Office. The initial date is significant because it begins the timetable for filing patents abroad. The limitation to file abroad is one year from the date on the U.S. application. When these patents are filed in other countries, the new patents claim priority to the date on the U.S. patent thus prevailing over others and competing with rights of other inventors. This priority is made possible due to the **Patent Cooperation Treaty.** Until the patents are processed abroad, companies can expect to expend money on prosecution and maintenance of patents here and abroad. To ensure a proper foundation for protecting inventions and preserving foreign filing options, attorneys must do a lot of homework. All international patent offices do not require the same information. A company can save a lot of time and money if its patent attorney knows what the other countries require and includes those items (such as metric measurements) in advance. After the patents are granted, they need to be reassessed to be sure they are still cost-effective options.

According to Minnesota patent attorney Philip Goldman of Fredrikson & Byron, P.A., global patent protection is important because patents are territorial in nature. "They only allow the patentee to prevent infringement that occurs within the country or region granting the patent. It is not unusual, therefore, for the owner of a process patent in one country to stand helplessly by as a competitor uses that process in another country (where the patentee has no protection), and imports the final product back into the first country to be sold" (Global, 1997, p. 23).

Treaties override all other domestic laws. The Constitution, Article VI, states, "all Treaties made or which shall be made, under the Authority of the United States shall be the supreme Law of the Land; and the Judges in every State shall be bound thereby, anything in the Constitution or Laws of any State to the contrary notwithstanding." Nations need to be cognizant of their sovereignty. They need to remember that all trade should be of mutual benefit and that treaties should be based on good science rather than on wishful thinking or bad politics (Bentacourt, 1997, p. 34).

Nonwritten Law

Often the interpretation of the law is very different between countries; for example, countries that communicate as high context would consider the situation as more important than the letter of the law. In a high-context culture, little emphasis would be given to the written word; the situation would determine whether to adhere to the law. The individual interpretation of the situation would be more important than external rules and regulations. Oral agreements would be considered binding, and written contracts would be considered flexible. Japan is an example of such a high-context culture. In a low-context culture, such as the United States, what is written is expected to be followed. Laws are binding and the situation is not considered. In the United States, laws determine how people respond to each other. In view of the difference in attitudes toward the law, it is not surprising that the United States and Japan have had their share of problems trying to understand each other in negotiations. While many agreements have been crystal clear to both sides, the enactment of the agreement generally gives rise to many problems.

Unwritten business laws are called **drawer regulations** in Brazil because they operate from unwritten operational codes rather than laws (Rachid, 1990).

China has written some joint venture law; however, the old ways are still controlling how the joint venture law is interpreted. Mexico's transfer of technology and foreign investment laws have been changeable; they were written in 1973 and changed in 1976, 1982, 1989, and 1991 and still have not been implemented (Rachid, 1990).

Sometimes the interpretation of the law can be a problem or solution depending on your position. An example of such a problem occurred when the EEC punished the United States for months of battling over trade matters. The EEC determined that U.S. meat inspection practices were not adequate, thereby halting U.S. sales of meat to the European community. Since Canada had said its meat inspection was equivalent to that of the United States, the EEC had to decide whether they should also cut off Canadian imports. The Canadian inspector offered them a way to distance Canada from the

FIGURE 12.1 Drawer Regulations

United States by saying *equivalent* meant *equal to* or *better than* thus allowing Canadian meat imports to continue.

Ethics and the Law

Since people throughout the world are culturally diverse, it is not surprising that what is considered ethical behavior in one culture may be seen as unethical in another culture. Missner (1980) cautions that when you are negotiating, it is important to understand the differences between ethics-based judgments and judgments based on concern and practicality.

Ethics judgments are based on some standard of moral behavior as to right and wrong. Practicality judgments are based on what is easiest, best, or most effective to achieve an objective. Lewicki and Litterer (1985) state that judgments are subjective, and the distinction between ethical or unethical is measured in degrees rather than absolutes; reasonable people disagree as to where the line is drawn between ethical and unethical acts.

In the business world, four motivations for unethical conduct exist: profit, competition, justice, and advertising (Missner, 1980). The three dimensions of negotiation ethics are means/ends, relativism/absolutism, and truth telling. The means/ends question is measured by utility. The moral value and worth of an act is judged by what is produced—the utility. The players in the negotiation game and the environment in which the negotiators are operating help to determine whether the negotiators can justify being exploitive, manipulative, or devious. The relative/absolute question considers two extremes: either everything is relative or everything is without deviation from the rule. Although most people are somewhere between the extremes of relative and absolute, they debate which point between the two extremes is correct. Of course, it is a matter of judgment as to what particular point on the continuum is correct.

Truth telling considers whether concealing information, conscious misstatements, exaggeration, or bluffing when you are in negotiations is dishonest. Judging how honest and candid one can be in negotiations and not be vulnerable is difficult.

Intercultural negotiations have the added problem of different business methods, different cultures, and different negotiation protocols. While the decision to be "unethical" may be made to increase power and control, whether the decision was made quickly, casually, after careful evaluation, or based on cultural values is important (Lewicki & Litterer, 1985).

The U.S. government has taken a strong stance concerning bribery and the accounting practices used in international business. The **Foreign Corrupt Practices Act of 1977** requires U.S. companies to account for and report international transactions accurately and prohibits bribes that are used to gain a business advantage. Bribes can include gifts and entertainment. A gift is a bribe when your firm is receiving something in return for the gift. A U.S. firm giving a Mexican utility official money "under the table" for the Mexican's personal use to speed up the installation of an electric line to a new construction site would be an example of bribery. This regulation often puts U.S. firms at a disadvantage when trying to compete with companies from cultures who have no problem with the practice of "gift giving," a practice which U.S. persons would call a bribe. Many U.S. companies take a hard line against bribery. Bill Pomeranz, a long-time employee with Hughes Space and Communications Company, indicated that over the years Hughes had lost only two contracts by failing to pay bribes. However, Pomeranz pointed out that they are the market leader and therefore are able to offer more than any other firm including those who would make payoffs. When asked why his company held the line on bribery, he said simply, "It's illegal. Whether it's the way somebody would want to do business or not, it's illegal—and the company has a rigid code of ethics that prohibits unlawful conduct." Many Fortune 500 companies share this company's view (Engholm & Rowland, 1996).

Because of the necessity of paying a commission in some countries to expedite business transactions, professional go-betweens are sometimes hired to assure that the proper persons are tipped to avoid delays in approvals and delivery. People of the United States cannot, of course, be involved in paying these commissions; this responsibility would be left with the local joint-venture partner or distributor (Engholm, 1991). The U.S. Department of Commerce's 1985 booklet, *Foreign Business Practices*, lists foreign laws by country and offers the following guidance on distributor agreements:

- What is legal in the United States may not be legal in another country.
- Translations should be checked for concise meanings.
- If possible, state the jurisdiction that will handle disagreements.
- Settle disagreements through an arbitrator; the arbitration body should be identified.
- Provisions of foreign laws that are to be waived should be stated.
- Benefits to both parties should be stated.
- The agreement should be in writing.

Another source of information to help distributors is *Export Administration Regulations*. A subscription is available by writing to the Superintendent of Documents, U.S. Government Printing Office, Washington, DC 20402.

The **Doctrine of Sovereign Compliance** is an international legal principle that can be used as a defense in your home country for work carried out in a host country when the two countries' legal positions are different. For example, a U.S. manager working in Canada may have to trade with Cuba; however, it is illegal to do so in the United States. If prosecuted, the manager could use the Doctrine of Sovereign Compliance as a defense. The defense is necessary because U.S. citizens or corporations are held accountable to U.S. law beyond the boundaries of the country through the Trading with the Enemy Act. The application of the act beyond the U.S. border is called **extraterritoriality.**

The **Export Trading Company Act of 1982** allows companies that normally would not be allowed to do joint ventures to develop trading companies similar to those in

Britain, The Netherlands, and Japan (Axtell, 1991). As an example of this act, General Motors, Ford, and Chrysler make parts with European and Japanese car manufacturers to jointly produce and sell cars.

How different countries view legal and ethical practices is best explained by an example used by Axtell (1991):

> A Latin businessman, commenting on the U.S. attitude toward morality in international business, once confronted me with this rather different perspective. Take the word "contraband," he said. Here in the United States, it is a very bad word. It suggests breaking the law by smuggling. However, in my country, the Spanish word is *contrabando.* It comes from the word contrabandido, which means literally, "against the bandits." When I was a child in the villages of my country, we were taught that the bandidos, the bandits, were the land and shop owners. I remember that even candy was illegally brought into our village and we were taught to favor that contraband candy because it was a way of fighting back against the bandidos. So, you see my culture was raised to view contraband as a good thing. That may help explain why there are differing values and differing perceptions of morality between our continents.

Intercultural business communication is affected by the laws of the countries in which companies do business and the growing body of international law. Because laws and rules develop from, and are a part of cultural beliefs, values, and assumptions, interpretation and discussion of legal issues can cause communication problems between intercultural business negotiators unless they are completely prepared.

International Travel and Law

Your passport is the most important document you can carry when traveling outside your native country. A **passport** is your proof of citizenship. To obtain a passport, you must apply in person with a copy of your birth certificate and current photo. As a precaution, make a copy of your passport so that if the original is lost or stolen, you can give the copy to the embassy to facilitate getting a replacement (Skabelund, 1991).

Citizenship is the state of being vested with certain rights and duties as a native or naturalized member of a state or country. Proof of citizenship may not be clear if you were born in another country, your parents are citizens of another country, or you are a naturalized citizen of the country that you consider your home country. If the country to which you are traveling considers you a citizen of their country (because it is the country of your birth or because your parents are citizens of the country), it may require you to do military service or pay income taxes (Skabelund, 1991).

A **visa** gives you the right to enter and stay in a country for a period of time for a specific purpose. If you are a tourist, most countries do not require a visa; however, for business purposes, a visa may be required. The country you are visiting issues the visa, and the visa may be obtained from the embassy or consulate of the country you wish to visit. A **consulate** is made up of individuals sent by the government to other countries to promote the commercial interests of their home country (Skabelund, 1991).

All countries have **customs** agents who enforce export and import laws of the country; they have the right to search and confiscate anything you may have with you. Be sure to get a list from your embassy of items that are illegal to bring back into your home country. The host country's embassy can provide a list of restricted items. When returning home, you will be asked to declare the value of items purchased that you are bringing home. Most countries have items for which they charge duties. **Duties** are an import tax. The host country's embassy can also give you immunization requirements and the verification needed for prescription drugs you may need to take. U.S. citizens should be aware that they cannot legally carry more than $10,000 out of the country without registering with U.S. customs officials before departing (Axtell, 1991).

To drive abroad, learn the type of license you may need and become familiar with the country's driving laws. If you obtain an international driver's license, it will help you learn international driving.

Past Rules, Present Problems

- The United States taxes foreign income of nonresident citizens; many countries exempt foreign business income.
- The IRS taxes corporate income at both corporate and stockholder levels; most countries integrate the two taxes.
- U.S. foreign tax credits are complicated; other countries have simplified systems.
- The United States treats foreign subsidiary loans to a domestic parent company as a dividend; other major industrialized nations do not.
- U.S. rules for allocating and apportioning expenses between domestic and foreign income conflict with other industrial countries.
- U.S. alternative minimum tax can cause a tax on foreign income already taxed abroad.
- U.S.-based multinational corporations (MNCs) cannot take advantage of host countries' tax incentives because they are not included in treaties with developing countries.
- If other nations defined qualified residents as narrowly as the United States, our United States-based MNCs would have trouble effectively competing in countries lacking tax treaties with the United States (Zelade, 1996, p. 6).

To be sure you do not break the law in other countries, the following tips can be beneficial (Axtell, 1990):

1. Because of political unrest in the world, register with the U.S. embassy or consulate when you arrive in a foreign country.
2. If you have any kind of trouble, turn to the embassy or consulate for legal, medical, or financial problems.
3. The U.S. consul can visit you in jail, give you a list of attorneys, notify family, and protest any mistreatment; however, the consul cannot get you released or provide for bonds or fines.
4. Remember that you are subject to the laws of the country you are visiting.
5. If you stay for a prolonged time period, you may need to register with the local authorities. You may be requested to leave your passport overnight or complete a data sheet.

6. Use authorized outlets for cashing checks and buying airline tickets; avoid the black market or street money changers that you will see in many countries.
7. Ask for permission before you photograph anything.
8. Notary publics in many countries have broader powers than those in the United States.
9. Common infractions of the law include trying to take historic artifacts or antiquities out of the country, customs violations, immigration violations, drunk and disorderly conduct, and business fraud.
10. If you need to drive, obtain an international driver's license. Travel agents can assist with this. Many countries require proof of insurance while driving.
11. Dealing in drugs is a serious offense in all countries. Penalties can be much more serious than in the United States and can include death.
12. Keep a list of credit card numbers and traveler's check numbers in a safe place in case they are lost or stolen.
13. Obtain a copy of *Know Before You Go* and *Customs Hints for Returning U.S. Residents* from the U.S. Customs Office, P. O. Box 7118, Washington, DC 20044. For foreign country customs information, write the Office of Passport Services, Department of State, Washington, DC 20514, for *Country Information Notices.*
14. Telephone numbers/addresses that may be beneficial include:
    The U.S. State Department, Washington, DC 202-635-5225 or 202-632-1512
    A copy of *Key Officers of Foreign Service Posts* available from the Superintendent of Documents, U.S. Government Printing Office, Washington, DC 20402
    Amnesty International, New York City, NY 212-807-8400
    International Legal Defense Counsel, 1420 Walnut Street, Suite 315, Philadelphia, PA 19102, 215-545-2428

Country-Specific Travel Tips

Before you travel to a foreign country, find out what documents are needed, what hotel accommodations and modes of transportation are available, what laws affect behavior (such as the legal drinking age), and other information to ensure personal safety and comfort so that your sojourn is a pleasant one. Books by Braganti and Devine (1992) and Devine and Braganti (1986, 1988) and Brigham Young University's *Culturgram* (1997) contain country-specific information that will make international travel easier. Because space does not permit an extensive examination of numerous countries, the following travel tips have been limited to the six countries with which the United States conducts a majority of its international trade.

CANADA

United States citizens need no passport when traveling to Canada from the United States but do need one when coming from another country. Although visas are not required for visits of up to 180 days, U.S. citizens need proof of citizenship such as a birth certificate or voter's registration card and identification containing a photograph.

Hotel accommodations in the large cities are comparable to those in the United States. Voltage connectors and plug adaptors are not needed for using small appliances.

Public transportation systems in Montréal and Québec City are very good. Montréal Metro system is one of the best subway systems in the world. The underground system includes miles of shopping malls; you can buy anything you want without going above ground. Since public transportation cannot accommodate the many isolated regions in the north, domestic air transportation is used to reach these areas. People who drive in Canada should remember to leave their radar detectors at home as they are illegal in that country and will be confiscated if detected.

Additional information about traveling in Canada can be obtained from:

Canadian Consulate General
1251 Avenue of the Americas
New York, NY 10020

Embassy of Canada
501 Pennsylvania Avenue, N.W.
Washington, DC 20001

GREAT BRITAIN

A valid passport is required for travel in Great Britain. U.S. citizens do not need a visa for visits lasting up to six months and vaccinations are not required.

If staying at a hotel, you may be asked if you would like early morning tea delivered to your room. Larger hotels may include a continental breakfast in the room price. Electrical converters and plug adaptors are needed to use small U.S. appliances in Great Britain.

Public transportation includes the underground (subway or tube) and taxis. To drive in Great Britain, you do not need an international driver's license but remember to drive on the left side of the road. In rural areas, gas stations may be scarce so fill your tank when you see a station.

The legal age for drinking in Great Britain is 18. The British police are known for being friendly and helpful; ask them for directions or assistance with travel-related problems (Braganti & Devine, 1992).

More information on traveling in Great Britain is available from:

British Tourist Authority
40 West 57th Street
New York, NY 10019

Embassy of the United Kingdom
3100 Massachusetts Avenue, N.W.
Washington, DC 20008

British Information Service
845 Third Avenue
New York, NY 10022

FRANCE

To travel in France, a valid passport is required, but U.S. citizens may travel in the country without a visa for up to three months. Vaccinations are not required.

Hotels in France do not always have a bath in the room nor are they always air conditioned. To use small appliances such as a hair dryer, you will need to have a voltage converter and plug adaptor.

Public transportation in France includes the Métro (subway), buses, streetcars, taxis, and the TGV (train à grande vitesse; a high-speed train connecting 36 European cities). Exercise care in choosing only an "official" taxi; unauthorized taxi drivers have no meters and charge whatever they wish. Driving a car in France does not require an international driver's license. Avoid honking the horn in cities since this is illegal; turning right on a red light is also not permitted.

The drinking age in France is 18. Women should exercise care when using the Métro at night since it is considered unsafe. Ask about other unsafe areas in France before exploring the locality (Braganti & Devine, 1992).

Additional information about traveling in France is available from:

French Government Tourist Office
610 Fifth Avenue
New York, NY 10010-2452

Embassy of France
4101 Reservoir Road
Washington, DC 20007-2185

GERMANY

A valid passport is required for travel in Germany; however, U.S. citizens do not need a visa to travel in the country for up to three months. Vaccinations are not required.

If you stay at a hotel, the price of the room generally includes a continental breakfast; heat may be an extra charge. When making your reservation, inquire about bathroom facilities; some rooms do not have a bath so you will use a communal facility. Electrical converters and plug adaptors are needed to use small appliances in hotels.

Public transportation includes buses, streetcars, subways, trains, and taxis. Tickets for mass transit are purchased in advance. Since the conductor often checks your ticket during the ride, have your ticket available for inspection. An international driver's license is required for driving in Germany. Except on the Autobahn (freeway), service stations in Germany are quite competitive, so shop around for the best prices on gasoline (Braganti & Devine, 1992).

Jaywalking is illegal in Germany. Biking, hiking, or hitchhiking along the Autobahn is illegal. Since the tapwater in towns along the Rhine contains dangerous chemicals, do not drink it. Always use bottled water instead.

More information on traveling in Germany is available from:

German National Tourist Office
747 Third Avenue
New York, NY 10017

Embassy of the Federal Republic of Germany
4645 Reservoir Road, N.W.
Washington, DC 20007-1998

JAPAN

Although no visa is needed for visits of less than 90 days, U.S. citizens need a valid passport when traveling to Japan. Vaccinations are not required.

Numerous western-style hotels are available in the large cities. They will probably have private baths but expect some differences in accommodations. Faucets and door handles, for example, operate in the opposite direction from what is considered the norm in the United States. Toilets are often for both genders and quite different from those people of the United States are accustomed to using. Small appliances usually work in Japanese electrical outlets.

Public transportation in Japan includes trains, subways, and buses. The "bullet train" which runs between major cities, offers regular and first-class service. Taxis are available at larger hotels and in commercial districts (Braganti & Devine, 1992).

Additional information about travel in Japan is available from:

Japan National Tourist Office
630 Fifth Avenue
New York, NY 10111

Embassy of Japan
2520 Massachusetts Avenue
Washington, DC 20008

MEXICO

U.S. citizens may stay up to three months in Mexico with no visa but need proof of citizenship. Although no vaccinations are required, they may be advisable when traveling in certain parts of the country.

Numerous excellent hotel accommodations are available in the resort towns and in larger cities. Since many people from the United States visit Mexico over the Christmas and Easter holidays, hotel reservations should be made well in advance.

Public transportation in Mexico is quite varied, from the subway of Mexico City to crowded buses. Trains are a good choice for longer distances such as between Mexico City and Monterrey. Driving a car in many parts of Mexico is not advisable. Driving can be hazardous, especially at night, because of bicycle riders, robbers, and problems receiving help should your car break down. In addition, you need to be aware that at various checkpoints, men dressed in military or police garb may stop you expecting money, cigarettes, or other bribes before permitting you to proceed. Failure to offer the bribe may result in lengthy delays while your car and luggage are searched (Braganti & Devine, 1992).

Additional information about traveling in Mexico is available from:

Mexican Government Tourist Office
405 Park Avenue, Suite 1002
New York, NY 10022

Embassy of Mexico
2827 Sixteenth Street, N.W.
Washington, DC 20009-4260

When traveling in other countries, the best advice is to obey the laws of the host country, be courteous and helpful to everyone you meet; and remember it is *their* country so if you cannot speak positively about the country, remain silent (Axtell, 1990).

Terms

- Act of State Doctrine
- Antidiversion requirement
- Antitrust laws
- Arms Export Control Act of 1968
- Berne Convention Implementation Act of 1988
- Bilateral governance
- Citizenship
- Consulate
- Contract
- Customs
- Doctrine of Sovereign Compliance
- Drawer regulations
- Duties
- Export Administration Act of 1985
- Export Trading Company Act of 1982

- Extraterritoriality
- Foreign Corrupt Practices Act of 1977
- Governance structure
- Home country laws
- Host country laws
- International Commercial Terms (Incoterms)
- International Chamber of Commerce
- International Court of Justice (World Court)
- International Emergency Economic Powers Act of 1977
- International Law Commission
- Macaulay's thesis
- Madrid Convention
- Market governance

- Passport
- Patent Cooperation Treaty
- Precedent
- Presidential Decree for the Development and Operation of the Maquiladora Industry Program, 1983
- Priority
- Quasi-international Laws
- Sanctions
- Thematization
- Trading with the Enemy Act of 1917
- Trilateral Governance
- Unified Governance
- Vienna Agreement
- Visa

EXERCISE 12.1

Match the following terms with their definition.

___ 1. Gives permission to stay in a country for a specified time and purpose

___ 2. Unwritten business laws

___ 3. Contract relationship

___ 4. Includes an arbitrator

___ 5. Nothing negotiated in advance; one party sets terms for both

___ 6. Persons sent to other countries to promote commercial interest

___ 7. Enforces export and import laws of the country

___ 8. Document that shows proof of citizenship

___ 9. Agreement between parties to do something that is enforceable by law

___ 10. Considers long-term cultural relationship more important than written legal contract

A. Bilateral governance

B. Consulate

C. Contract

D. Customs

E. Drawer regulations

F. Host country laws

G. Macaulay's thesis

H. Market governance

I. Passport

J. Trilateral governance

K. Unified governance

L. Visa

EXERCISE 12.2

Match the laws with their major provisions

___ 1. Prohibits bribes to gain a business advantage

___ 2. Prohibits transfer of information on military materials

___ 3. Legal right of each nation to do as it wishes within its own boundaries

___ 4. Protects trademarks of countries who are signatories

___ 5. Requires federal licensing of technical information in business correspondence

___ 6. Recognizes copyrights of signatory nations

___ 7. Prevents research-oriented information from being communicated to foreigners

___ 8. Affect exporters involved in mergers/acquisitions of foreign firms

___ 9. United Nations body involved in laws on international commerce

___ 10. Regulates differing legal positions of home and host country

A. Act of State Doctrine

B. Berne Convention Implementation Act

C. Corrupt Practices Act

D. Doctrine of Sovereign Compliance

E. Export Administration Act

F. International Emergency Economic Powers Act

G. International Law Commission

H. Madrid Convention

I. Trading with the Enemy Act

J. U.S. antitrust law

Questions and Cases for Discussion

1. Explain the difference between home country and host country laws.
2. Describe how a low-context and a high-context culture view a contract.
3. Are ethics the same around the world? Explain how they may vary.
4. Explain differences among the four governance structures.
5. Why are nonwritten laws difficult to learn before going to another country to do business?
6. Explain the importance of citizenship. Include in your answer how differences between countries in interpretation of citizenship could affect an individual.
7. What is the difference between a passport and a visa?
8. Who governs a multinational corporation's operations?
9. Why is legal counsel important when doing business in a foreign country?
10. Which act prohibits a corporation or individual from circumventing the Arms Export Control Act of 1968?

CASE 1

A famous doctor's parents emigrated from Russia in the early 1900s before he was born but eventually became naturalized citizens after all their children were born. They also changed their last name to an English-sounding name. The doctor practiced medicine during the 1950s and 1960s. The doctor spoke and wrote seven different languages and was very involved in research and education in his field of study. As the doctor became sought after for educational seminars around the world, he was invited to Russia to speak. The doctor refused to go. What are the legal, cultural, and political issues that could have caused him to reach this decision?

CASE 2

Your corporation has sent you to another country to build a manufacturing facility. A representative of the government informs you it will take six months to get the necessary permits to allow work to begin. You explain that you have a deadline to begin manufacturing in nine months and that three months is not sufficient time. He explains that certain people, if compensated, may be willing to help things progress at a faster pace. You must determine if it is illegal to do this. How would you respond? Explain why you have chosen your answer and whose laws you are considering.

CASE 3

Aerobus, a French airplane manufacturer, and Boeing, a U.S. airplane manufacturer, have reached an agreement to jointly manufacture a new airplane to carry 600 people. Which country's laws will govern the manufacturing of the plane? Where will litigation of any disagreements take place? What form of thematization will be used? What should the governance structure be?

CASE 4

A major corporation uses a large quantity of a derivative from high-grade petroleum. Because of the cost of the high-grade petroleum and a decrease in the use of other derivatives that come from the cracking process, the cost of the derivative is going to increase. Substitute products are available if the cost increases sufficiently to make those products cost efficient. The purchasing agent for the corporation, without the direction of his superiors, has verbally agreed with his supplier to purchase a six-month supply of the derivative at the current cost. In the meantime, the research department has found a cheaper substitute that can be available for shipment in two months. The purchasing agent is told to begin purchasing the substitute in two months. What are the legal ramifications concerning the four extra months of the derivative that has been ordered and that the supplier has already begun to produce?

Activities

1. Bring to class an example of a critical incident related to international law.
2. Secure forms for obtaining passports and visas for a country of your choice. How will you learn the nonwritten laws of this country before you travel there?
3. Interview students from another culture; ask them to identify at least one law in their own country that differs from that in the United States.

4. Ask a professor of international law to address the class on variations in contracts in various cultures.
5. Prepare a list of books or journal articles related to international law.

References

Axtell, R. (1990). *The do's and taboos of hosting international visitors.* New York: John Wiley & Sons, Inc.

Axtell, R. (1991). *The do's and taboos of international trade.* New York: John Wiley & Sons, Inc., 111–135.

Bentacourt, P. (1997, November 10). Tread carefully with international treaties; they override all law. *Business Journal Serving Fresno & the Central San Joaquin Valley, (322223),* 34.

Blankenburg, E. (1988, October). *Zum Begriff "Rechtskultur."* Paper presented at the 24th meeting of the German Sociological Association, Zurich, Switzerland.

Blegvad, B. (1990). Commercial relations, contract, and litigation in Denmark: A discussion of Macaulay's theories. *Law and Society Review, 24*(2), 397–411.

Bowler, M. (7 July 1997). Keeping up with international law. *San Diego Business Journal, 18*(27), 1A, 2p.

Braganti, N. L., & Devine, E. (1992). *European customs and manners.* New York: Meadowbrook Press.

Devine, E., & Braganti, N. L. (1986). *The traveler's guide to Asian customs and manners.* New York: St. Martin's Press.

Devine, E., & Braganti, N. L. (1988). *The traveler's guide to Latin American customs and manners.* New York: St. Martin's Press.

Engholm, C. (1991). *When business East meets business West.* New York: John Wiley & Sons, Inc.

Engholm, C., & Rowland, D. (1996). *International excellence.* New York: Kodansha International.

Fisher, G. (1997). *Mindsets: The role of culture and perception in international relations.* Yarmouth, ME: Intercultural Press.

Global patent protection can be cost-effective, achievable. (1997). *New Hampshire Business Review, 19*(9), 23.

Jarvis, S. S. (1990). Preparing employees to work south of the border. *Personnel,* 59–63.

Kroll, H. (1989). Property rights and the Soviet enterprise: Evidence from the law of contract. *Journal of Comparative Economics, 13,* 115–133.

Lewicki, R. J., & Litterer, J. A. (1985). *Negotiation.* Homewood, IL: Irwin.

Macaulay, S. (1976). An empirical view of contract. *Wisconsin Law Review,* 465–82.

McCubbins, T. F. (1994). Three legal traps for small businesses engaged in international commerce. *Journal of Small Business Management, 32*(3), 95–103.

Missner, M. (1980). *Ethics of the business system.* Sherman Oaks, CA: Alfred Publishing Company.

Murray, J. E. (1992, March 19). What exactly is a contract? *Purchasing, 25,* 27, 29.

Murray, M. E., & Evans, D. (1992). United States laws affecting business communication at home and abroad. In Lesikar, R.V., Pettit, J. O., Jr., & Flatley, M. E., *Basic business communication.* Homewood, IL: Irwin.

Presner, L. A. (1991). *The international business dictionary and reference.* New York: John Wiley & Sons, Inc.

Rachid, R. (1990, June 15). Unwritten laws govern business in some nations. *The Journal of Commerce, 384*(27250), 5A (1).

Roberts, P. C. (1997, November 24). A growing menace to free trade: U.S. sanctions. *Business Week, 3554,* 28.

Skabelund, G. P. (Ed.). (1991). *InfoGram: Travel and international law.* Provo, UT: Brigham Young University.

Zelade, R. (1996). Past rules, present problems. *International business: Strategies for the global marketplace, 9*(10), 6.

Appendix A
Glossary

Acculturation the process of adapting to a new and different culture.

Acronyms words formed from the initial letters or groups of letters and pronounced as one word.

Act of State Doctrine doctrine that states each nation can do as it wishes within its borders.

Antiboycott regulations regulations that prohibit U.S. firms or employees from refusing to do business with friendly nations.

Antidiversion requirement a requirement that states a bill of lading and invoice must clearly display that the carrier cannot direct the shipment to a U.S.-restricted country.

Antitrust laws laws that affect the merger or acquisition of foreign firms, raw material, licenses, and distribution channels.

Area training model (also called the simulation model) an approach to intercultural training that emphasizes affective goals, culture specific content, and experiential processes.

Argot a vocabulary of a particular group; it is often regional.

Arms Export Control Act of 1968 an act of the U.S. Congress that prohibits transfer of military or defense-related materials.

AsiaShock a special kind of cultural shock experienced by U.S. people when traveling to Asian countries.

Associative a cultural quality also called geminscheft; includes the smaller ethnic groups within the large abstractive society.

Attitudes likes (or affinities) and dislikes (or aversions) to certain people, objects, or situations.

Attribution the ability to look at social behavior from another culture's view.

Attribution training training style that focuses on explanations of behavior from the point of view of a person in the host country.

Authority the power to give commands and make decisions.

Back translation the concept of written work translated to a second language, then having another person translate the work back into the first language to determine if the translations are equivalent.

Backstage culture cultural information that is concealed from outsiders.

Berne Convention Implementation Act of 1988 established an international system of national treatment to protect intellectual property of authors.

Bernstein Hypothesis a hypothesis that explains how social structure affects language; speech emerges in restricted or elaborated codes.

Bilateral governance strong recognition of a continuing economic relationship.

Bribery to give or promise to give something, often money, to influence someone's actions.

Buffer a paragraph used to begin a bad news letter; tells what the letter is about, is pleasant, but says neither yes nor no.

Caste system rigid system of class in India; a person is determined to belong to a certain caste by birth. Each caste has its status, rights, and duties.

Chitchat small talk or light conversation.

Chromatics use of color to communicate nonverbally.

Chronemics use of time to communicate nonverbally.

Citizenship the state of being vested with certain rights and duties as a native or naturalized member of a state or country.

Cognates words that sound the same and have the same meaning.

Collectivism emphasizes common interests, conformity, cooperation, and interdependence.

Colloquialism informal words or phrases often associated with regions of the country.

Communication barriers obstacles to effective communication.

Compromise Agreement negotiation strategy agreement reached when two parties find a common ground between their individual wishes which results in lower joint benefit.

Consulate made up of individuals sent to other countries to promote commercial interests.

Connotative meanings emotional meanings of words.

Continental style of eating a manner of eating; place the fork in the left hand and knife in the right; use the knife to push food onto the back of the fork then move the food into the mouth with the tines of the fork down.

Contract an agreement between parties to do something that is oral, written, or implied through conduct.

Conversation taboos topics considered inappropriate for conversation with people in certain cultures or groups.

Cultural Awareness Model includes a comparison of values and behaviors of people in the home country and the host country.

Cultural heritage body of customary beliefs, social forms, material traits, thoughts, speech, and the artistic and intellectual traditions of a society.

Cultural noise anything that would distract or interfere with the message being communicated.

Cultural synergy when people of different cultures absorb a significant number of each others' cultural differences and have a number of similarities that merge to form a stronger overriding culture.

Cultural shock the trauma a person experiences when he or she moves into a culture different from his or her home culture; a communication problem that involves the frustrations that accompany a lack of understanding of the verbal and nonverbal communication of the host culture, its customs, and value systems.

Cultural universals formed out of the common problems all cultures have.

Cultural symbol word or object that represents something in the culture.

Culture the structure through which the communication is formulated and interpreted; deals with the way people live.

Customs socially acceptable ways of behaving; also refers to enforcement of export and import laws of a country.

Deductive method problem solving that goes from broad categories or observations to specific examples to determine the facts and then the solution to the problem.

Demeanor conduct, behavior, and deportment.

Denotative meanings definition meanings of words.

Diffusion process by which two cultures learn and adapt materials and adapt practices from each other.

Directional model negotiation process that is based on the prediction that tough or soft moves will be reciprocated by the other negotiating party.

Dissing an e-mail term meaning to speak ill of someone.

Doctrine of Sovereign Compliance international legal principle used as a defense in your home country for work carried out in a host country.

Drawer regulations unwritten laws.

Duties import taxes.

Ebonics distinctive language of African Americans.

Economic system the way in which the material needs of the people are produced, distributed, and consumed.

Elaborated codes messages low in predictability; verbal transmission is important.

Emoticons computer symbols used to convey emotions within e-mail messages.

Enculturation adapting to the cultural patterns of one's society.

Ethical standards guidelines established to convey what is perceived to be correct or incorrect behavior by most people in a society.

Ethnocentric management management that occurs when a firm is located in one country and all its sales are also in the same country; does not account for cultural differences in the workforce.

Ethnocentrism the belief that your own cultural background, including ways of analyzing problems, language, verbal and nonverbal communication, is correct.

Etiquette manners and behavior considered acceptable in social and business situations.

Euphemisms inoffensive expressions that are used in place of offensive words or words with negative connotations.

European Economic Community (EEC) a free trade zone in Europe currently involving 15 countries.

Exports goods sent out of the country.

Exports Administration Act of 1985 an act of U.S. Congress that requires federal licensing of technical information in business correspondence.

Export Trading Company Act of 1982 an act of U.S. Congress that permits trading between competitors normally prohibited from association by antitrust laws.

Extended family unit consisting of grandparents, uncles, aunts, and cousins.

Extraterritoriality application of laws, such as the Trading with the Enemy Act, beyond the U.S. border.

Figurative meanings descriptive meanings of words.

Flaming sending vicious, insulting messages via e-mail.

Foreign Corrupt Practices Act of 1977 U.S. law that prohibits bribes that are used to gain business advantage.

Formality degree of preciseness, regularity or conformity expected within the society.

Free trade zones areas of international commerce where foreign or domestic merchandise may enter without formal customs entry or customs duties.

Frontstage culture cultural information that you are willing to share with outsiders.

Gemeinschaft (also called associative) cultural quality; the smaller ethnic groups within the larger abstractive society.

General Agreement of Tariffs and Trade (GATT) multinational trade agreement of which the United States is a member; deals with intellectual property, services, national treatment for services, market access for services, foreign investment, antidumping, subsidies, textiles, agriculture, market access, dispute settlement, and telecommunications.

Geocentric management type of management that requires a common framework with enough freedom for individual locations to operate regionally in order to meet the cultural needs of the workers; a synergy of ideas from different countries of operation.

Gesellscheft large abstract society.

Globalization the ability of a corporation to take a product and market it anywhere in the world.

Governance structure how parties maintain their relationship over time.

Grammarians people who study how a language is governed, its grammatical forms, roots, and endings.

Group Decision Support Systems (GDSS) a business conference software package.

Haptics use of touch to communicate nonverbally.

High-context language communication that transmits little in the explicit message; nonverbal aspects are important.

Home country laws laws of the nation in which your corporation is headquartered.

Homonyms words that sound alike and have different meanings.

Host country laws laws of the nation in which you are conducting business.

Host Language native language of the country.

Imports goods brought into the country.

Individualism the attitude of valuing ourselves as individuals responsible for our own destiny and actions.

Inductive Method problem solving that starts with facts or observations and goes to generalizations.

Integrative agreement a negotiation strategy in which two parties reconcile their interests to yield a high joint benefit.

Intellectual model (also called the classroom model) an approach to intercultural training in which participants are given facts about the host country using a variety of instructional methods such as lectures, group discussions, and video tapes.

Interaction approach interaction with people in the host country, either nationals or U.S. persons who have been in the host country for some time.

Interaction model negotiation process that includes environment, atmosphere, parties, and process.

Intercultural business communication communication within and between businesses that involves people from more than one culture.

Intercultural communication communication between persons of different cultures.

Intercultural negotiation discussion between persons of different cultural backgrounds who work toward mutual agreement.

Intermediaries people who act as go-betweens with other people.

International Chamber of Commerce international organization headquartered in Paris, France, that establishes a consensus on matters such as trading practices and procedures for handling trade disputes.

International Commercial Terms (Incoterms) standard definitions of international terms of sale.

International communication communication between nations and governments rather than individuals; quite formal and ritualized.

International Court of Justice (World Court) specialized body of the United Nations that provides a means to settle international disputes between countries.

International English a limited vocabulary for international businesses using the 3,000 to 4,000 most common English words.

International Emergency Economic Powers Act of 1977 an act of the U.S. Congress that governs research-oriented information from being communicated to foreigners.

International Law Commission body of the United Nations that works toward laws of international commerce.

Intimate zone one of four zones of physical distance between people in the United States; is less than 18 inches; reserved for close friends.

Intracultural communication communication between and among members of the same culture.

Jargon technical terminology used within specialized groups.

Johari Window named for its creators, Joseph and Harrington; a method of considering a person's inner world. It includes panes that represent the self that is known and unknown to oneself and the self that is known and unknown to others.

Keiretsu system a company group formed by the principal company and the partner companies that supply parts, equipment, financial support, or distribution of the final products.

Kinesics term used for various types of body language including facial expressions, gestures, posture and stance, and other mannerisms used to communicate or to accompany verbal messages.

Lexical errors language content errors.

Linear language language that has a beginning and an end; logical and object oriented.

Linguistic determinism the assumption that a person's view of reality stems mainly from his or her language.

Linguists people who study the phonetic aspects of language and define language by the sounds speakers produce and listeners receive.

Low-context language communication explicitly coded and given in more than one way to be sure it is understood by the receiver.

Macaulay's thesis thesis stating intercultural business cultures are developing that consider long-term, mutually beneficial relationships more important than written contracts.

Macroculture the larger society or culture.

Madrid Convention treaty signed by 22 countries to protect intellectual property.

Market governance contract-based relationship.

Marriage and family system attitudes, beliefs, and practices related to marriage and the family that are held by people in a particular culture; importance placed on marriage and the family in a society.

Matriarchal family that is mother oriented.

Mediation the use of a third party in the negotiation process.

Melting pot a sociocultural assimilation of people of differing backgrounds and nationalities; being or becoming the same.

Metacommunication the intentional or unintentional implied meaning of a message.

Microculture a subculture; a group of people possessing characteristic traits that distinguish them from others within the macroculture or larger culture.

Mindset a way of being that allows you to see, perceive, and reason through your own cultural awareness.

Monochronic a system of time that allows for performing only one major activity at a time.

Monogamy family system that includes one spouse at a time.

Multicultural learning more than one culture and being able to move between two cultures comfortably.

Multidimensional approach an approach to intercultural training based on the concept that using any single approach is not as effective as using an approach that attempts to combine cognitive, affective, and behavioral aspects of training.

Multinational firm corporation with operations and subsidiaries in many foreign countries.

Negotiation strategies plans organized to achieve a desired working relationship.

Netiquette cyberspace or network etiquette.

Network a group formed with personal ties and involves an exchange of assistance.

Nonlinear language language that is circular; subjective; traditional orientation.

Nonverbal communication nonword messages such as gestures, facial expressions, interpersonal distance, touch, eye contact, smell, and silence.

Norms culturally ingrained principles of correct and incorrect behaviors, which, if broken, carry a form of overt or covert penalty.

North American Free Trade Agreement (NAFTA) an expansion of the free trade zone concept; deals with trade in goods, technical barriers to trade, government procurement, investment, services and related matters, intellectual property, and administrative and institutional provisions. Members include the United States, Canada, and Mexico.

Novelists people who believe that language is a series of words arranged to produce harmonious sounds or to have a logical effect.

Nuclear family family consisting of the father, mother, and children.

Oculesics use of eye contact as a way of communicating nonverbally.

Olfactics use of smell to communicate nonverbally.

Package deal model negotiation process that includes background factors, process, atmosphere, and outcome.

Parable story to convey a truth or moral lesson.

Paralanguage the linguistic elements of speech such as pitch, loudness, quality, rate, or dialect that interrupt or temporarily take the place of speech and affects the meaning of a message.

Parochialism same as ethnocentrism.

Passport a document that shows proof of citizenship.

Patent Cooperation Treaty a treaty that recognizes the patents of the 49 signatory nations.

Patois a nonstandard form of English developed by a U.S. associative culture.

Patriarchal a family that is father oriented.

Perception the learned meaning of sensory images.

Personal constructs individual belief systems and attitudes that are different for different cultures.

Personal zone zone of physical distance between people in the United States; from 18 inches to 4 feet; used for giving instructions to others or working closely with another person.

Platinum Rule do unto others as they would have done unto them (i.e., follow the practices of the host culture).

Political system the governing system of the country that can be based on dictatorship, inherited rights, election procedures, consensus, or conquest.

Polyandry one woman with many husbands.

Polycentric management type of management that considers the culture of the country in which the firm is located.

Polychronic a system of time that allows for performing several activities simultaneously.

Polygamy one man with many wives.

Power the ability to influence others.

Precedent interpretation of the law in previous court decisions.

Presidential Decree for the Development and Operation of the Maquiladora Industry Program, 1983 a Mexican program that allows duty-free import of equipment, machinery, and materials to assemble parts of products that are returned to the home country.

Principles model (comparative model) a model that assumes that the negotiators are problem solvers and that they share a goal that they wish to reach efficiently and amicably; the people are separate from the problem; the focus is on interests; the options have mutual gains; and the criteria used to judge the gains are objective.

Property something that is or may be possessed.

Protocol customs and regulations dealing with diplomatic etiquette and courtesies expected in official dealings with persons in various cultures.

Proverb saying that expresses a commonplace truth.

Proxemics communicating through the use of space.

Public distance zone of physical distance between people in the United States of about 12 to 25 feet.

Quasi-international law rules for the relationship between legal entities and states that do not have national status.

Reentry Shock sometimes called reverse cultural shock; problems with readjustment to the home culture.

Regiocentric Management type of management that considers the region rather than the country in which the firm is located, realizing that countries can and often have many different cultural backgrounds.

Repartee conversation a conversation in which the parties take turns speaking and talk only for short time periods.

Restricted codes include highly predictable messages; use oral, nonverbal, and paralinguistic transmission channels.

Ritual conversation communication that involves standard replies and comments for a given situation, with little meaning attached to what is said.

Roles behavioral expectations of a position within a culture and are affected by norms and rules.

Rules formed to clarify cloudy areas of norms.

Sanction prohibits U.S. firms from doing business in targeted countries.

Sapir-Whorf Hypothesis hypothesis that language functions as a way of shaping one's experiences; includes structural and semantic aspects of a language.

Self-awareness model an approach to intercultural training also called the human relations model; it is based on the assumption that the trainee with self-understanding will adapt to the new culture better and will therefore be more effective in the overseas assignment.

Semanticists people who study the meaning of words and where and how the words developed.

Semantics the study of the ways behavior is influenced by the use of words and other symbols used to communicate.

Sensitivity training one element used in the self-awareness approach to intercultural training; includes training exercises in which people are told in a group setting why their behavior is inappropriate.

Serial monogamy family system that includes a number of different monogamous marriages through divorce or death.

Shouting typing a message via e-mail in all capital letters.

Slang idioms and other informal language vocabulary.

Social hierarchies structure of a culture.

Social interaction what is acceptable and unacceptable communication between people in a culture.

Social reciprocity refers to the way formal and informal obligations are handled, ranging from the belief that people are forever indebted to others to those who feel no obligation to others.

Social zone in the United States, a zone of physical distance between people from 4 to

12 feet; used for business situations in which people interact in a more formal, impersonal way.

Sociolinguistics effects of social and cultural differences upon a language.

Socio-psychological model a negotiation process that involves the goals the parties want to reach, the communication and actions leading to the negotiations, the expected outcomes for each, the pre-existing relationship and cultural factors of both parties, and the conditions under which the negotiations are conducted.

Spamming the cyberspace term for mass mailings of commercial advertisements or material cross-posted to numerous newsgroups.

Stereotypes perceptions about certain groups of people or nationalities.

Subculture group of people possessing characteristic traits that set apart and distinguish them from others within a larger society (macroculture).

Subgroup groups with which the macroculture does not agree and has problems communicating.

Subjective interpretation interpretation placed on a message that is affected by thought processes; influenced by personal judgment, state of mind, or temperament of a person.

Subnationalism a condition that exists when a political body attempts to unite diverse people under one government.

Supernationalism extending authority over more than one nation.

Superstitions beliefs that are inconsistent with the known laws of science or what a society considers to be true and rational.

Syntactic errors errors in language meaning.

Syntactic rules rules that govern how words are arranged in a sentence.

Taboos practices or verbal expressions considered by a society or culture as improper or unacceptable.

Tactic any maneuver used for gaining advantage or success.

Thematization process by which a framework for mutual communication and satisfaction is reached.

Trade agreements laws under which U.S. businesses must function when exporting.

Trading with the Enemy Act of 1917 an act of U.S. Congress that prohibits the transfer of information on military material or defense-related materials.

Transnational corporations that cross the borders of countries in conducting their business.

Trilateral governance negotiation method that allows for later redetermination of terms by using an arbitrator.

Uncertainty-reduction theory creation of proactive predictions and retroactive explanations about our own behavior, beliefs, and attitudes and those of others.

Unified governance no advance negotiations; provides maximum flexibility; terms for both parties controlled by one party.

U.S. style of eating zigzag style of eating used by people in the United States: cutting the meat with the knife held in the right hand and the fork in the left, then placing the knife on the plate, shifting the fork to the right hand, and eating.

Values social principles, goals, or standards accepted by persons in a culture.

Verbal dueling a friendly type of argument or debate.

Vienna Agreement a multilateral treaty signed by states to protect intellectual property.

Visa written permission to enter and stay in a country for a specified time and purpose.

World culture a developing culture that involves the breaking down of traditional barriers among people of differing cultures, emphasizing the commonality of human needs.

Work mental or physical activities directed to socially productive accomplishments.

Work attitudes how people of a culture view work.

Work ethic the attitude that work is applauded and rewarded, while failure to work is viewed negatively.

Appendix B
Answers to Exercises

Chapter 1

MATCHING
1. D
2. C
3. I
4. B
5. A
6. H
7. F
8. G
9. K
10. J

Chapter 2

TRUE/FALSE
1. F
2. T
3. F
4. F
5. F
6. T
7. T
8. T
9. F
10. F

MATCHING
1. A
2. H
3. C
4. A
5. K
6. G
7. D
8. I
9. L
10. F

Chapter 3

TRUE/FALSE
1. T
2. F
3. T
4. T
5. F
6. F
7. F
8. F
9. T
10. T

Chapter 4

TRUE/FALSE
1. T
2. T
3. F
4. T
5. T
6. T
7. T
8. T
9. F
10. F

Chapter 5

TRUE/FALSE
1. F
2. T
3. F
4. T
5. T
6. T
7. F
8. T
9. T
10. T

Chapter 6

IDENTIFICATION
A. determination
B. happiness
C. interest
D. disgust
E. anger
F. contempt
G. surprise
H. sadness

TRUE/FALSE
1. F
2. F
3. F
4. T
5. F
6. F
7. F
8. F
9. T
10. F

MATCHING
1. K
2. F
3. I
4. H
5. G
6. E
7. B
8. A
9. J
10. D

Chapter 7

TRUE/FALSE
1. F
2. F
3. F
4. T
5. F
6. T
7. F
8. T
9. T
10. T

Chapter 8

TRUE/FALSE
1. T
2. F
3. T
4. T
5. T
6. T
7. F
8. F
9. F
10. F

Chapter 9

TRUE/FALSE
1. T
2. F
3. F
4. F
5. T
6. T
7. F
8. T
9. F
10. T

Chapter 10

TRUE/FALSE
1. T
2. T
3. F
4. F
5. T
6. F
7. T
8. T
9. T
10. T

Chapter 11

MULTIPLE CHOICE
1. C

TRUE/FALSE
1. T
2. F
3. T
4. F
5. T
6. F
7. T
8. F
9. T
10. F

Chapter 12

MATCHING
1. L
2. E
3. H
4. J
5. K
6. B
7. D
8. I
9. C
10. G

MATCHING
1. C
2. I
3. A
4. H
5. E
6. B
7. F
8. J
9. G
10. D

Index